Neuropsychological Aspects of Brain Injury Litigation

This accessible handbook focuses on the importance of neuropsychological evidence and the role of the neuropsychologist as expert witness in brain injury litigation.

This thorough, evidence-based resource fosters discussion between the legal profession and expert neuropsychological witnesses. The chapters reflect collaborations between leading personal injury lawyers and neuropsychologists in the UK. The key issues in brain injury litigation that are addressed are essential to an understanding of the role of the neuropsychologist as expert witness and of neuropsychological evidence for the courts. These include neuropsychological testing, assessment of quantum, vocational rehabilitation, mental capacity, forensic outcomes, the frontal paradox, mild traumatic brain injury and more.

Combining the scientific and legal background with practical tips and case examples, this book is valuable reading for legal professionals, particularly those working in personal injury and clinical negligence, as well as trainees, students and clinicians in the field of neuropsychology, neurorehabilitation and clinical psychology.

Phil S. Moore is a HCPC registered Consultant Neuropsychologist & Clinical Psychologist and Director of Medicolegal-Psychology-Neuropsychology Ltd. He has over twenty years' experience of working clinically and previously worked for 15 years within the NHS. He has had over ten years' experience of completing medicolegal expert witness work in brain injury.

Shereen Brifcani is a Consultant Clinical Psychologist, who has worked in the NHS and private sector healthcare since 2003. She continues to work clinically with people with various neurological conditions, has conducted medicolegal assessments since 2013, and provides psychological intervention for claimants with acquired brain injury.

Andrew Worthington is a Consultant Clinical Neuropsychologist and Clinical Psychologist with over 30 years' experience in brain injury. He is honorary Professor in the Faculty of Medicine, Health and Life Science, Swansea University, UK. An internationally recognized expert in neuropsychological rehabilitation, he has provided medicolegal services since 1995.

Neuropsychological Aspects of Brain Injury Litigation

A Medicolegal Handbook for Lawyers and Clinicians

Edited by
Phil S. Moore, Shereen Brifcani
and Andrew Worthington

LONDON AND NEW YORK

Cover credit: Cover image by B Wooley

First published 2022
by Routledge
2 Park Square, Milton Park, Abingdon, Oxon OX14 4RN

and by Routledge
605 Third Avenue, New York, NY 10158

Routledge is an imprint of the Taylor & Francis Group, an informa business

© 2022 selection and editorial matter, Phil S. Moore, Shereen Brifcani and Andrew Worthington; individual chapters, the contributors

The right of Phil S. Moore, Shereen Brifcani and Andrew Worthington to be identified as the authors of the editorial material, and of the authors for their individual chapters, has been asserted in accordance with sections 77 and 78 of the Copyright, Designs and Patents Act 1988.

All rights reserved. No part of this book may be reprinted or reproduced or utilised in any form or by any electronic, mechanical, or other means, now known or hereafter invented, including photocopying and recording, or in any information storage or retrieval system, without permission in writing from the publishers.

Trademark notice: Product or corporate names may be trademarks or registered trademarks, and are used only for identification and explanation without intent to infringe.

British Library Cataloguing-in-Publication Data
A catalogue record for this book is available from the British Library

Library of Congress Cataloging-in-Publication Data
Names: Moore, Phil S., 1980- editor. | Brifcani, Shereen, 1980- editor. | Worthington, Andrew, editor.
Title: Neuropsychological aspects of brain injury litigation : a medicolegal handbook for lawyers and clinicians / edited by Phil S. Moore, Shereen Brifcani, and Andrew Worthington.
Identifiers: LCCN 2021031495 (print) | LCCN 2021031496 (ebook) | ISBN 9780367569587 (paperback) | ISBN 9780367616274 (hardback) | ISBN 9781003105763 (ebook)
Subjects: LCSH: Personal injuries—England—Trial practice. | Forensic neuropsychology—England. | Evidence, Expert—England. | Medical jurisprudence—England. | Brain damage—Psychological aspects. | Brain—Wounds and injuries. | Neuropsychology.
Classification: LCC KD1954 .N48 2021 (print) | LCC KD1954 (ebook) | DDC 346.4203/23—dc23
LC record available at https://lccn.loc.gov/2021031495
LC ebook record available at https://lccn.loc.gov/2021031496

ISBN: 978-036-7616274 (hbk)
ISBN: 978-036-7569587 (pbk)
ISBN: 978-100-3105763 (ebk)

DOI: 10.4324/9781003105763

Typeset in Bembo
by codeMantra

Phil S. Moore: For Stevie.
Shereen Brifcani: For Sofia and Noah.
Andrew Worthington: In memory of Dr Maria A. Wyke.
For Lara, Steph and Amber.

Contents

List of contributors ix
Acknowledgements xi

1 Introduction: neuropsychological aspects of brain injury litigation: a medicolegal handbook for lawyers and clinicians 1
   PHIL S. MOORE, SHEREEN BRIFCANI AND ANDREW WORTHINGTON

2 Legal principles in litigation 4
   HENRY F. CHARLES AND RUTH JOHNSON

PART 1
'But for' the brain injury and causation 19

3 Premorbid abilities: cognition, emotion and behaviour 21
   MARTIN BUNNAGE WITH MARC WILLEMS QC

4 Neuropsychological testing in brain injury litigation: a critical part of the expert neuropsychological examination 35
   ANDREW WORTHINGTON AND PHIL S. MOORE

5 Paediatric outcomes after traumatic brain injury: social and forensic risk management in multidisciplinary treatment approaches 64
   HOPE KENT, JAMES TONKS AND HUW WILLIAMS WITH IAN BROWNHILL

PART 2
Current condition — 87

6 Effort testing, performance validity, and the importance of context and consistency — 89
SIMON GERHAND, CHRIS A. JONES AND DAVID HACKER

7 Mild traumatic brain injury and persistent neuropsychological symptoms — 116
ANDREW WORTHINGTON AND PHIL S. MOORE

8 The frontal lobe paradox — 140
SAMANTHA FISHER-HICKS, RODGER LL. WOOD AND BILL BRAITHWAITE QC

9 Assessing mental capacity in brain injury litigation — 158
IAN P. BROWNHILL

PART 3
Loss, disability and impact — 169

10 Legal principles of quantum — 171
WILLIAM LATIMER-SAYER QC

11 Practical applications of quantum principles — 195
ANDREW WORTHINGTON, WILLIAM LATIMER-SAYER AND ANDY TYERMAN

12 Conclusion: formulating neuropsychological opinion in brain injury — 221
PHIL. S. MOORE, SHEREEN BRIFCANI AND ANDREW WORTHINGTON

Index — 227

Contributors

Bill Braithwaite QC	Exchange Chambers
Shereen Brifcani	St Peter's Hospital, Ludlow Street Healthcare
Ian P. Brownhill	39 Essex Chambers
Martin Bunnage	North Bristol NHS Trust
Henry F. Charles QC	12 Kings Bench Walk
Simon Gerhand	Hywel Dda Health Board and Brain Injury Rehabilitation Trust
David Hacker	University Hospital Birmingham
Samantha Fisher-Hicks	Swansea University
Ruth Johnson	Irwin Mitchell
Chris A. Jones	University Hospital Birmingham and School of Psychology Birmingham University
Hope Kent	The University of Exeter
Phil S. Moore	Medicolegal-Psychology-Neuropsychology Ltd
William Latimer-Sayer QC	Cloisters
James Tonks	The University of Exeter
Andy Tyerman	Community Head Injury Service, Buckinghamshire Healthcare NHS Trust
Marc Willems QC	Cobden House Chambers
Huw Williams	The University of Exeter
Rodger Ll. Wood	Swansea University
Andrew Worthington	Headwise

Acknowledgements

I would like to thank Marzena for her unwavering support, and my parents and family who never failed to support my ambitions within psychology and beyond. I am fortunate to have worked with some great psychologists along the way, some starting out, some still practising and some sadly passed away. A special thank you to David Hughes, who saw something in me 25 years ago and still calls his student with learned advice to this day.

Phil S. Moore

To my many current and previous colleagues and mentors, thank you for your support and encouragement over the years, and for the ongoing opportunities for learning that you have provided. To my family for your unrelenting belief in me, with a special acknowledgement of my mother and my late father who sparked my curiosity in science, reasoning and ethics from a young age. Working with people, means that we will always be presented with novelty and challenge. I am ever thankful for being privileged to share in people's stories, and to witness the resilience of individuals and families during some of their most difficult times.

Shereen Brifcani

I have been extremely fortunate to work with some truly inspiring clinicians in neuropsychology, neurology, neuropsychiatry and rehabilitation medicine. Their influence in shaping my thinking and practice is probably greater than I am aware. Over 25 years of medicolegal experience has also introduced me to many impressive lawyers whose empathy, dedication and commitment has been a privilege to witness. Finally, and ultimately, I have learned much from the many claimants and their families who have shown me both the frailties and strength of human spirit and taught me to appreciate life come what may.

Andrew Worthington

To everyone who has contributed to and supported the development of this book. We appreciate the time, thought and effort you have all dedicated, the ideas you've shared, and the stimulating conversations we have had. These have already, and will continue to inform our practice. Thank you.

From the editors

1 Introduction

Neuropsychological aspects of brain injury litigation: a medicolegal handbook for lawyers and clinicians

Phil S. Moore, Shereen Brifcani and Andrew Worthington

Opportune gap

For some time, the editors have been aware of the paucity of accessible medicolegal-based neuropsychological literature. Much of the existing literature is US focused and not entirely applicable to medicolegal neuropsychology practice in the UK. There have been many successful high-quality, professional development brain injury events between lawyers, neuropsychologists and other clinicians. Yet there are few accessible handbooks which cover brain injury from the perspectives of both lawyers and neuropsychologists. This opportune gap in the literature generated enthusiasm from both professions. As editors we have learned a great deal from these collaborations and although we have had to prioritise the focus of the book to the title in hand, we consider the main topics provide good breadth. Along with a dual legal-neuropsychology authorship, the book aims to attract a broad readership, with the content being of interest to the wider range of professionals working in brain injury litigation.

Central themes

Many neuropsychologists refrain from referencing literature within medicolegal reports because it often seems that every written word can be critiqued, sometimes correctly, sometimes unfairly. The clinical literature has developed to the point where almost any opinion can be countered by a brief Google Scholar review. Therefore, it is important to appreciate that the opinions in this book are a considered, balanced interpretation, true to the author at the time of writing and no more. There will continue to be differences of opinion amongst lawyers and experts within their own professions and beyond, and where possible we have tried to reflect this range of opinion within the chapters which follow, aided by exploring differences of view between authors in the process of writing the book. Opinions are not immutable and this will be apparent in some chapters that explain how ideas in the literature have developed over time. Opinions are, however, what matters to court and the

DOI: 10.4324/9781003105763-1

book is united by a few central themes: impartiality, balance, evidence-based reasoning and the biopsychosocial framework.

As we shall explore within this book, the UK civil legal system is inherently adversarial. This means that neuropsychologists acting as experts must constantly adhere to the highest professional standards, deploying complete independence and impartiality in an increasingly accountable system. The contributors of this book were carefully chosen on this basis. Each chapter has been edited to ensure an evidential approach, reflecting a critical and balanced review of the available literature. The perspective of the book takes a biopsychosocial view of brain injuries and the people who sustain them.

Chapter structure and contributors

The book starts with a legal introduction co-written by Henry Charles QC of 12 Kings Bench Walk and Ruth Johnson of Irwin Mitchell Solicitors. This brings to life the fundaments of the law as it applies to litigation and how the expert neuropsychologist contributes to this process. The book is then arranged into three parts which should be familiar to seasoned expert neuropsychologists and lawyers: Part 1: "'But for' the brain injury and causation"; Part 2: "Current condition"; and Part 3: "Loss, disability and impact". Case examples have been used to illustrate certain points, basing relevant arguments on real-life cases from personal injury and clinical negligence.

Part 1: 'But for' the brain injury and causation

The 'but for' starts with the neuropsychological-based topic of premorbid ability, expertly described and critiqued by Professor Martin Bunnage, who is joined by Marc Willems QC of Cobden House Chambers to traverse the legal implications. There follows a critical examination of neuropsychological tests by Professor Andrew Worthington and Dr Phil S. Moore. Finally, Hope Kent, Dr James Tonks and Associate Professor Huw Williams frame our understanding of paediatric outcomes after traumatic brain injury discussing social and forensic risk management in multidisciplinary treatment approaches with Ian Brownhill of 39 Essex Chambers providing special interest legal commentary.

Part 2: Current condition

This part starts with Dr Simon Gerhand then tackling the topic of symptom validity with Dr Chris Jones and Dr David Hacker. They discuss its importance in contextualising the role of different factors where a person's effort or symptom severity may be under question. Professor Andrew Worthington and Dr Phil S. Moore then take the growing issue of mild traumatic brain injury and critically explore persistent symptoms which can often accompany litigation claims. The frontal paradox phenomenon is critically reviewed by

Dr Samantha Fisher-Hicks and Professor Rodger Ll Wood, who are joined by Bill Braithwaite QC of Exchange Chambers to provide some legal context. Ian Brownhill of 39 Essex Chambers concludes part 2 by providing expertise in his law-led chapter on the very important issue of capacity, including the two aspects central to brain injury litigation: financial decisions and litigation decisions.

Part 3: Loss, disability and impact

Principles of quantum are methodically described by William Latimer-Sayer QC of Cloisters in the first chapter within this section. This is followed by a chapter which addresses the application of these principles in practice, authored by Professor Andrew Worthington William Latimer-Sayer QC, and Dr Andy Tyerman.

The editors finish by synthesising the content of the book. A framework for medicolegal formulation is proposed to draw together chapter content as it applies to understanding brain injury sequelae. Key points from chapters are identified, along with those areas that require further exploration.

2 Legal principles in litigation

Henry F. Charles and Ruth Johnson

What the lawyers want to know, and when

Lawyers work to a template: How to prove a case at trial (claimant), or conversely, how to prevent a claimant proving his or her case at trial (defendant).

It never hurts to remember that the claimant must prove his or her case on the balance of probabilities, but that within that scenario there is a process akin to legal ping-pong. If the claimant's team put forward a respectable case on, say, capacity, and the defendant puts an equally respectable case in reply, then the claimant's team have work to do.

In a brain injury case the lawyers will want to know:

a   The claimant's pre-injury capability for work, including future career prospects
b   Whether the claimant had any pre-existing impairments, the extent of such impairments, and how they impacted upon day-to-day life
c   In comparison, what the claimant's prospects for work/future career are now
d   Any care or case management needs flowing from the brain injury
e   Whether the claimant has capacity to litigate and whether the claimant has capacity to manage his or her affairs going forwards

There will be a significant pressure upon the lawyers for the claimant to acquire this knowledge as quickly as possible. The defendant will have the option of making an early offer to settle,[1] and the claimant's lawyers will want to scope out what evidence is likely to be needed so that when proceedings are issued they are in a position to drive the litigation forwards.

Before even that stage of issuing and serving proceedings the claimant will be expected to set out its case in a pre-action protocol letter. The letter should contain the date and details of the decision, act or omission being challenged, a clear summary of the facts and the legal basis for the claim. It should also

---

1   Although in serious cases the Serious Injury Protocol will in theory ease the pressure.

DOI: 10.4324/9781003105763-2

contain the details of any information that the claimant is seeking and an explanation of why this is considered relevant.

Where neuropsychological evidence fits in practice

Assuming that the injury is of some significance then the neurologists will start by identifying the brain injury using medical knowledge, and will typically rely upon neuropsychologists to provide an opinion regarding the validity, nature and extent of neuropsychological injury, and impact upon the claimant's functioning, prognosis, capacity and psychological wellbeing. This includes the claimant's pre-injury status, current functioning, and recommendations for treatment. A neuropsychiatrist's opinion may also be sought when there is a potential significant interaction with psychiatric issues, historical and/or current, but will similarly rely on neuropsychological opinion.

The cases involving severe injury are relatively straightforward, so long as there were no neurological or psychiatric issues prior to the brain injury being acquired, and the victim was in settled employment.

The cases that really cause difficulty are the mild traumatic brain injury (TBI) cases. These have grown more prevalent and prominent in the last decade or so. The diagnostic difficulties attached to a number of these cases, the developing scientific literature, the potential for overlap/confusion with psychiatric injury and the potentially adverse impact of telling someone he or she has a brain injury mean that any objective information is critical. Neuropsychological assessment can provide at least some improved clarity with regard to cases involving entangled causation.

So the golden thread is that causation is key.

Some basic legal principles

The court makes findings on the balance of probabilities.[2] Once breach of duty has been established: the focus turns to causation, i.e. what the result of the breach of duty has been.

An award of damages is intended to compensate the claimant for pecuniary and non-pecuniary losses resulting from the defendant's tort (i.e. wrongdoing). The aim is to award a sum of money that will put the injured party into the same position as she or he would have been if she or he had not sustained the wrong for which compensation is being awarded.[3]

---

2 As ever with law, this is nuanced: so where the question is one of past facts then mere balance of probabilities is the test, where the question is one of what hypothetically might have been then to the extent that the chance of an event falls significantly below 100% the award will be discounted.
3 Perhaps the best known statement of the principle was from Lord Blackburn in *Livingstone v Rawyards Coal Co* [1880] 5 App Cas. 25.

The basic test is the 'but for' test, in which the defendant will be liable only if the claimant's damage would not have occurred 'but for' his negligence. Neuropsychology can be helpful in establishing the 'but for' position and if there are factors which superimpose a brain injury.

Establishing the 'but for' counterfactual position has given the courts huge difficulty as a matter of law and practice.

Firstly, what is the position where someone was very vulnerable, perhaps exquisitely vulnerable, to a brain injury, for example due to having a thin skull? A person committing the wrong has to take the victim as found: the so-called eggshell skull rule – which is not limited to eggshell skulls. For example in *Smith v Leech Brain & Co*[4] a factory worker was splashed with molten metal, burning his lip. His lip happened to have pre-malignant cells, malignancy was triggered, the factory worker died, the defendant had to pay up.

If a claimant – having been knocked off a bicycle – suffers much greater neurological damage than the 'ordinary' person, that is the defendant's misfortune. That said, in eggshell skull cases, a defendant might try and prove that sooner or later the claimant would have suffered some or equivalent damage.

Neuropsychological evidence is less likely to be involved on such matters, but it takes centre stage where there was already damage.

In *Reaney v University Hospital of North Staffordshire NHS Trust & Another*[5] the claimant went into hospital suffering T7 paraplegia. Plainly this permanent condition caused various care and care-related requirements – a few hours of care per week rising to 31.5 hours of care per week after the age of 75 would have given her a largely independent life. Unfortunately, whilst in hospital she developed grade 4 pressure sores, with very adverse effect. There was no dispute that the claimant was going to have increased care and related needs because of the impact of the pressure sores (which should not have developed, and in respect of which the hospital had accepted liability).

The High Court Judge (Foskett J) held that the claimant now essentially needed 24-hour care. He further held that the hospital was liable in respect of all future care needs, even though the claimant would have required care in the future, irrespective of the development of the pressure sores. His logic was that the wrongdoer must take the victim as he finds him and if that involved making the current damaged condition worse, then the wrongdoer had to fully compensate the worsened condition. Thus being totally deaf was far worse than being half deaf, so an otherwise modest negligently caused additional hearing loss might have a disproportionate effect. In other words, 2 + 2 can equal 5.

Foskett J held that the additional damage of the pressure sores meant that Mrs Reaney's care needs were now materially different. He also invoked an

---

4 [1962] 2QB 405.
5 [2015] EWCA Civ 1119.

alternative argument, to which we shall return shortly: the hospital had 'materially contributed' to the overall condition.

The Court of Appeal disagreed with Foskett J, holding that if the additional care required by reason of the pressure sores could be characterised as more of the same then the wrongdoer was only liable to compensate for the increased portion of care. So, given an overall care need of, say, 14 hours per day, with 5 hours per day being the original level of care required but for the defendant's negligence, then the defendant had to compensate 14–5 = 9. Mrs Reaney's case was such a case, on the facts, said the Court of Appeal.

Nonetheless the Court of Appeal accepted that there would be cases where the outcome of a defendant's negligence superimposed on pre-existing injury would lead to a qualitatively different situation.

In doing so they noted the case of *Sklair v Haycock*[6] where the claimant required some care from his father but was basically independent. He was involved in a road traffic accident, the injuries sustained in that accident meaning that he required round-the-clock care. The trial judge had allowed Mr Sklair the full cost of the round-the-clock care package without deduction in respect of the care previously being provided by Mr Sklair's father.

We need not look at how the trial judge got there, but it is sufficient to note that the Court of Appeal in Reaney noted the outcome in Sklair as an example of a case wherein the care package required following the accident, was qualitatively different from what had been previously required.

So, where a claimant has care needs prior to the index brain injury the claimant's lawyers are going to be keen to see whether it can be shown that what is now required is qualitatively different. The defendant's interests will lie in the opposite direction. Neuropsychological evidence may be a key part of the determination.

However we now need to return to the concept of material contribution. This is a form of 'legal winner takes all'. The defendant can be responsible for causing an injury if it can be proved that such a defendant has materially contributed to the claimant sustaining such an injury, even if the defendant's breach of duty is not the sole, or indeed even the most significant, cause of the injury.

In *Reaney* the Court of Appeal also rejected Foskett J's material contribution alternative finding. They noted that in *Bailey v MOD*[7] [2009] it was held that the material contribution test was appropriate where medical science cannot establish the probability that 'but for' an act of negligence the injury would not have happened, but can establish that the contribution of the negligent cause was more than negligible. In Mrs Reaney's case it was very clear what the hospital's negligence had caused.

Needless to say it is often not quite that simple.

6 [2009] EWHC 3328 (QB).
7 [2009] 1 WLR 1052.

8   *Legal principles in litigation*

In *Dickins v O2*[8] the Court of Appeal were faced with a workplace stress claim in which the identified employer's breach of duty had made a material contribution to the severe psychiatric condition the Claimant suffered. There were multiple factors involved: a vulnerable personality, a relationship issue, perhaps IBS. The trial judge followed workplace stress claim guidance from the Court of Appeal in *Sutherland v Hatton*[9] and apportioned damages as 50% due to the employer's wrongdoing and 50% by reason of the non-negligent matters. In Dickins, Janet Smith LJ, in remarks which were obiter (i.e. non-binding) felt that in a case where the wrongdoer had caused material i.e. significant (as opposed to insignificant) damage and where it was not scientifically possible to say how much that contribution was, and where the injury to which it led was indivisible it would be inappropriate to apportion damages. However, it could be appropriate to make allowance for future events likely to have taken place in any event irrespective of the employer's negligence.

The significance of *Dickins v O2* is its willingness to look at psychiatric injury as being indivisible. In brain injury cases where there is an element of psychiatric injury and a pre-injury psychiatric condition and/or the brain injury has mediated the pre-injury psychiatric condition the neuropsychologist may become pivotal in determining whether divisibility can be achieved.

In practice the courts are usually reluctant to find on the basis of material contribution if apportionment can be achieved. Expert evidence does not always help the courts. That was illustrated in *Thaine v London School of Economics*[10] in which Keith J held:

> If we know – and we do know, for by the end of the case it was no longer seriously in dispute that a substantial part of the impairment took place before the defendants were in breach, why, in fairness, should they have been made to pay for it? The fact that precise quantification is impossible should not alter the position. The whole exercise of assessing damages is shot through with imprecision … I see no reason why the present impossibility of making a precise apportionment of impairment and disability in terms of time, should in justice lead to the result that the defendants are adjudged liable to pay in full, when it is known that only part of the damage was their fault. What justice does demand, to my mind, is that the court should make the best estimate which it can, in the light of the evidence, making the fullest allowances in favour of the plaintiffs for the uncertainties known to be involved in any apportionment.

The case of *BAE v Konczak*[11] approved *Thaine v London School of Economics* and, importantly, emphasises that the experts' role is to assist the court by

---

8 [2008] EWCA Civ 1144.
9 [2002] EWCA Civ. 76.
10 [2010] ICR 1422.
11 [2017] EWCA Civ 1188.

carefully mapping out the factors enabling an assessment of whether or not an injury is divisible or otherwise, and whether in cases of indivisibility the pre-existing state may not nevertheless demonstrate a high degree of vulnerability to, and the probability of, future injury: if not today, then tomorrow (Irwin LJ, paragraphs 92 and 93).

The Dickins, Thaine and BAE cases involved workplace stress-related causes, a type of case where particular guidance had been laid down (see *Sutherland v Hatton*, above), but the approach, particularly in *BAE v Konzcak* should impinge upon the wide run of cases engaging similar issues. For more detail on the issue of material contribution see the masterful exposition of the law by HH Judge Auerbach in *Davies v Frimley Health NHS Foundation Trust*.[12]

The role of the neuropsychologist in cases involving a psychological/psychiatric element and/or interaction with pre-accident brain damage (whether congenital or acquired) or atypical neurology will therefore be critical both directly and as an enabler for the other experts.

We will now turn to the heads of loss supporting a claim where the neuropsychological assessment may be pivotal.

Loss of earnings

Future losses, including earnings, are dealt with on a heavily actuarially based approach via the Ogden Tables (now in their 8th Edition).

As practitioners will know, the approach is to work out what the claimant would have earned but for the index accident, then assess what the claimant will earn.

As to what the claimant would have earned, if the claimant was aged say 59 at accident, in good health and likely to have remained in good health, had held the same job for 30 years and that job was secure – vanishingly rare now – then the neuropsychologist will not be terribly important in assessing 'but for' earning capacity.

Now contrast that with a claimant who was 19 at accident, on a gap year, with middling exam results, maybe suitable for an apprenticeship, maybe suitable for university and it will be readily appreciated that an assessment of the pre-morbid state is becoming more important.

Let us further add in a history of behavioural problems and the importance of the neuropsychological assessment becomes ever more clear. What would the claimant have been capable of? Critically, given the Ogden basis of assessment of future losses, would the Claimant have been classified as disabled? Will the Claimant now be classified as disabled? Those issues really matter.

The process of identifying and classifying disability is not, currently, ideal.

Ogden 8. stresses the requirements for disability with reference to the Disability Discrimination Act 1995.

12 [2021] EWHC 169 (QB).

10 *Legal principles in litigation*

A claimant has to satisfy these three requirements to count as disabled:

i   The person has an illness or a disability which has or is expected to last for over a year or is a progressive illness; and
ii The DDA1995 definition is satisfied in that the impact of the disability has a substantial adverse effect on the person's ability to carry out normal day-to-day activities; and
iii The effects of impairment limit either the kind **or** the amount of paid work he/she can do;
iv The introduction to Ogden 8 cites the 1995 Act guidance notes. As a whole they give a flavour for the threshold for disability:

Mobility – for example, unable to travel short journeys as a passenger in a car, unable to walk other than at a slow pace or with jerky movements, difficulty in negotiating stairs, unable to use one or more forms of public transport, unable to go out of doors unaccompanied.

Manual dexterity – for example, loss of functioning in one or both hands, inability to use a knife and fork at the same time, or difficulty in pressing buttons on a keyboard.

Physical co-ordination – for example, the inability to feed or dress oneself; or to pour liquid from one vessel to another except with unusual slowness or concentration.

Problems with bowel/bladder control – for example, frequent or regular loss of control of the bladder or bowel. Occasional bedwetting is not considered a disability.

Ability to lift, carry or otherwise move everyday objects (for example, books, kettles, light furniture) – for example, inability to pick up a weight with one hand, or to carry a tray steadily.

Speech – for example, unable to communicate (clearly) orally with others, taking significantly longer to say things. However, a minor stutter, difficulty in speaking in front of an audience, or inability to speak a foreign language would not be considered impairments.

Hearing – for example, not being able to hear without the use of a hearing aid, the inability to understand speech under normal conditions or over the telephone.

Eyesight – for example, whilst wearing spectacles or contact lenses – being unable to pass the standard driving eyesight test, total inability to distinguish colours (excluding ordinary red/green colour blindness), or inability to read newsprint.

Memory or ability to concentrate, learn or understand – for example, intermittent loss of consciousness or confused behaviour, inability to remember names of family or friends, unable to write a cheque without assistance, or an inability to follow a recipe.

Perception of risk of physical danger – for example, reckless behaviour putting oneself or others at risk, mobility impairment(s) that reduce ability to cross the road safely. This excludes (significant) fear of heights or underestimating risk of dangerous hobbies.

However the Guidance Notes were dropped from the Equality Act 2010.

The Court of Appeal provided some guidance as to what classified as disability and how to approach quantification in *Billett v MOD*[13]. There are two essential issues here: firstly whether the claimant is disabled and secondly, even if the claimant is disabled, whether the information is there to formulate a future loss calculation. The two are theoretically different issues, in practice they are different levels of the same trifle.

So in Billett Jackson LJ approved the definition of disability given in *Aderemi v London & South Eastern Railway Ltd*[14] *[2013] ICR 59* as being a 'substantial adverse effect' on a person's 'ability to carry out normal day to day activities'. However 'substantial' simply means more than insignificant. Mr Billett certainly had significant limitations in his home and leisure life but in his work he had only very limited hindrance. Nonetheless he qualified as disabled albeit at the outer fringe. However Jackson LJ felt that there would be no rational basis for adjusting the standard contingency factors for disability and that in the circumstances the use of the Ogden tables would be inappropriate.

Those issues highlight the importance of a thorough neuropsychological evaluation as a tool for assessing whether the claimant was disabled for Ogden purposes in any event from a neuropsychological perspective, and whether the claimant will be disabled for Ogden purposes, and in both cases the extent of that disability. The stakes can be high. Consider the example of a non-disabled 25-year-old male with educational/vocational attainment below GCSE level but employed, at the time of his accident, as a process operator in a factory on £15,000 net per annum doing heavy work. His lifetime earnings to retirement age 65 would have been £15,000 x a multiplier of 37.31, i.e. £559,560. If he had been disabled prior to the accident by reason of congenital brain damage, the calculation would become £15,000 x 23.37 being £350,550. So if by dint of an acquired brain injury he could no longer work at all the insurers would be nearly £250,000 better off, all other things being equal.

In the example above the claimant's likely progression may have been limited. The neuropsychological assessment of the position pre-accident becomes particularly important if that claimant argues that he had been marking time on the labour market for a particular reason (for example, looking after an elderly relative) but would have obtained further qualifications and aimed to become an engineer in Formula 1.

Alternatively the claimant may present a range of potential employment scenarios. The younger the claimant, the more likely that is. At the time of writing

---

13 [2015] EWCA Civ 773.
14 [2013] ICR 59.

Covid-19 is looking likely to import great uncertainty in some fields for a number of years, and it seems possible that claimants will have to start to look at providing multiple scenarios. There has already been case law on the question of multiple scenarios: *X, Y, Z v Portsmouth Hospitals NHS Trust* [2011] EWHC 243. The trial judge was faced with an assessment of how the claimant's business career would have gone: he might have successfully launched a multi-million pound business, it might have been less successful, there might have been an equity partner. The court calculated out each of the models and applied a percentage likelihood to each, thus achieving an overall figure. It is not difficult to see how in suitable cases a neuropsychological assessment could underpin such a calculation and for that matter prospects following a brain injury.

A claimant is under a duty to reasonably mitigate losses. So, for example, if a brain injury causes a claimant to resign as a senior investment banker because of difficulties managing the immediacy and pressure of such a role but she still has the capability to be an analyst, working at a more predictable and gentle pressure, then she would be expected to do so, all assuming such a job was likely to be available. Even if the claimant could obtain a similar investment banker position she would not be expected to do so. The neuropsychological assessments will underpin the parties' contentions. The assessments may, for example, indicate that problems are likely to be primarily psychiatric, and therefore potentially 'fixable'.

Care/therapies

The importance of neuropsychological input here relates principally to two aspects:

a   Where there were neuropsychological issues prior to the index accident, what care/support/case management/therapies would have been required,
b   Looking forwards, what care/support/case management/therapies might the claimant require?

So, for example, neuropsychological assessment might indicate the need (or suggest that the need would have been there in any event) for memory aids. It may indicate a need for neuropsychological therapies. It may indicate that some potential therapies are not going to be of value.

Sometimes the neuropsychological assessment may reveal underlying problems independent of the index brain injury that might have in effect extinguished any effect of a more subtle brain injury: for example Wernicke-Korsakoff syndrome, a life threatening illness caused by thiamine deficiency sometimes indicative of an alcohol issue: the prognosis might be dreadful, equally the treatment modalities might well need to be addressed in the context of the acquired brain injury for which the defendant is responsible, say by provision of support to absolutely ensure medication is taken.

Capacity

Finally we come to the issue of capacity to conduct litigation and capacity to manage property and affairs.

Capacity is assessed in relation to the decision or activity in question.

Section 2 of the Mental Capacity Act 2005 provides that a person lacks capacity in relation to a matter if at the material time he is unable to make a decision for himself in relation to the matter because of an 'impairment of, or a disturbance in the functioning of, the mind or brain'.

Note that pursuant to section 1(3) of the 2005 Act a person is not to be treated as unable to make a decision unless all practicable steps to help him to do so have been taken without success.

Pursuant to section 3 of the 2005 Act a person is unable to make a decision for himself if he is unable to

1. understand the information relevant to the decision
2. retain that information
3. use or weigh that information as part of the process of making the decision
4. communicate his decision (whether by talking, using sign language or any other means).

It is provided that information relevant to a decision includes information about the reasonably foreseeable consequences of deciding one way or another, or of failing to make the decision.

Note that making an unwise decision does not mean that someone is to be treated as not being able to make a decision.

The expert has to assess whether the person being assessed has an impairment of the mind or brain, or whether there is some sort of disturbance affecting the way their mind or brain works, whether the impairment or disturbance is temporary or permanent. Then, if so, does that impairment/disturbance mean that the person is unable to make the decision in question at the time it needs to be made? Four sub-assessments follow:

a. Does the person have a general understanding of what decision they need to make and why they need to make it?
b. Does the person have a general understanding of the likely consequences of making, or not making, this decision?
c. Is the person able to understand, retain, use and weigh up the information relevant to this decision?
d. Can the person communicate his or her decision?

Time and again these tests throw up problems ranging from the banal (a difficult, long journey to the assessment) to unspoken crises or concerns (an example of which can be worries about what will happen to children in consequence of the assessment) via inadequate time for the assessment and accidental failure to take non-psychiatric medication or even diabetic issues. It really is incumbent on the assessor to take a careful and wide look so far as possible.

Capacity also needs to be in the neuropsychologist's mind and indeed the legal team's mind where there has been a lasting power of attorney. Sadly the authors' experience is that all too often LPAs[15] are advised and executed with inadequate consideration as to capacity, and whilst the specific issue based 2005 Act test may well pose a lower threshold for a decision to have an LPA in favour (for example) of a family friend or relative, in fact – where there is litigation afoot – the decision may be complex. Equally, where there has been a brain injury to someone in the late years of life it may be the case that there was not capacity to enter into an LPA even before the index accident.

It is absolutely essential that the neuropsychological assessment sets out the background to the assessment and the train of logic with regard to capacity in detail. That is particularly important for cases on the cusp of capacity because insurers will rightly be concerned about the costs of deputyship, particularly where there is a long life expectancy and that can escalate into a position where settlement becomes difficult. There may be particular problems where capacity is likely to fluctuate, or where there is presently capacity but a concern as to the long term.

Supporting the neuropsychologist

As noted at the outset, the neuropsychologist does not act in a vacuum.
The lawyers can help in several ways. These are outlined below.
Firstly, calm reflection:

a   Ascertaining the nature of the injury to the head particularly in mild TBI cases.
b   If the accident involved impact to the head and/or high deceleration forces; might there have been a TBI?
c   Obtaining contemporaneous notes of the accident – both medical and non-medical – and reviewing carefully can assist. Ambulance and Helicopter Emergency Medical Service notes can be particularly helpful in capturing details of the accident circumstances. In respect of non-medical notes, police reports in RTAs, accident book entries and the file from the Health and Safety Executive (HSE) in accident at work cases can all help to build up a picture of the mechanism of the accident that can assist the medical experts.
d   Do the medical records and history suggest some pre-accident problems?

Lawyers should start thinking about financial losses at the outset of the claim. In relation to loss of earnings if the claimant cannot give a history and his/

---

15 Lasting Power of Attorney.

her own assessment of prospects, what is the family background? Are there individuals that the injured person worked with pre-accident that can assist and provide witness evidence? Clearly, there can be a very substantial overlap with psychiatric injury, but the core questions of what happened in the index accident (or if, for example, by clinical negligence then intra-operatively) are critical to the investigation process and formulating the questions for the experts identified as being required.

The next issue is obtaining documentation. Obviously, some items in the list below will be more or less relevant to the individual case, and whether you are acting for claimant or defendant.

a   Medical records – make sure they are continuous and full, and also ascertain if there has been a problem in terms of either a GP being dismissive or the client not feeling able to discuss matters with his or her doctor? Consider having a medical chronology and prepare to highlight any notes or scans that may be missing. Have the notes then paginated to assist the medics with easy reference within reports.
b   Therapy records – these may be very difficult to obtain from psychotherapists, and experience tells that the quality of records ranges from the abominable to the exquisite. Many are handwritten, and they need to be reviewed on receipt in case help is needed to decipher them. These records are also often destroyed early – particularly psychotherapy records – so there is no time to waste.
c   School records/LEA records: including up to date reports and projections. Where pre-accident behaviour/capability is an issue, just because a child about whom you have concerns has not been statemented, does not mean that there is not a problem. S/he may have been educated at a school specialising for example in behavioural issues, and so was never statemented.
d   Social Services records (which may lead to Multidisciplinary Team records, and possible Police involvement).
e   Employment records. Note that increasingly these may not show the full story – when did you last see an adverse reference? Or a highly critical (reasoned) assessment? Equally there may be a slant to the records which the claimant or his her family can explain, so there needs to be discussion.
f   Housing records.
g   MOT records: it is sometimes the case that a claimant will maintain that he or she is no longer able to drive or drive far. If you have the registration number of the vehicle you can simply go online (google MOT history and the DVLA site will come up) from where you can check the annual mileage.
h   If applicable, case management records, and carer records.
i   Freedom of information requests are often useful methods for finding out a wealth of information, such as: how likely a young person may have been successful in their career aspirations, or if a claimant was likely to have received health and social care before the brain injury.

16 *Legal principles in litigation*

Witness statements need a lot of work to do justice to a case. They should paint a picture of how the claimant was before the index accident in full detail and how they are now. View them as the opportunity for the Claimant and his/her family to tell the court and the Defendants how day-to-day life has been affected.

a   Firstly identify who you want to take statements from and indeed who is willing to provide a statement. This will be shaped by the issues in the case but can range from close family to wider family and friends. If there is an issue as to employment path, look to get statements from school teachers (where the claimant is young enough to be remembered), former employers, former colleagues. Ask the employer if career progression data including earnings is available. Some – for example the armed services – may be able to provide decent projections. Some former colleagues may be able to give statements as comparators if they have progressed in their career as the Claimant says they would have done.

b   Consider how to take those statements whether that be in person, over the telephone or virtually. How will you get the best evidence from your witness? Normally this flows from establishing an environment of trust and also if they come prepared to speak to you. It is helpful to give people notice and time to reflect, before taking the statement and explaining the purpose of it to them.

c   You want to encompass within the statement, a look at family life and interactions with friends, hobbies, and habits. Set out the Claimant's education history and track it through to the employment (if relevant) at the time of the accident. Within that, draw out anything that is relevant about school history, medical conditions and future employment prospects.

d   Contrast the pre-accident life with the post-accident life, what the claimant now enjoys, what is difficult, hopes and fears, whether family and friend interactions have been kept up and if so how, if not how and why things went wrong.

e   Look at decision making in everyday life – e.g. money management, how information is stored/filed by the claimant. Identify positive and negative stimuli, identify fatigue and engagement levels. Set out the medication history.

f   With all of the above, examples are key.

g   Allow time to reflect back on witness statements following an initial discussion with the identified witnesses. Cross reference evidence with the disclosure you have received which may then lead to second and even third discussions to explore points further to truly build up a full and complete picture of what life was like and is like.

All of this information is going to assist the neuropsychologist.

If you are defending a claim then you are going to lack primary source material but you may have the advantage of being able to step back and decide what disclosure should exist, and match that against what disclosure the claimant's lawyers are providing. Where the indications are, for example, that the claimant may have a troubled background involving brushes with the law be prepared to require the claimant to apply for criminal records. Where there are indications of pre-index accident claims, insist on disclosure of medical evidence, witness statements, pleadings and orders and any terms of settlement. Always ask yourself whether you are being given the disclosure you might expect to be out there.

The opportunities to obtain witness evidence as a defendant will be limited.

Where there are concerns as to a claimant's bona fides then you will need to consider full social media intelligence reports. It is quite remarkable what emerges of use, whether directly or indirectly. An example: an allegedly significantly brain injured claimant pictured in a rowing boat in busy tidal waters, well out from shore with his children. Someone with a significant brain injury may still be capable of rowing, but if his partner took the picture for social media why would she have let the claimant be doing this?

The defendant will also need to consider surveillance. The surveillance may act just as much as a confirmation of the scale of the claim as undermine it, and may be of value if it does provide confirmation.

On receipt of the report

On receipt of the report, obviously check carefully but compare the report against what you know. Are there omissions? Do the findings and conclusions reflect expectations?

Whether acting for claimants or defendants, try to bear in mind the need to have a time difference in the assessments of the parties – opinions vary but in our experience never less than four months and usually six months. That will impact on court timetables. Of course, the neuropsychologists should be invited to share data.

Finally, we come to the issue of credibility. The neuropsychological tests can be telling here: whilst psychiatric issues can and do affect effort testing, sometimes the claimant's results are simply unreliable or uninterpretable. Another thing to look out for is a mismatch between reported limitations and what the neuropsychological testing reveals. Go through the individual test outcomes.

Concluding remarks

This chapter has set out core legal principles and practical issues surrounding and underpinning the management of brain injury cases with an emphasis on the neuropsychological perspective. Issues such as mental capacity, quantum and central other medicolegal issues to the neuropsychologist are explored within this handbook.

Part 1

'But for' the brain injury and causation

3 Premorbid abilities

Cognition, emotion and behaviour

Martin Bunnage with Marc Willems QC

In a typical personal injury claim it is necessary to prove, on the balance of probabilities, that the event(s) giving rise to the claim have, in some way, affected the person bringing the claim, and those effects have had a negative consequence for that person in their life.

The person bringing the claim needs to prove they are different after the event(s) compared with how they were before the event(s).

To be able to confidently assert someone is different now from how they were before it is necessary to understand what that person is like now and of course what they were like before. This methodology is most relevant when trying to determine changes in adults, i.e. people in whom we expect a relatively stable cognitive, emotional and behavioural/personality picture because they have completed neurodevelopment. This chapter is focused on these comparisons in adults, as distinct from the comparisons that need to be made when considering a developing child or young adult (see chapter by Kent, Tonks, Williams & Brownhill et al in this volume). For these latter comparisons, where neurodevelopment is still in progress when an injury takes place, it would be more accurate to describe the comparison as one between where the person is now and where they were expected to be now if the injury had not occurred, and their developmental trajectory had continued as anticipated.

In clinical neuropsychology practice how the person was, and now is, with respect to their cognitive skills and abilities, their emotions and their behaviour/personality is commonly the focus of attention, these facets potentially being affected by brain damage.

In clinical neuropsychology there are many well researched and theoretically grounded tools and approaches that allow for the detailed characterisation of what someone is like *now* in terms of their cognitive function, emotional/psychological function and behaviour/personality. There are also some specific methods within clinical neuropsychology designed to help determine what someone was like before in terms of their cognitive function. In typical clinical or medico-legal work these specific methods are usually combined with the other commonly available approaches to understanding the past, i.e. records and self/other report, to arrive at an estimate of how someone was likely performing historically.

DOI: 10.4324/9781003105763-4

In both a clinical and medico-legal context it is necessary to try and understand how someone was functioning before they presented to healthcare. In both contexts this allows for a better understanding of the person's pre-injury context and what has likely changed, if anything. How any changes or problems might relate to what happened to someone and/or their pre-injury context can then be considered, ultimately leading to hypotheses about what the best approach(s) might be for improving things for the person concerned. In clinical neuropsychology the above process is broadly represented by the idea of a 'formulation' of what is going on in a particular case. The accuracy of a formulation is dependent upon the accuracy of the information feeding into the formulation, the quality of the research evidence base regarding the issues at hand, and the thoughtfulness and experience of the clinician involved.

Clinical Neuropsychology is most commonly focused on the cognitive, emotional and behavioural/personality effects of damage, disease or dysfunction affecting the brain. Typically then understanding how someone was functioning prior to and subsequent to the event in question in terms of their cognitive ability, emotional function and behaviour/personality is uppermost in the mind of the clinician. The broader context of functioning, to include for example, a person's physical capacity, is of course also relevant but less commonly the detailed focus of attention.

Broadly speaking there are different sources of evidence commonly considered by clinicians when trying to understand the question of how someone was functioning before. These include:

1. Current 'self-report' and 'others-report' about the past, i.e. what someone tells you now about how they were functioning before, or what someone else tells you now about how the person was functioning before. This evidence is commonly obtained through an interview with the person and / or significant others or through witness statements.
2. Past contemporary report / record, i.e. what was documented at times in the past about the person's ability or functioning. This evidence is commonly obtained through records, such as medical records, educational records or social services records, for example.
3. Statistical probability, i.e. what the most common state is in the population of people to which the person belongs. This evidence is commonly derived from empirical sources and the research evidence base.
4. Scientifically predicted, i.e. what someone's ability is predicted to have been in the past based on empirical correlation data relating a currently measurable entity to the area(s) of functioning from the past we are interested in.

In a typical clinical or medico-legal encounter all of these sources are evidence that are relied upon to varying degrees when estimating a person's pre-injury neuropsychological function. Each source of evidence has strengths and weaknesses which will be explored below.

Current 'self-report' and 'others-report' about the past

A key advantage of evidence from this source is it is usually readily available and highly contextualised. Asking people what is different now, compared with how they were before will often result in a host of symptoms, changes or problems being reported. This is very helpful in appreciating the person's perspective/perception of what is different for them or their life now compared with before.

However, such report of a person's past is subject to a host of potential biases that can potentially affect both what is reported and its accuracy (Stone et al, 2000).

It cannot be assumed there is always complete agreement of understanding between the person asking and the person answering questions as to what specific questions or terms mean. The interpretation of even apparently simple questions is somewhat subjective and would therefore influence what is reported. The order in which questions are asked and how they are asked influences what is reported and the subjective interpretation of terms such as 'serious' or 'significant' can also influence whether something is reported or not. Furthermore, the normal way in which human memory systems work also influences what is remembered and subsequently recalled.

For example, in their study, Don and Carragee (2009) compared the report of past symptoms of pain, past drug and alcohol use, past psychological diagnoses and the past pre-existing medical conditions of diabetes or hypertension with the actual historic medical records of a group of 335 patients, of which approximately 65% were in litigation. Overall their findings indicated that 76% of the subjects who were found to have one or more pre-existing comorbid conditions at record audit (alcohol abuse, illicit drugs use and psychological diagnosis) did not report this in the post-accident history. This percentage was increased to 89% in the subgroup that perceived the accident in which they were involved to be the fault of someone else.

Current mood state can affect what is reported, including in relation to the past. Someone who is depressed at the time they are being interviewed, for example, will potentially, amongst other memory effects, report things in a more negative light than would be the case if they were not depressed (Clark and Teasedale, 1982).

As well as past symptoms, problems and experiences Clinical Neuropsychologists will commonly ask about a person's pre-injury educational and employment history. The reason for this is because of the association that exists between attainment in these areas and a person's level of cognitive ability. Methods founded on these associations are noted in more detail below, but at this juncture it is worth observing the potential unreliability of the self-report of key pieces of information, such as education attainment, that feed into these methods. Kuncel et al (2005), for example, compared actual educational attainment (grade point averages) with report of the same by healthy individuals. In a group of 640 people reporting their college level GPA, 34%

over-estimated their level of achievement, and 9% under-estimated it. Accuracy of report was better when looking at high-school GPA, where only 12% reported a higher performance. Within the context of litigation, however, the study of Greiffenstein et al (2002), noted an over-estimate of educational attainment by more than 1 GPA in 39% of a litigating head injury group compared with only 3% of a control group.

The report from others about how someone was before is sometimes also available. This can be a useful additional perspective on the past, but it is important to also recognise the subjective nature of such report and the potential biases and motivations that could influence what is reported.

So the report of a person about their past is a helpful source of evidence in understanding what someone was like before, providing a context and richness like no other source. It should not be assumed, however, that such a report is reliable in every respect without, wherever possible, independent corroboration of what is reported because it is normal for there to be biases and errors in a person's recall of how they were in the past.

Case example

The most common 'mistake' made with regard to self-report and other's report in relation to trying to understand a person's past is to accept uncritically all that has been said. Doing so, without consideration of the above issues, leads to a situation where there is an increased chance of conflating an individual's perception of their past with an externally verifiable 'truth' of their past.

An example would be the report of an individual following an injury, that in organic and psychological terms was very minor/mild, that indicated they felt they currently had a host of problems which they did not have in the past. Their report of their past was that they were always happy, never anxious and always able to concentrate and remember things. Such a report might be accurate, but more likely probably reflects the consequences of a somewhat biased perception of the past, akin to the 'good old days' bias, where things in the past are seen more favourably than the present (Iverson et al, 2010).

Past contemporary report/record

Records are commonly available both in clinical and medico-legal encounters. Usually the breadth and depth of records available within a litigation context is greater than those routinely available in a clinical context.

A key advantage of this source of evidence in relation to how a person was functioning in the past is that it benefits from having been created contemporaneously in the past, and usually by someone other than the patient/ claimant. These advantages mean it is assumed the content of the records will more accurately reflect what occurred at the time because there was little opportunity for things to have been forgotten or miss-recalled. It is further presumed, usually, that the records will be a less biased reflection of what happened because they were created prior to whatever reason the patient/claimant is now presenting.

Experience shows, however, that contemporary records are not infallible (Aaronson and Burman, 1994) and commonly lack a contextual narrative that allows for a full understanding of the meaning of what has been written. Comments such as "depression", "anxiety" or "memory problems" written in the medical records have an ambiguous meaning, potentially reflecting a severe level of psychopathology or cognitive impairment or a very ordinary level of emotional distress and everyday forgetfulness. Corroboration by the patient/claimant of what is written in the records is usually helpful in properly contextualising the information.

What is written in a medical record, also, to some extent reflects the priorities of the time and the preferences and interpretations made by the person during the encounter. To that extent they may be biased in that they reflect a snapshot of what was judged by the person writing them to be the most relevant and pertinent aspects of the encounter.

Lastly, the absence of entries in the records should not be assumed to reflect the absence of any problems or issues in the past. Records will only be created if an encounter occurs, and this will only happen if the person perceived themselves to have a problem of sufficient severity to seek help. Even then *where* someone seeks help from will vary depending on individual preferences and perceptions regarding the role of professionals of the kind that keep records, such as healthcare professionals.

So while the records relating to a person's past are a helpful source of evidence in understanding what someone was like before, providing independence and contemporaneousness, like no other source, they should not be assumed to be infallible or 'complete'. They reflect the biases of the specific author who generated them and the context in which they were generated. In cases where little or nothing has been noted in the records it is helpful to remember that an absence of evidence is not the same as evidence of an absence. As before, corroboration of the information derived from the records is often helpful.

Case example

The most common 'mistakes' made with regard to past report/record is to presume an interpretation of information that is actually somewhat ambiguous and/or to interpret the absence of evidence as evidence of absence.

An example would be to interpret the two entries in the GP record labelled 'depression' as indicating a person had a severe mental health difficulty with mood. While this is a possibility it could also be possible the records reflected a GP's shorthand summary of a person's unhappiness and low mood occurring within the context of divorce, for example. Contextualising the record is usually needed in order to disambiguate commonly used shorthand terminology such as 'depression' or 'memory problems'.

Statistical probability

When thinking about how someone was in the past, particularly when considering how they would have performed on a metric of any sort, such as a measure of memory ability, or intellectual ability, it is helpful to observe the mathematics that typically underpin the measurement of psychological phenomenon in a clinical encounter.

In clinical neuropsychology it is common to make use of a psychometric approach to sampling a patient/claimant's current functioning in terms of cognitive, emotional and other psychological processes. This typically involves the reliable measurement of a theoretically supported psychological construct, such as memory for example, using a standardised tool. The use of a standardised tool allows for the derivation of a metric, i.e. memory performance, which can be compared with the performance of others who have also taken the same test. Clinically valuable measures have usually been given to many other people to derive a representative 'normative' dataset against which to compare an obtained score.

A typical cognitive test given to a large representative sample of people of interest, commonly a 'normal'/non-clinical group, will yield a range of scores across individuals within the group. Some will score better than others, some worse and the vast majority will be somewhere in the middle. The resulting distribution of scores is called a 'normal distribution', or sometimes a 'bell curve'. Within this distribution there are different ways to describe 'average', i.e. the modal values within the distribution. Using the labels presented within Wechsler tests (Wechsler, 2008) 'average' reflects a score that falls between 90 and 109, which corresponds to the middle 50% of the population sampled. An alternative definition of average reflects a score falling within one standard deviation either side of the mean score of the population. With this definition 68% of people would be considered average.

These facts may, at first, not appear to be a source of evidence at all in relation to a particular person's likely standing, pre-event, on a test. However, what these statistical properties suggest is, when knowing nothing else about a person, you are more often right than wrong if you say the person was likely to have been average. When using the first definition 50% of people are average and 25% are above and 25% are below average. So suggesting average each time would be correct ½ of the time, whereas saying someone was above or below average would be correct ¼ of the time. In the second definition even more people fall within the average range, 68%, with 16% above and 16% below average. So, when using this definition, saying somewhat was likely to have been average will be right approximately 7 out of 10 times.

Therefore, absent any evidence to the contrary, assuming someone was average, from a psychometric point of view, is likely to be a rational way of estimating pre-event ability much of the time.

Case example

A common 'mistake' is to forget that 'average' is the most common state, by definition, and to conflate terminology such that psychometrically average performance on a cognitive test is considered synonymous with an individual *being* average.

Scientifically predicted

The last area to be discussed in relation to knowing what someone was probably like before is effectively an elaboration upon, and refinement of, the above 'statistical probability' proposition. Two different approaches can be used. In one approach performance on a contemporaneously measured word-reading test is used to predict likely past performance on other tests of cognitive ability, usually an IQ test. In the other approach key demographic data, sometimes with the addition of contemporaneously measured cognitive performance, is used to predict past performance on other tests of cognitive function, again usually an IQ test.

With regard to the word-reading test approach, performance on a test of reading of irregularly spelled words is undertaken post-injury. This performance is assumed to be the same post-injury as it would have been in the past, based on early research showing the lack of an effect of brain damage on this ability. The correlation between performance on this measure and performance on other measures of cognitive ability is then used to 'predict' the likely level of past performance on the other tests, given the obtained performance on the word-reading test.

More contemporary research has, however, challenged the assumption that performance is not affected by brain damage and a number of studies show that it can be in some situations, i.e. with dementia and with traumatic brain injury in some circumstances (McFarlane et al, 2006; Cockburn et al, 2000; Freeman et al, 2001; Morris et al, 2005). Additionally it is important to appreciate the limited validity of a word-reading test-based approach in people with development or acquired language problems, in people with atypical access to education and in people for whom English is not their dominant language.

Furthermore, most of the research using this method has focused on predicting performance on an IQ test, rather than on a full range of different cognitive abilities. The research that has been done also shows a variable degree of correlation between word-reading test performance and performance in the areas sampled by an IQ test. As a consequence, this method is likely better at predicting verbal crystallised abilities than it is at predicting some other abilities (Law and O'Carroll, 1998; Watt and O'Carroll, 1999).

In addition, the magnitude of the correlations between word-reading performance and performance in other areas of cognitive ability suggests the confidence intervals (i.e. the statistical certainty of the prediction, or put another way the margin of error/uncertainty around the prediction) associated with the predictions are likely to be relatively large, indicating a range of likely prior ability levels, rather than a confident prediction of ability within just a narrow range of scores.

With regard to the demographic approach the correlation between facets of an individual and their cognitive ability level is used as the basis for a prediction equation. Educational attainment and occupational level are typically used as important predictors (Crawford and Allan, 1997). However, as with the word-reading test approach, the confidence intervals around the predictions derived from these equations is relatively large, i.e. a *range* of likely scores is predicted. Furthermore, as noted earlier, the self-report of a person's educational history, which is typically included in these prediction equations, may be imperfect which can also affect the accuracy of the prediction.

Finally, while these methods and approaches have their merits it is important to remember the correlations that form the basis of the predictions are not perfect and there will be people who have combinations of educational experience, employment experience, and underlying cognitive ability who deviate from the typical. For example, there are people who have very high levels of cognitive ability, but for one reason or another have not engaged well with formal education. Possibly, for example, because of a specific learning difficulty like dyslexia, or because of parental mental health difficulties while they were growing up, which resulted in them achieving school exam results below their true ability and consequently led to them being under-employed.

So while the more statistically based methods noted above are a helpful source of evidence in understanding what someone was like before, from a cognitive perspective, they predict some areas of ability better than others, and typically predict a *range* of possible premorbid scores on a test/area of function, rather than a single score. As with all the approaches noted above, corroboration of the information derived from these statistical methods is usually helpful.

Case examples

The most common 'mistakes' with regard to this methodology are to forget/ignore the margin of error associated with the predictions, and/or to ignore relevant contextual details, or to include irrelevant contextual details, which impact on the accuracy of any predictions.

An example of the former would be to declare an individual's pre-injury IQ to be 110 and then to assume their performance on all other cognitive tests administered should fall at this level and any deviation from this level must reflect a deterioration. Doing so ignores the margin of error associated with the prediction (i.e. the person's pre-injury level is not an IQ of 110 but rather is, for example, an IQ somewhere between 95 and 125). It also ignores the different degree to which different cognitive abilities are associated with IQ/word-reading test performance. For example, verbal crystallised intellectual skills are more closely correlated with word-reading performance, and therefore should be more reliably predicted (i.e. with a smaller confidence interval), than some other abilities, like memory, for example. Scores on tests of the latter may therefore, in the above example, deviate further from the predicted IQ score of 110 without necessarily reflecting a decline in ability (i.e. because of the larger confidence interval of prediction).

One example of the latter would be to declare an individual's pre-injury cognitive ability to be low on the basis of the prediction made using a word-reading test without acknowledging they had a pre-existing history of dyslexia and self-declared lack of interest in reading books. These would arguably likely reduce their vocabulary for more obscure words without necessarily reflecting their level of cognitive ability in areas other than reading.

A further example of the latter, but in the other direction, would be to declare an individual's pre-injury cognitive ability to be high on the basis of their salary, despite their average performance in education and on a word-reading test, and their chosen employment being one that is not heavily dependent on cognitive skills.

Conclusion

Creating a reliable picture of what someone was like before in terms of their cognitive function, emotions and behaviour/personality is difficult.

There are different approaches to understanding what a person was like in the past, each with strengths and weaknesses.

The prediction of pre-injury cognitive function is currently more scientifically advanced within clinical neuropsychology than the prediction of other areas of function/ability.

The use of multiple methods corroborating one another increases the chances of obtaining a reliable picture of what someone was like before. Even then, estimates of prior function are likely to encompass a degree of uncertainty.

Where different sources of evidence diverge or disagree it is important to appreciate the inherent strengths and limitations associated with each source of evidence.

When there is a discrepancy between the self-reported history and all other sources of evidence, particularly when those other sources are consistent, it is important to consider the basis for such biased reporting, noting that biases in the recall of information happen for a host of potential reasons.

Legal perspective provided by Marc Willems QC of Cobden House Chambers

The litigation process following a head injury and/or a brain injury, when compensatory damages are required to return an individual to the position that they would have been in but for the accident, necessarily involves careful analysis of an individual's premorbid cognition, emotion and behaviour with a comparison to post-accident presentation and abilities.

The litigation process most typically benefits from a combination of the use of psychometric testing to evaluate premorbid cognitive ability and functioning with a comparison to post-accident ability and functioning. The more serious the brain injury, the more useful modern radiological techniques such as CT scanning, Magnetic Resonance Imaging scanning (MRI) and PET scans (Positron Emission Topography) are to this assessment. Counterintuitively the more seriously injured an individual is, the easier it is to establish a causative link between the accident and the Claimant's increased needs arising from that injury. The most complex cases arise with the walking wounded head injured who encounter subtle difficulties after an accident and where neuroradiology provides less or even no assistance. In the latter type of cases, the report of others in the form of witness statements is frequently the best if not the only source of evidence upon which a Court can make an assessment of the effects of an accident event.

Perhaps the most complex litigation cases are those where brain damage is expected to result from a head injury, but radiology does not support this expectation. These cases can initially lead those clinically treating and legally representing an individual with a head injury to conclude that the symptoms exhibited are the effects of brain damage when they are in fact more closely linked to a neuropsychiatric/neuropsychological reaction to the life-threatening event. On occasion symptomatology out of proportion to the actual life-threatening nature of the event is seen. In this situation psychometric testing can pick up levels of anxiety while identifying a modest impact upon cognitive ability and working memory. It is here that witness evidence is essential in establishing profound changes in the individual out of proportion to the actual organic damage visible on brain scanning. It is also here that the most hostile litigation battles occur. Defendants who are backed by litigation sceptical insurance companies often question the veracity of such claims. Concerns are raised that the Claimant's lawyers have rushed to put in place clinical rehabilitation aimed at treating a brain injury when no such damage has occurred thereby convincing the Claimant that they are brain damaged and perpetuating their suffering and as a result their claim.

Another smaller cohort of individuals who can present with consequences which are seemingly out of proportion to the level of damage occasioned are those functioning at particularly high levels such as athletes and successful professionals. A modest reduction in function of single digit percentage levels can lead a high-functioning individual to no longer be or perceive themselves to be the best in their field with disproportionate and occasionally catastrophic reductions in functional ability.

A case study of a high-functioning professional financial adviser[1] involved a Claimant who suffered a serious head injury when a goalpost fell upon him while watching a rugby match causing a fractured skull but suffered no

---

1 *Morrow -v- Shrewsbury Rugby Union Football Club Limited* [2020] EWHC 379.

organic brain damage and no loss of cognitive ability based upon the psychometric testing performed. Nevertheless, the accident and the stress of being unable to work and return to a particularly demanding but rewarding post caused an increase in anxiety and a fear that the individual's self-identity as a successful financial adviser would be lost forever. The initial fear following the fractured skull was that a significant brain injury had been suffered but when exhaustive radiological examination and psychometric testing identified that this was not the case, the individual concerned who had been treated with cognitive behavioural therapy on the basis that he suffered a brain injury was left with the almost similarly devastating diagnosis that he was no longer able to function as a result of a psychological injury and the psychiatric effects of the accident and its consequent stress being imposed upon a vulnerable personality.

The individual in question had pre-existing, but controlled, epilepsy which the Court accepted was reactivated as a result of the build-up of stress caused by not being able to work. In addition he was diagnosed as having an anankastic personality which allowed him to function particularly successfully in his chosen field because he was able to channel his obsessive characteristics into his work. The examination of the evidence identified that the individual had long downplayed his anxiety levels and a pre-existing somatoform disorder prior to the head injury in order to maintain his position in the workplace. He was deemed, correctly, to be vulnerable pre-accident to such trauma having an 'eggshell skull personality'.[2] The analysis by the Court of neuropsychological and neuropsychiatric evidence presented on both sides led the Court to conclude that the individual would not have been able to suppress the pre-existing somatoform disorder and anankastic personality for the remainder of his career because, as he progressed through his career, the work stresses upon him would increase and the ageing process would reduce his coping abilities such that he would, eventually, have been unable to deal with the work demands upon him. The anankastic personality that preceded the accident was what enabled the individual Claimant to reach the heights of a demanding career but ironically would also inevitably lead to the point at which the individual could not maintain the emotional and psychological effort required to function at continued high levels.

The Court was assisted in this situation from the evidence of previous work colleagues and could see from earning levels and the nature of the work involved that the Claimant was using all available energy and emotional resources to maintain his high-standing position within the business. Hence his vulnerability to any further insult or trauma such as the fractured skull sustained in the accident.

---

2 The legal concept of taking a victim as you find him allows those with an eggshell skull personality who suffer disproportionate effects arising from another's negligence to be fully compensated despite occasionally suffering relatively minor initial injury.

Other cases involving vulnerable individuals who respond unusually and sometimes catastrophically to head injury without the radiologically identified organic brain damage upon scanning to justify the loss of function are reasonably common in civil litigation. Conditions such as conversion disorder in extreme cases can arise but more typically the effect of a head injury will merely amplify pre-existing characteristics and courts are sympathetic to the notion that an individual who previously may have had below average cognitive ability would have fewer resources to draw upon in order to compensate in the face of a subsequent brain injury. In the case of *Killilea -v- Aviva Insurance UK Limited* (2018) the individual had a history of behavioural problems with antisocial and challenging behaviours from an early age at school with multiple school exclusions and was described by the neuropsychologists as a young man of limited intellectual ability with a premorbid intellectual ability which was probably below average. Post-accident the neuropsychologists agreed through psychometric testing and based upon the witness statements available that there was neuro-behavioural disturbance/personality change which compounded his previous difficulties.

In such a case as the latter, the impact of an accident upon an individual's earning capacity may be relatively limited because the pre-accident prospects were themselves limited and the need for increased care and/or support in order to live independently may be relatively modest but the effect of the accident may be such that their capacity to litigate in itself and their capacity to manage their property and affairs may be reduced such that they could never manage the award of damages which is a result of the litigation.

The Claimant lawyer will therefore need to obtain witness evidence from those who knew the individual before an accident and, if possible, those who know the individual post-accident. This is not always as straightforward as it may seem. Brain injured individuals will often lose social groups and networks and are not always themselves in a position to assist in identifying potential witnesses or their losses and needs. The family members, if available, are usually a better source of information. The evidence of witnesses is not only of assistance in establishing the functional losses and needs created by the impact of the accident but does also assist the Court in identifying whether an individual has capacity to manage their property and affairs. This has become a significant issue in litigation because of the increasing actual cost of requiring a Financial Deputy and the services of the Court of Protection for the remainder of an individual's life.

The assessment of an individual's earning capacity but for an accident is also fraught with difficulty when an individual does not have a straightforward or easily predicable career path. An assessment of personality as well as cognitive ability and pre-accident function is required to assist in identifying the motivation, employability and eventual earning capacity of individuals who may have only just embarked upon any chosen career path. Brain injury in school children increases the complexity of this evaluation and assessment of loss.

To summarise and conclude, the litigation lawyer needs to be able to evaluate an individual's pre-accident cognitive ability, emotional situation and behaviour in order to be able to compare it to the post-accident situation and the likely future situation. To that end the litigation lawyer's understanding of how someone was functioning prior to and subsequent to the event in question in terms of their cognitive ability, emotional function and behaviour/personality is identical to that of the clinician. The understanding of the post-accident cognitive ability, emotional function and behaviour/personality allows an assessment of an individual's needs. This in turn permits a financial evaluation of those increased needs both current and life long, since such injuries are rarely self-correcting. All this occurs in an adversarial litigation process where the Claimant is lawfully attempting to maximise the damages recoverable based upon the medico-legal evidence obtained and the Defendant, equally lawfully, is attempting to minimise the damages recoverable.

It is the challenges implicit in this process that create the acknowledged complexity of brain injury litigation. The psychology of the litigation battle would merit a chapter to itself.

References

Aaronson, L.S. and Burman, M.E. (1994). Use of health records in research: reliability and validity issues. *Research in Nursing and Health*, 17 (1), 67–73.

Clark, D.M. and Teasedale, J.D. (1982). Diurnal variation in clinical depression and accessibility of memories of positive and negative experiences. *Journal of Abnormal Psychology*, 91 (2), 87–95.

Cockburn, J., Keene, J., Hope, T. and Smith, P. (2000). Progressive decline in NART scores with increasing dementia severity. *Journal of Clinical and Experimental Neuropsychology*, 22 (4), 508–517.

Crawford, J.R. and Allan, K.M. (1997). Estimating premorbid WAIS-R IQ with demographic variables: Regression equations derived from a UK sample. *The Clinical Neuropsychologist*, 11 (2), 192–197.

Don, A.S. and Carragee, E.J (2009). Is the self-reported history accurate in patients with persistent axial pain after a motor vehicle accident? *The Spine Journal*, 9, 4–12.

Freeman, J., Godfrey, H.P.D., Harris, J.K.J. and Partridge, F.M. (2001). Utility of a demographic equation in detecting impaired NART performance after TBI. *British Journal of Clinical Psychology*, 40, 221–224.

Greiffenstein, M.F., Baker, W.J. and Johnson-Greene, D. (2002). Actual versus self-reported scholastic achievement of litigating postconcussion and severe closed head injury claimants. *Psychological Assessment*, 14 (2), 202–208.

Iverson, G.L., Lange, R.T., Brooks, B.L. and Rennison, V.L.A. (2010). "Good old days" bias following mild traumatic brain injury. *The Clinical Neuropsychologist*, 24 (1), 17–37.

Kuncel, N.R., Crede, M. and Thomas, L.L. (2005). The validity of self-reported grade point averages, class ranks, and test scores: A meta-analysis and review of the literature. *Review of Educational Research*, 75 (1), 63–82.

Law, R. and O'Carroll, R.E. (1998). A comparison of three measures of estimating premorbid intellectual level in dementia of the Alzheimer type. *International Journal of Geriatric Psychiatry, 13*, 727–730.

McFarlane, J., Welch, J. and Rogers, J. (2006). Severity of Alzheimer's disease and effect on premorbid measures of intelligence. *British Journal of Clinical Psychology, 45*, 453–463.

Morris, P.G., Wilson, J.T.L., Dunn, L.T. and Teasdale, G.M. (2005). Premorbid intelligence and brain injury. *British Journal of Clinical Psychology, 44*, 209–214.

Stone, A.A., Turkkan, J.S., Bachrach, C.A., Jobe, J.B., Kurtzman, H.S. and Cain, V.S. (2000). *The Science of Self-Report Implications for Research and Practice*, Lawrence Erlbaum Associates, Inc.NJ.

Watt, K.J. and O'Carroll, R.W. (1999). Evaluating methods for estimating premorbid intellectual ability in closed head injury. *Journal of Neurology, Neurosurgery and Psychiatry, 66*, 474–479.

Wechsler, D. (2008). *Wechsler Adult Intelligence Scale – Fourth Edition, Technical and Interpretive Manual*, NCS Pearson Inc.

4 Neuropsychological testing in brain injury litigation

A critical part of the expert neuropsychological examination

Andrew Worthington and Phil S. Moore

'Man is the measure of all things'

Protagoras (c.490–420 BCE)

Introduction

The courts recognise the important role of neuropsychological evidence in brain injury litigation and the central place within that evidence of neuropsychological testing, which includes not only formal tests of cognitive function but also other measures which have been developed to identify or quantify aspects of cognition, emotion, motivation or behaviour. The neuropsychologist provides an expert opinion based upon a broad-based assessment of documentary evidence, interviews and psychometric evaluation which involves objective and standardised tests and inventories based upon psychometric theory that aim to measure domains of neuropsychological function. These clinical tools, when administered correctly and interpreted carefully can help establish opinion on the nature and extent of neurocognitive change, differentiation between brain injury and other factors, relationships between neurocognitive factors and difficulties in daily functioning. Rather than focused on a research or clinical question, the medicolegal neuropsychological assessment is guided by the legal instruction. Opinion often extends to care and treatment, prognosis and mental capacity.

Following a review of the rationale and principles underlying neuropsychological testing, this chapter will consider the five most common uses of formal psychometric tests as part of the broader neuropsychological examination. Key issues highlighted in the subsequent discussion will be the use of flexible versus fixed batteries, older versus newer tests, appropriate intervals between testing, intra-individual variability in test scores and the recording of neuropsychological examinations. Issues in the assessment of complex cases such as dysphasia, apraxia, visual or hearing-impaired, minimal conscious state and non-English-speaking claimants are also raised.

Cognitive principles underlying neuropsychological testing

The dominant cognitive paradigm underpinning neuropsychological testing is that of modularity, whereby different domains of cognition work in harmony but are essentially separable components. This stands in contrast to all regions of the brain contributing in equal measure to cognitive function which would mean brain injury caused a general depletion of cognitive resources in proportion to the severity of injury. Evidently this does not happen and studies of patients with discrete brain lesion that cause highly specific deficits have contributed greatly to the popularity of modularity as an organising principle (Shallice, 1988), though for a dissenting voice see Plaut (1995). In his seminal monograph Fodor (1983) distinguished between modules which represent computationally autonomous units with limited processing capabilities from non-modular processes (central systems) required for integrating modular information for action. Specialised modular systems rely on general purpose processing resources such as effort and motivation which will also affect performance (see the chapter by Gerhand, Jones and Hacker). In a litigation context this notion of functionally separable information processing modules has to be interpreted in light of any evidence of brain injury in order that a relationship of causation can be established.

There is no rigid prescription of what should be included in a neuropsychological evaluation and it is not the purpose of this chapter to recommend specific tests which will depend on the claimant's condition, test availability and the issues to be addressed. Some specific matters that arise in assessing complex cases are considered later in the chapter. A comprehensive assessment does not involve testing every aspect of cognitive function in minute detail but should encompass the following broad areas which are loosely based on the notion of modular cognition: general intellectual function, attention, information processing, working memory, anterograde memory and learning, language, visuospatial ability and executive skills. Some areas may need assessing in greater detail according to their clinical presentation. Literacy and numeracy may be assessed further with specialist tests, especially in paediatric cases or people with a prior history of such difficulties. Some test batteries will also include measures of motor speed and dexterity. DSM 5 also includes social cognition amongst the domains of relevance for a diagnosis of neurocognitive disorder, although tasks of this nature tend to be research-based and not adequate for medicolegal evidence. Instead, some of the standardised neurobehavioural inventories may be utilised.

Neurological basis of cognitive functions

Lawyers will often ask a neuropsychologist whether the pattern of test results is consistent with the areas of damage on a brain scan. This means trying to equate a functional impairment with a structural lesion which is rarely a straightforward exercise. Research in cognitive neuroscience, aided by the latest brain imaging techniques, has informed understanding of how cognitive modules may be organised in the brain at neural level (see Shallice & Cooper (2011) for a review). Cognitive abilities do not reside in discrete brain compartments and it is more accurate to consider brain functions as being laid out in an overlapping pattern of networks (Catani, 2006). Damage to brain cells (grey matter) after brain injury is not random but follows identifiable network-like patterns (Cauda et al., 2011). This means that damage in one area may affect several functions and damage in different areas may affect the same function. In neuroscience this has led to a revival of interest in disconnection syndromes (Catani, 2005) although the term rarely finds its way into medicolegal reports.

Psychometric principles underlying neuropsychological testing

A basic grasp of the key psychometric principles serves as a refresher for neuropsychologists and is important for lawyers in order to understand (and challenge) the statistical basis of experts' clinical interpretations. The origins of measurement of psychological constructs date from the nineteenth century reflecting a coalescence of varied influences in Europe and the United States in experimental methodology, individual differences, child development and military recruitment. Concepts and tests evolve but modern neuropsychological testing is still influenced by statistical methods developed over a century or more and many of the challenges that face practitioners today would not be unfamiliar to psychological scientists of past generations. Unique amongst medical examinations carried out for the courts, the very practical task of neuropsychological testing is founded on statistical and cognitive principles which make up test theory. Neuropsychological tests are sometimes referred to as psychometric tests because they possess established psychometric properties, which are essential for their interpretation. Crocker and Algina (1986) identified five challenges which test theory seeks to address:

- No single approach to measurement of a construct is universally accepted
- Psychological measurement is based on limited samples of behaviour
- Measurement is always subject to error
- Units of measurement are often poorly defined
- Psychological constructs cannot be defined only in terms of operational definitions but must also have demonstrable relationships to other constructs or observable behaviour

It is axiomatic that the relationship between tests and the functions they measure is imperfect. Implicit in many psychometric tests is the classical notion of a *true score*, a notion associated with the psychologist and statistician Charles Spearman (Levy, 1995) whereas a test score can only ever get close to a true score and is in effect a *random variable* which occurs according to a set of probabilities. There are therefore three elements to assessing a cognitive function as illustrated in Figure 4.1 below: the thing to be measured (underlying construct), the measuring tool and the process of measurement. The ideal neuropsychological test is one in which there is strong correspondence to the cognitive construct it is intended to assess, the cognitive test is robust and reliable, and the process of measurement is uncontaminated by extraneous factors so that the result is a pure measure of the cognitive domain under scrutiny. The challenges of meeting these standards will form the basis for much of what follows in the chapter.

Central to test theory is the notion that the distribution of psychological attributes and abilities in the population conforms to a normal distribution, with most people demonstrating a skill or trait in moderation and fewer people showing very high or very low levels (see Figure 4.2). From this core assumption it is possible to determine a person's position relative to the population as a whole or a specific sub-population (typically people of the same demographic or clinical condition). Data from neuropsychological measures which do not conform to this distribution are often mathematically transformed in order to do so as this aids interpretation and makes it easier to compare across cognitive domains where different tests are used, as theoretically the same metric is being used. For accurate interpretation the person being tested must reasonably be considered to be a member of the population from which the normative sample was drawn. Thus, where the normative data is obtained from a 'healthy' sample which is representative of the general population, the neuropsychologist has to determine whether the obtained scores indicate that individual is a member of that population. In practice this means that if the person was previously assumed to be of average ability the test scores will indicate whether they still belong to that subgroup of the population which scores in the average range.

Comparison with healthy controls assists the court in understanding how far a test score deviates from the population average in order to determine whether it is in some sense abnormal. This is done by converting test scores (raw scores) into a conventional metric (known as a standard score) representing the amount of deviation from the population mean. The most common of these is the standard deviation (SD) which, for the mathematically inclined, is the square root of the variance. Once the standard deviation is known it follows that approximately 68% of scores lie within one SD above

Figure 4.1 The Basis of Neuropsychometric Testing
Source: A. Worthington.

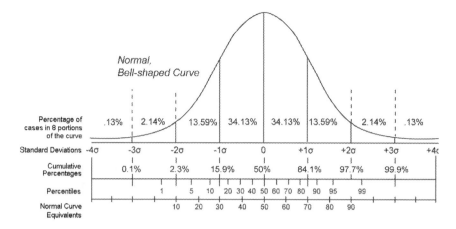

Figure 4.2 The Normal Distribution

and below the population mean and 95% of scores lie within two SDs either side of the mean. Standard scores can therefore be converted to percentiles which is recommended for clinical interpretation (Crawford & Garthwaite, 2009) and the easiest way for non-specialists to understand the distribution of scores. Sometimes by way of shorthand test scores are referred to as impaired or deficient but this is not strictly accurate, a score can only be low or high and low scores may or may not correspond to a deficit. In an attempt to overcome inconsistency in how scores are described in different tests and by different neuropsychologists the American Academy of Clinical Neuropsychology produced a consensus conference statement on uniform labelling (Guilmette et al., 2020). A conversion table of test scores to percentiles using the recommended descriptors is included in an Appendix at the end of the chapter.

Neuropsychologists also use the Standard Error of Measurement (SEM) in calculating the significance of scores and establishing a confidence interval. The SEM shows how far the sample mean is likely to be from the true score if there was no inherent measurement error. Where possible scores should be reported with confidence intervals as this provides an indication of the accuracy of the test score (Crawford & Garthwaite, 2009). A 95% Confidence Interval (95% C.I.) is calculated as 1.96 x SEM, the interval increasing as the SEM increases and also varying between tests and according to age.

Interpretation of clinically meaningful test scores

There are a number of important factors that need to be considered before interpreting any low score as indicative of a deficit and attributing it to a specific cause.

Reliability of test scores

All things being equal, the examinee needs to be confident that a test score obtained on one day will not differ widely from the score obtained if the same were administered on another day or by a different neuropsychologist. This does not mean an identical score would be expected every time but the degree of variation should be minimal and known in advance. Determining reliability during test development can be affected by practice effects and some tests are more susceptible to such influence than others. Neuropsychologists may therefore need to consult data on inter-rater reliability and test/re-test reliability. This will vary from test to test and sometimes according to age, especially in children. It would not usually be incorporated into a medicolegal report unless it raises an important evidential point such as whether a person has really recovered or simply done a test so many times they have learned how to pass.

Premorbid (pre-injury) function

Comparison of test scores with the population average will be misleading for people who were formerly functioning well below or well above this level. Lawyers often ask medical experts to consider the 'but for' scenario, inviting the expert to reflect on a range of pre-existing factors that would have influenced the claimant's life trajectory for better or worse absent the index event. Neuropsychologists are particularly well placed to consider the consequences of any prior cognitive difficulties and to estimate premorbid function (see Bunnage & Willems in this volume). Failure to take this into account increases the risk of missing genuine deficits (false negative errors) in higher functioning examinees. Conversely it raises the risk of false positive errors in lower functioning individuals who are more likely to demonstrate inconsistent domain performances and supposed 'deficits' (Diaz-Asper et al., 2004).

Normal variability

The neuropsychologist also has to determine how likely it is that low scores are clinically significant given that there is a significant number of people who demonstrate 'abnormal' results compared to the population average in one domain and a smaller minority who do so in two domains (Schretlen et al., 2003). Within-person variability is also common; more than 70% of individuals on the Wechsler Adult Intelligence Scale (WAIS)-IV normative sample had at last one of four principal index scores that differed significantly from their index score average (Gregoire, Coalson & Zhu, 2011) though multivariate analysis provides a useful means of evaluating the abnormality of WAIS-IV index sores (Crawford et al., 2012).

The more tests administered, the more low scores one might observe leading to criticism that some experts might engage in 'fishing' for findings (Parker & Szymanski, 1992). Higher IQ also leaves open more room for greater within-person subtest variability (Binder & Binder, 2011). Thus even when differences between test scores are statistically significant such disparities may be quite common and are therefore not clinically meaningful. Neuropsychologists where possible should make explicit reference to base rates of low scores as well as test norms although this information is often lacking. Data in test manuals on the statistical abnormality of test scores is based on univariate analysis, that is, the probability that a particular low score on a test would occur by chance. This does not take account of the fact that such scores are usually obtained alongside many other tests and it is important to know how many low scores are likely when multiple tests are administered. Neuropsychologists should be mindful of multivariate data available for different thresholds of low scores for the Wechsler Memory Scale (WMS)-IV and WAIS-IV batteries (Brooks, Holdnack & Iverson, 2011) and the Delis-Kaplan Executive Function System (D-KEFS) battery of executive function tests (Karr et al., 2018). This is especially helpful for executive tasks as these tend to correlate with intelligence. Thus the authors demonstrate that if two scores from a four-test battery lie at or below the 9th percentile this may be significant for someone of above average functioning as only 6.1% of the normative sample obtained two or more scores at or below this level.

Actuarial data have to be interpreted in clinical context. The same observation of two D-KEFS scores at or below the 9th percentile in a person with no history to suggest cognitive impairment could be considered normal variation because 28.2% of the normative sample showed this pattern (Karr et al., 2018). Importantly, whereas use of base rate data on low scores assumes that incidental low scores will occur randomly across a series of tests, if the overall number of low scores is within the normal range but the distribution seems to cluster around key domains then this may well be clinically significant. For example, the interpretation of results from a claimant of average pre-injury intelligence who shows low scores on 40% of his tests will be different if the low scores occur amidst good scores on a range of cognitive domains than if they occur on every processing speed and working memory test administered in the context of good scores on all other measures.

This highlights another issue rarely addressed which is that normal variation for a given IQ, for example an average IQ of 100, should include some scores higher and lower than this value. If the number of low scores below 100 is within the expected range but no scores are above 100 the neuropsychologist has to consider whether this too represents an unusual result. This requires base rate data on the normal frequency of high scores (i.e. how often will a person of overall average ability obtain a score above this level on a given subtest). Initial data for the D-KEFS battery show high scores are more common the more subtests are administered but even with just three tests 24% of people had at least one test score at the 95th percentile or higher (Karr et al., 2020).

Test specificity and sensitivity

In order to consider the clinical significance of a test score the examiner will usually compare a person's score with a normal sample to determine the deviation from the mean (using the SD or z score) and evaluate the score in terms of its proximity to a hypothetical true score (based on the SEM). The clinician also needs to consider the test score in terms of its classification accuracy, that is how well the test identifies a deficit (such as memory impairment) in people who are genuinely memory impaired and differentiates from healthy people. If it is too easy the test will not be very *sensitive* to memory problems. If it is too difficult even healthy people will perform poorly so in that case low scores will not be *specific* to genuine memory impairment. As Kay (1999) noted, 'those tests most sensitive to any type of brain damage – tests of attention (especially complex attention), concentration, and short term memory are also those least specific to brain damage' (p.149). This applies just as much to identifying genuine deficits as to invalid or non-credible scores (see chapter by Gerhand, Jones and Hacker).

Whilst a specific isolable mental process can be conceptualised in abstract fashion, the reality of assessment is that it cannot be tested in a cognitive vacuum. Take for example a visual memory test involving objects or faces. Even assuming satisfactory sensory function, in order to perform well an examinee has first to be able to understand what the test requires of them, be it in the form of spoken or written instructions. A claimant with receptive dysphasia and/or dyslexia may already be having difficulties. They must be able to perceive the material presented, drawing on the requisite face or object processing skills. A claimant with prosopagnosic impairment or visual form agnosia would fail at this stage. They may need to be able to identify the object in the picture, which would be difficult for someone with an associative agnosia. They must be able to attend throughout the time it takes to present perhaps 50 stimulus items. This could be problematic for a very distractible examinee, one whose mind tended to wander without external on-task prompts or someone preoccupied with their own anxious internal ruminations. Finally, having been presented with all the stimuli the examinee has to be able to demonstrate the recollection the test is designed to assess. But even at this stage there may be problems, not due to memory impairment. If the recognition phase is in the form of a two- or three-way multiple-choice format, any tendency to impulsive behaviour may evoke hasty responses without the examinee first considering and weighing up each option. If the stimuli are presented one at a time a propensity to perseveration may cause the same yes or no answer, repeatedly. An examinee with lateralised inattention may not attend to stimuli on one side of the response booklet. An examinee who responds affirmatively to most items will score high on positive hits but also show a high number of false positive errors. This is different from an examinee who forgets many of the items and consequently shows numerous false negative errors.

Before a test can be considered representative of the cognitive ability it is purported to measure, the neuropsychologist has to take into account the above factors, the overall clinical presentation and nature and location (if known) of the injury. The nature of a person's performance, including type of errors, provides clues to the underlying deficit. Evidence obtained from a variety of tests and other sources must be considered as to the likely impact of confounding sensory and cognitive influences on overall attainment.

Influence of psychological and general health conditions

Neuropsychologists have to apply the same discipline to the effects of general health conditions which may affect cognition as well as mood disturbance or other psychological or psychiatric disorder. Whilst the topic lies outside the scope of the present chapter there are a range of health problems that can have direct cognitive effects. These include diabetes (McCrimmon et al., 2012) chronic kidney disease (Elias et al. (2013), respiratory illness (Dodd et al., (2010) and cardiac disease (Eggermont et al., 2012). In the context of litigation, whilst physical health problems may be attributable to injuries sustained in the index event, they may alternatively reflect premorbid chronic illness and the potential contribution to current cognitive status has to be acknowledged.

Similarly with psychological disorder, whether longstanding or arising since the index injury or illness, the likely effect on cognitive test scores must be considered. The literature in this area is complex and it is difficult to draw clear conclusions. Much depends on the nature of the psychological disorder, its severity and the specific test under scrutiny. Arnett (2013) provides a comprehensive review of the field. Conversely neuropsychological analysis can help to shed light on the nature of neuropsychiatric disturbance (Halligan & Marshall, 1996).

The special case of executive functions

The notion of executive functions refers to a diverse range of higher-level cognitive processes involved in cognitive organisation and behavioural regulation. These include concept acquisition, planning, reasoning, judgment and problem solving, attention control and mental flexibility, as well as behavioural skills of initiation, inhibition, self-monitoring and social-emotional skills. As articulated by Priestley et al. (2013), presenting evidence of executive dysfunction in court can be challenging yet many disabling neurobehavioural disturbances after brain injury are underpinned by executive dysfunction (see Wood & Worthington, 2017). Although sometimes alternatively referred to as 'frontal lobe functions' executive processes rely on subcortical networks outside the frontal lobes and can therefore be disrupted without structural damage to the frontal lobes. Strictly, executive functions are associated with the prefrontal cortex, the largest part of the frontal lobes, and most commonly with the dorsolateral prefrontal region. Different models of executive function emphasise different core characteristics such as attention (Shallice & Burgess, 1991), working memory (Baddeley, 2002), knowledge representation (Wood & Grafman, 2003) and voluntary action (Passingham, 1993). Stuss (2011) has argued for the functional distinction between left dorsolateral (task setting) and right dorsolateral (task monitoring) in addition to a dorso-medial 'energizing' function and ventro-medial/orbital role in emotional and behavioural regulation. These brain regions do not fully mature until the third decade of life and therefore any inferences drawn about status of executive abilities has to take the claimant's age into account.

Tests designed to measure executive functions also rely on integrity of lower-order functions. A concept attainment task, for example, assumes an understanding of the task demands. A word inhibition test entails adequate reading and speaking ability. A verbal fluency task requires good word retrieval in normal circumstances such as conversation or confrontation naming. Executive tasks therefore have what Burgess (1993) described as *task impurity*, for which reason some tests also include a baseline task to assess that the requisite lower-order function is intact. As executive skills depend on integrity of more basic underlying cognitive skills, it is very difficult to identify specific executive deficits against a background of poor performance more broadly and it may be inappropriate to attempt to do so.

Neuropsychologists differ in how accurately they believe executive deficits can be identified in a structured clinical examination. Cognitive testing is intended to be carried out in a quiet, distraction-free environment, involving only one task at a time with a high degree of cueing. Much effort is taken to put the examinee at their ease; they may be given positive encouragement and feedback, and they can usually request clarification of instructions or take a break when they feel the need. Tests administered in this way can be very useful in identifying or ruling out any major underlying cognitive impairment in many domains, but are less well equipped to elicit certain key features of executive dysfunction such as initiative, planning, prioritising and multi-tasking. This is especially important after a traumatic brain injury (TBI) where the brunt of the injury is often to the frontal lobes, but is relevant in any situation where the expert is instructed to give an opinion on the impact of an injury on everyday activities including employment capability. In this regard attention should be paid to the disparity sometimes reported between intact executive test scores and difficulties in daily life which characterises the *frontal paradox* (see Fisher-Hicks, Wood, & Braithwaite this volume).

Most common uses of formal neuropsychological tests

There are five common uses of neuropsychological testing in a litigation context. In some cases the neuropsychologist will be able to provide an expert opinion in all of these areas, in other cases they may be specifically instructed to address one aspect only such as establishing whether there is any cognitive impairment or evaluating mental capacity. As noted above, test scores cannot be interpreted in isolation and must be seen as one part of the neuropsychological evaluation. For each situation outlined below, the results of formal testing have to be interpreted within the broader clinical context and other available evidence.

To identify nature and extent of cognitive impairment

Neuropsychological evidence is frequently used to identify the nature and extent of deficits in cognition, emotion and behaviour. This is a central aspect of any quantum argument and may also be important where liability is contended in clinical negligence claims. Claimant lawyers place great store by this and certainly the correspondence of a pattern of attainment on formal testing and a known area of cerebral pathology can be compelling. As the relationship between tests and brain regions is imprecise and the degree of brain injury needed to produce a given level of deficit can also be uncertain, there is often scope for different views. Specific cognitive deficits are often easier to correlate with evidence of localised injury such as a haematoma or infarction than with diffuse brain injury.

To provide objective corroboration of a claimant's symptoms

Whilst symptoms are inevitably subjective, they tend to carry more weight as evidence if they can be corroborated objectively by the results of some investigation. Standardised neuropsychological tests and psychometrically valid inventories can provide valuable information to support reports from a claimant (or third party) about their difficulties. Equally importantly, neuropsychological tests may show no underlying impairment to justify the reported symptoms or disability. This does not necessarily invalidate such reports but may well lead to alternative interpretation about their likely aetiology and extent. This is often central to understanding cases of mild TBI (see chapter by Worthington and Moore this volume) but brain injury of any severity may produce symptoms that are part neurological and partly due to other factors.

To provide an estimate of recovery and a prognosis

In their role as expert the neuropsychologist is often instructed to comment on the treatment a person has received, their progress to date and to give a prognosis. Neuropsychological data can provide a useful basis for such judgements, for example by contrasting current ability with estimated premorbid function or comparing current performance with attainment on testing earlier in recovery. In the latter instance, if no significant change is observed then, depending on time since injury, there may be good reason to consider a person has reached a plateau in their neuropsychological recovery. The likely timescale for reaching maximum recovery potential will depend on type and severity of injury. Even if impairments are unlikely to change it may be possible to ameliorate the associated disability with skilled support and rehabilitation.

To identify profile of strengths and weaknesses

By assessing a range of cognitive domains the neuropsychologist will arrive at a profile of relative strengths and weaknesses. This may reflect a longstanding pattern and careful note should be made when taking a history of any areas of difficulty as well as any particular interests or aptitudes. A person's work or hobbies can be a useful guide to possible pre-existing traits, though occasionally one is surprised to find a person scoring much better or much worse on a test than would have been expected based on their employment. By analysing the cognitive profile and identifying areas of difficulty likely to be attributable to the index injury, the neuropsychologist can make informed recommendations for therapy and rehabilitation. Cognitive functions shown to be preserved can be capitalised upon therapy. For example, a person with specific visual memory problems can learn verbal encoding strategies, whilst a verbal memory deficit may be amenable to visualisation techniques.

To inform judgment of mental capacity

In England and Wales a lack of mental capacity ('incapacity' in Scotland) is a functional test which requires demonstration of impairment of brain or mind. Leaving aside the questionable philosophical basis for this distinction neuropsychological testing can identify impaired cognitive function in an objective and reliable way regardless of whether there is any recognisable brain damage on a scan. Neuropsychological evidence is not determinative of capacity and the use of neuropsychological tests in this manner at times is straining the limits of their usefulness. Most such tests are not particularly sensitive to decision making impairments especially as they are designed to be shorn of the emotional influences on performance, which often drive decisions in normal life (see Worthington, 2019). The neuropsychologist should consider not just the level of attainment, but also how this is achieved. A person responding impulsively on a multiple-choice test for example may be lacking the ability to carefully weigh up the information. This can be helpful in identifying whether similar behaviour is apparent in everyday decision making. Conversely, a claimant who scored very poorly on a sentence repetition task (a short-term memory test) did so because they were unable to repeat sentences verbatim but retained the gist of the meaning which may well be sufficient to exercise capacity.

Issues in forensic neuropsychological assessment

Use of flexible versus fixed test batteries

Set against the lengthy time it takes to administer a fixed battery, an advantage of undertaking all the tests in a battery is greater depth and breadth of assessment. Repeated administration of the same tests on multiple examinees also provides a basis for evaluating statistical patterns for potential significance (Russell, 1994). By contrast in a flexible battery the neuropsychologist selects from a wide range of possible tests from different sources, offering greater sensitivity to the uniqueness of the individual claimant, though it can also be seen as subjective and idiosyncratic. Although certain lawyers in the US have argued that only the fixed battery should be admissible as the only 'scientifically validated' approach, this attitude has been criticised as being inflexible and impervious to new developments in cognitive and clinical neuroscience (Bigler, 2007) and research has shown both approaches to be comprehensive and sensitive to brain injury (Larrabee, 2008).

In the UK there is no tradition of using single comprehensive test batteries to encompass all aspects of the neuropsychological examination as there is in the US and parts of Eastern Europe, reflecting in part historical differences between the psychometric and cognitive approaches to neuropsychology. Whilst some test batteries are widely used (notably the Wechsler batteries) these provide broad-based measures of a restricted domain of function. In the UK test batteries like the Wechsler intelligence and memory scales or D-KEFS executive function system are supplemented with additional tests to assess a wider range of cognitive functions.

The debate may be considered sterile in the UK because there is almost universal adoption of the flexible battery approach but a version of the same argument applies even though it is rarely articulated. Whereas use of a standard battery allows test performance to be compared on the same metric over time and by different neuropsychologists, the flexible battery can inadvertently result in a claimant being examined by two neuropsychologists on two entirely different test batteries. Abstruse and esoteric debate amongst experts as to the relative merits of their chosen tests are unhelpful to the court and unlikely to serve the expert's primary purpose. Different experts will have their preferred measures, but most neuropsychologists adopt a pragmatic approach, relying on a core set of well-validated tests as much as possible with additional tests according to the claimant's specific symptoms or level of disability. What is important is that the expert understands the strengths and limitations of their tests and is able to justify their use.

Older versus newer neuropsychological tests

Many neuropsychologists have favoured tests which have served them well and which they are understandably reluctant to dispense with. Yet there is a powerful impetus to purchase new tests, often driven by test publishers but also the desire of neuropsychologists (and perhaps an expectation amongst lawyers) to examine claimants using the latest tests. Indeed, experts may feel they will be subject to criticism if this is not the case, with neuropsychologists unwittingly engaging in a kind of 'arms race' with their colleagues to ensure they have the most up-to-date tests. Acquisition of the latest revision or version of a test however is not only expensive, but also from a scientific perspective, unnecessary.

Inevitably neuropsychological tests have to evolve. Sometimes the test material and questions need updating. Revised tests also benefit from practitioner's experiences of previous versions to allow a more efficient or comprehensive examination. Many new tests may incorporate advances in psychological knowledge and technology. Russell (2010) however argued valid tests do not lose their validity due to improvements in methodology or knowledge and premature abandonment of an older valid test does a disservice to neuropsychology. Although some test publishers have suggested the use of the newest version of tests within 6 to 12 months of publication, older tests will have been subject to more research and field-testing. There is likely to be independent evidence of their utility across a far wider range of conditions and scenarios than any test publisher will have carried out with a novel test (Bush, 2010). Such a rich source of data may be extremely useful in a medicolegal setting. Bush et al. (2018) made recommendations for justifying selection of revised and new tests which include (i) improvements in ease of use (ii) enhanced classification accuracy, (iii) opportunity to assess additional or new constructs, (iv) inclusion of special populations of interest in normative studies, and (v) significant cohort changes to in part to address the potential 'Flynn effect' of rising intellectual attainment (Trahan et al., 2014) though not all tests show this (Dickinson & Hiscock, 2011).

Repeat assessments and appropriate intervals between testing

When undertaking an examination, the neuropsychologist must be mindful of any testing carried out previously. This is important in order to make comparisons of performance over time but it may also affect interpretation of the results if the examinee can recall how to solve a problem (thereby losing its novelty), or remember material from an earlier assessment. Lawyers should be alert to this possibility and make every effort to establish what testing has been carried out clinically and by other experts. It is wasteful and disruptive to begin testing only for the claimant to report they saw another doctor a month earlier who did the same testing. If examined in a clinic it may be possible to substitute alternative tests, but this will not be practical if the examination is being undertaken at home. Where possible the previous examiner should be contacted and the results requested (if necessary emailing over the claimant's signed consent). If the results are unavailable (and they may not be disclosable at that stage) then a list of tests previously administered is helpful. Sometimes testing has been carried out by a treating neuropsychologist although practitioners should be aware of the potential of any assessment carried out clinically to compromise the medicolegal examination and should enquire whether an assessment for the claim is planned. The respective neuropsychologists can then agree on what tests each will undertake. Similarly, where two neuropsychology experts are due to examine a claimant around the same time, subject to the agreement of legal parties, they can agree that one will share data with the other or – if seen very close together – they may divide up the testing between the two of them.

Whilst there are practical reasons why it is undesirable to test a claimant twice in close succession the common assumption that testing should not be repeated within six months on a priori grounds is a myth (Greiffenstein, 2009). It poses interpretative challenges, but signs of learning can be a useful indicator. Practice effects vary from test to test and where they are reported in test manuals they are often based upon relatively small samples of healthy adults, tested no more than twice and over specified time intervals. From this data it is difficult to extrapolate to a brain-injured claimant tested twice over a different time period. One might consider memory impaired examinees to show fewer practice effects but some claimants may have been tested three or four times over the course of a claim. The matter is further complicated because normative population studies used in test development will have presumed stable neuropsychological status, but this will not be the case for assessments which take place during periods of recovery from brain injury. Variability in test scores over time is not always a property of the tests and may be complicated by variability within the person. This is particularly common in young children (Alibali & Sidney, 2015) but variability in performance over time is also seen after frontal brain injury and can in itself be a pathognomic sign (Stuss et al., 2003). One solution if it is not possible to delay an evaluation is to incorporate into the assessment a combination of (i) tests undertaken previously and (ii) additional novel measures of the same cognitive domains in an attempt to distinguish between task familiarity and true level of cognitive ability.

Ecological validity

The importance of neuropsychometric data lies not only in the relationship to brain injury but also in the ability to explain difficulties in daily life (functional disability) and to predict future functioning. Claimants (and some lawyers) may question how a test with no obvious resemblance to any kind of activity a competent person would be expected to do in normal life can have any value in litigation. Thus, tests are often criticised for lack of 'ecological' validity. This is not a psychometric term and is used inconsistently, but essentially it means that tests do not resemble the real-life situations in which the measured skills would be deployed (verisimilitude) or that results do not generalise well to normal life (veridicality). This is relevant insofar as tests should inform judgments about skills and behaviour outside the testing environment but what is important is that they do this in a scientifically valid fashion rather than how they appear. A test which measures inhibition or impulsiveness may appear quite artificial but may encapsulate problems which manifest in a wide range of situations. Similarly, slow processing responses on a cancellation task may account for mental fatigue, attention lapses on a target detection task may explain errors in the workplace or a host of misplaced personal items, a list-learning memory test may reveal an impairment of auditory memory which explains forgotten names and unrecalled conversations.

Research continues to explore means of improving the ecological validity of neuropsychological assessment (see Dawson & Marcotte, 2017). Whilst neuropsychology cannot rest on its laurels, the conclusion of Chaytor and Schmitter-Edgecombe (2003) is still pertinent: 'If we take into account that the relationship between tests and everyday outcome is far from perfect, then it seems reasonable to conclude that many neuropsychological tests are moderately related to everyday performance' (p.193).

It might be argued that the closer tests resemble normal tasks the better they will be at predicting everyday function. Taking this view to its extreme one could omit formal testing and base opinion solely on behavioural observation. In fact, structured observations can be extremely helpful alongside standardised psychometric tests but not as a substitute for formal testing. The purpose is quite different; whilst some tests have a more obvious link to real-life tasks this does not make them better at identifying core neuropsychological impairments. The best tests should be sensitive to the presence or absence of a specific function whereas real-life tasks involve multiple cognitive operations and impairment on such tasks does not illuminate the underlying cognitive processes responsible. As noted above, no test is immune to multiple confounding influences but no test is interpreted in isolation. The neuropsychological examination involves a careful analysis of patterns of performance to reach an accurate interpretation.

Recording of neuropsychological examinations

Whilst recoding of consultations has much to commend it in a clinical setting, it can be problematic in a medicolegal context where information is legally privileged and not disclosed until accompanied by a signed declaration and statement of truth. Certain lawyers however have encouraged claimants to record the examinations. Amongst neuropsychologists there is understandable concern about the ethics of this practice and potential for undermining test integrity and copyright infringement if testing is recorded. For some experts recording a clinical interview represents a threat to the integrity of the process and betrayal of trust, particularly if undertaken covertly. Conversely it may be seen as a means of ensuring the expert's report accurately reflects the consultation. Experts should be familiar with the judgment in *Mustard v Flower et al*[1] in which the trial judge accepted covert recording of the neuropsychological examination as probative, noting that covert video surveillance is commonly accepted.

Yet neuropsychological examination is quite different from surveillance and whilst experts of all disciplines should welcome transparency, justice is not served by measures that would compromise the expert's examination however well-intentioned. This includes the presence of a third party

1 *Mustard v Flower et al* [2019] EWHC 2623

observer who may be a relative or a professional. The courts need to be guided by evidence. In a meta-analysis Eastvold et al. (2012) reported that the tests most likely to be negatively affected by the presence of an observer were measures of attention, learning and delayed recall. There are concerns in the United States that the use of observers has become a tactic designed to limit the value of neuropsychological evidence in court (Glen et al., 2021).

The need to establish a professional position on the matter has become essential given the increased number of examinations taking place remotely. Recent guidance (British Psychological Society Division of Neuropsychology, 2021) is that covert recording in the medicolegal setting should not take place and could result in termination of the examination. In some circumstances recording of an interview may proceed if agreed in advance. This is consistent with the position of neuropsychologists in the United States that there should be no covert recording of testing or interviews (Bush et al., 2009).

The British Psychological Society Guidance also recognises the contaminating effect on test results and disclosure at interview that a third party observer may have. The expert has a decision to make in cases of very disabled adults and the assessment of children for whom the background presence of a relative may be a prerequisite to carrying out formal testing. For non-English speaking claimants an interpreter may be essential (see below). As the influence of a third party presence is unknown every effort should be made to conduct neuropsychological testing with the claimant alone (see also Lewandoski et al., 2019). Where a third party is present this should always be clearly identified in the report.

Integrating evidence from the neuropsychological examination

Information obtained from psychometric tests must be integrated within the broader framework of material obtained directly from the assessment and documentary evidence provided to assist the expert in reaching their opinion. This triangulation of source material is illustrated in Figure 4.3 and is important in all expert examinations, though the neuropsychologist will find it particularly helpful in complex cases where evidence is inconsistent or conflicting and expert opinion is sharply divided.

A neuropsychological examination should also include some or all of the following:

i   Behavioural observations made during the examination
ii Semi-structured clinical interview with the claimant
iii Interview with an immediate relative or close friend
iv Structured self-report measures
v   Measures of performance validity and validity of symptom report

52 'But for' the brain injury and causation

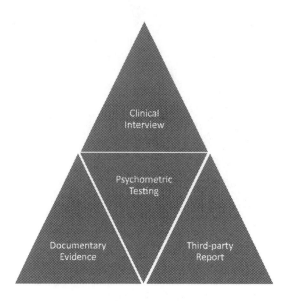

Figure 4.3 Triangulation of Evidence from Expert Neuropsychological Examination

In addition, depending on the nature of the claim and circumstances of the claimant, the expert should have access to (or may otherwise request to see) the following:

  i Hospital medical records
  ii General practitioner records
  iii Private clinical records (including case management and therapy records)
  iv Social care and welfare records
  v Police or other criminal records
  vi Educational (School/College/University) records
  vii Employment records including Human Resources and Personnel files
  viii Witness statements (e.g. from family, friends, a teacher, an employer, work colleagues)
  ix Other expert evidence from neuropsychology and experts in other fields

In light of the above the neuropsychologist needs to consider many questions of which the following are typical:

  i Is the claimant's general presentation in keeping with their documented condition?
  ii Are the claimant's reported symptoms in keeping with the nature of their injury at the time of examination?
  iii Is the claimant consistent in what they have reported at different times and to different professionals?

iv Have valid and reliable results been obtained with formal neuropsychological testing?
v If so, do the results fit with the problems reported by the claimant and/or other parties?
vi Do the results fit with what is known about the nature and extent of the claimant's injury?
vii If results are not valid or credible, what are the likely factors responsible?
viii How far can the problems identified on examination be attributable to the index incident and consequences thereof?
ix Is there evidence of pre-existing conditions that have been aggravated or accelerated by the index events?
x Will the claimant recover; to what extent and within what time-frame?
xi If there is any residual disability, what impact will this have on their personal, social, domestic, recreational and work life?
xii Would the claimant benefit from neuropsychological or other therapies?
xiii What would be the impact of therapy or rehabilitation on their longer-term prognosis?
xiv Does the neuropsychological evidence raise concerns about lack of mental capacity, especially their ability to litigate and to manage their property and affairs (other issues may also be relevant)?

Assessment of complex cases

There are occasions where a claimant's presentation makes it difficult to administer standardised tests due to a very low level of cognitive function or due to sensory/motor impairments. The neuropsychologist has to select which tests will best provide the court with evidence as to a person's cognitive strengths and weaknesses. As far as possible this should be based upon appropriately normed tests although descriptive tasks may provide additional information where these are limited. Whilst not the purpose of the chapter to recommend specific tests, as these will change over time and according to circumstance, complex cases necessitate additional considerations for both neuropsychologist and their instructing parties.

Aphasia

Receptive aphasia may affect the comprehension of spoken task instructions and test materials. Where language is known to be compromised it is good practice to establish a level of comprehension first before moving onto other tests. Written instructions may provide a practical substitute to spoken instructions, but reading also needs to be formally assessed where feasible. Word reading and word comprehension may dissociate so ideally both need to be considered. This is especially relevant in paediatric assessments, but also whenever an acquired language impairment is suspected. Neuropsychologists vary in their familiarity with models of language and assessments and there may be evidence from an Educational Psychologist or Speech and Language Therapist which assists, but the neuropsychologist should be prepared to carry out their own evaluation relevant to their assessment as a whole in order to be able to interpret their results.

Severe expressive aphasia usually precludes administration of tests requiring a verbal response. It may be accompanied by difficulties with reading (dyslexia) and/or writing (dysgraphia) so it is important to assess these alternative modalities of response before proceeding to further testing in other domains such as memory. A variety of symbol, gesture or picture responses may prove the most effective response mode but additional care needs to be taken to ensure this is a reliable outlet, for example by repeating a series of easy questions initially.

Apraxia

Defined by Goldenberg (2013) as a disturbance of the mental control of deliberate motor actions, apraxia may co-occur with receptive aphasia and can interfere with gesture production for communication. The neuropsychologist should be also mindful of the potential for apraxia to undermine performance on manual tasks, including writing and drawing and construction. Apraxia can be assessed directly using a variety of descriptive tasks and standardised batteries. In doing so care should be taken to assess performance and imitation of gestures, pantomiming object use and using real objects (see Bickerton et al., 2012). Apraxia can manifest with multiple objects despite normal performance on examination with single objects (Foundas et al., 1995) so it is important to ask about everyday object use where praxis difficulties are suspected rather than rely solely on structured assessment.

Vision or hearing impairment

It is common practice when examining hearing-impaired claimants to rely on visual tests and with visually-impaired claimants to focus on focus on spoken tasks. This has long been recognised as unsatisfactory, Domino (1968) for example highlighted the need for a non-verbal intelligence measure for blind adults as important in understanding their interaction with the environment. Efforts to develop condition-specific measures of intellectual ability have shown only modest correlations with standard scales (e.g. Nelson, Dial & Joyce, 2002). Examination usually relies upon the neuropsychologist using similar adaptations they may undertake for communication-impaired examinees, for example by writing down instructions for people with impaired hearing. The effect of deviations from standard instructions is rarely investigated (Hill-Briggs et al., 2007) and due caution needs to be expressed when interpreting results obtained in a manner which either deviates from the standard instructions or is based upon an unrepresentative normative sample. Few neuropsychological instruments in common use have been specifically validated on sensory-impaired populations. A recent exception is research by Chovaz et al. (2021), suggesting the TOMM remains valid amongst deaf people who communicate using sign language.

Minimal conscious state

Neuropsychologists are sometimes called upon to assist the court to determine the status of people with a prolonged disorder of consciousness. The prognosis for such conditions can have a major bearing on a claim, one recent study of 50 patients reporting 46% emerged after a median of 200 days, and people in a minimally conscious state (MCS) were more likely to demonstrate neurobehavioural recovery over time (Lee et al., 2020). Whilst in the future, neurodiagnostic imaging may play an increasing role, central to the diagnosis of MCS is the presence of behavioural evidence of consciousness awareness. Neuropsychologists have been instrumental in the development of relevant behavioural measures (e.g. Wilson, et al., 1996; Shiel et al., 2000) and an expert neuropsychological evaluation may be called upon to support or challenge a neurological opinion. Some of the issues raised in conducting an independent examination in low awareness states are discussed by Zasler (2005) and a review of useful clinical measures was published by Seel et al. (2010). Probably more so than in any other situation the neuropsychologist must interpret their own observations in the context of the reliability of behavioural reports from family, carers and therapists.

Non-English-speaking claimants

Most tests in common use in the UK and US are standardised on a representative sample of the respective populations. Increasingly however test development lags behind changing demographics. Whilst ideally claimants would be examined by a neuropsychologist in their first language this may be less important than the expertise of the clinician and does not circumvent the limitations of the test material and normative data. Professional interpreters are commonly used as an intermediary, but their role complicates the evaluation. The neuropsychologist being unsure whether assessment in a claimant's second (or third) language would be more valid than via an interpreter will find little evidence-based guidance. Much depends on the linguistic fluency of the examiner and examinee in another language, the claimant's cognitive level and available tests.

Whilst in many tests the norms are manipulated to ensure appropriate demographic and cultural diversity (Howieson, 2019) others may be available in translation but without adequate accompanying norms. Attitudes to testing and to disability more generally may have a bearing on the examination, as may the way cognitive concepts are construed. For example Nisbett and Miyamoto (2005) discussed how cultural differences in analytic versus holistic perspectives influence perceptual processing. Another study comparing US and Russian examinees suggested that different attitudes to time and familiarity with timed procedures affected results on timed tasks (Agranovich, Panter & Touradji, 2011). Fernandez and Abe (2018) set out how these problems can be overcome with considerable time and effort but for the foreseeable future neuropsychologists and lawyers will need to recognise the limits of formal psychometric evidence obtained from claimants from culturally and linguistically diverse communities.

Conclusion

The application of cognitive and psychometric theory to the measurement of cognitive functions is a key part of the expert neuropsychologist's role in personal injury litigation. Neuropsychological sequelae are not limited to changes in cognitive function although standardised neuropsychological tests can be very useful in quantifying such changes where they occur. Accurate interpretation of data obtained from standardised tests requires appreciation of the strengths and limitations of the measures used. In order to formulate their opinion, the expert has to take account of all the available evidence. Inconsistencies between test results and everyday life can arise in either direction: everyday function can be poorer than would be expected from individual tests due to other contributory factors and conversely, tests can reveal underlying cognitive difficulties that are masked in normal life due to habitual routines and effective compensation. Difficulties associated with executive function may be more evident in daily life than on formal testing so test results must always be interpreted as part of the picture but not the final word on the presence or absence of cognitive dysfunction in daily life. Whilst outside the scope of the present chapter on testing, other aspects of executive function involved in appraisal of emotional events, social cognition and emotional control are not readily encapsulated in neuropsychological assessment, but these can cause significant distress and disability. At its best neuropsychological testing provides the court with an objective, scientifically grounded basis for the nature and extent of cognitive impairment which informs an understanding of the case but as the trial judge noted in *Ali v Caton [2013]* 'the presence of reliable test results is useful but not determinative'.[2]

References

Agranovich, A. V., Panter, A., & Touradji, P. (2011) The culture of time in neuropsychological assessment: Exploring the effects of culture-specific time attitudes on timed test performance in Russian and American samples. *Journal of the International Neuropsychological Society* 17: 692–701.

Alibali, M., & Sidney, P. (2015) The role of intraindividual variability in learning and cognitive development. In: Diehl, M., Hooker, K., & Sliwinski, M. J. (Eds)

---

[2] *Ali v Caton* [2013] EWHC 1730 QB.

Handbook of Intraindividual Variability Across the Life Span. Routledge, New York: 84–102.

Arnett, P. (2013) (Ed) *Secondary Influences on Neuropsychological Test Performance*. New York: Oxford University Press, 427pp.

Baddeley, A. (2002) Fractionating the Central Executive. In: Stuss, D., & Knight, R. (Eds) *Principles of Frontal Lobe Function*. New York: Oxford University Press, 246–260.

Bickerton, W., Riddoch, M. J., Samson, D., Balani, A. B., Mistry, B., & Humphreys, G. W. (2012) Systematic assessment of apraxia and functional predictions from the Birmingham cognitive screen. *Journal of Neurology, Neurosurgery and Neuropsychiatry 83*: 513–521.

Bigler, E. (2007) A motion to exclude and the 'fixed' versus 'flexible' battery in 'forensic' neuropsychology: Challenges to the practice of clinical neuropsychology. *Archives of Clinical Neuropsychology 22*: 45–51.

Binder L., & Binder A. (2011). Relative subset scatter in the WAIS-IV Standardization Sample. *The Clinical Neuropsychologist 25 (1)*: 62–71.

British Psychological Society Division of Neuropsychology (2021) *Guidance on the Recording of Neuropsychological Testing in Medicolegal Settings*. Leicester: British Psychological Society.

Brooks, B., Holdnack, J., & Iverson, G. L. (2011). Advanced clinical interpretation of the WAIS-IV and WMS-IV: Prevalence of low scores varies by level of intelligence and years of education. *Assessment 18 (2)*: 156–167.

Burgess, P. (1993) Theory and methodology in executive function research. In: Rabbit, P. (Ed) *Methodology of Frontal and Executive Function*. Hove: Psychology Press, 81–116.

Bush, S. S. (2010) Determining whether or when to adopt new versions of psychological and neuropsychological tests: Ethical and professional considerations. *The Clinical Neuropsychologist 24 (1)*: 7–16.

Bush, S. H., Pimental, P. A., Ruff, R. M., Iverson, G. L., Barth, J. T., & Broshek, D. K. (2009) Secretive recording of neuropsychological testing and interviewing: Official position of the National Academy of Neuropsychology. *Archives of Clinical Neuropsychology 24*: 1–2.

Bush, S. S., Sweet, J. J., Bianchini, K. J., Johnson-Greene, D., Dean, P. M., & Schoenberg, M. R. (2018). Deciding to adopt revised and new psychological and neuropsychological tests: An inter-organizational position paper. *The Clinical Neuropsychologist, 32 (3)*: 319–325.

Catani, M. (2005) The rises and falls of disconnection syndromes. *Brain 128*: 2224–2239.

Catani, M. (2006). Diffusion tensor magnetic resonance imaging tractography in cognitive disorders. *Current Opinion in Neurology 19*: 599–606.

Cauda, F., Nani, A., Manuello, J., Prem, I. E., Palermo, S., Tatu, K., Duca, S., Fox, P., & Costa, T. (2011) Brain structural alterations are distributed following functional, anatomic and genetic connectivity. *Brain 141*: 3211–3232.

Chaytor, N., & Schmitter-Edgecombe M (2003) The ecological validity of neuropsychological tests: A review of the literature on everyday cognitive skills. *Neuropsychology Review 13 (4)*: 181–197.

Chovaz, C. J., Rennison, V. L. A., & Chorostecki, D. O. (2021) The validity of the test of memory malingering (TOMM) with deaf individuals. *The Clinical Neuropsychologist 35 (3)*: 597–614.

Crawford, S., & Garthwaite, P. (2009). Percentiles please: The case for expressing neuropsychological test scores and accompanying confidence limits as percentile ranks. *The Clinical Neuropsychologist, 23* (2): 193–204.

Crawford, J., Garthwaite, P., Longman, R., & Batty, A. (2012). Some supplementary methods for the analysis of WAIS-IV index scores in neuropsychological assessment. *Journal of Neuropsychology 6*: 192–211.

Crocker, L. & Algina, J. (1986) *Introduction to Classical and Modern Test Theory.* New York: Holt, Rinehart and Winston.

Dawson D., & Marcotte, T. (Eds) (2017) Special issue: Ecological validity and cognitive assessment. *Neuropsychological Rehabilitation 27* (5).

Diaz-Asper, C. M., Schretlen, D. J., & Pearlson, G. D. (2004). How well does IQ predict neuropsychological test performance in normal adults? *Journal of the International Neuropsychological Society 10* (1): 82–90.

Dickinson, M. D., & Hiscock, M. (2011) The Flynn Effect in neuropsychological assessment. *Applied Neuropsychology 18*: 136–142.

Dodd, J., Getov, V., & Jones, P. (2010) Cognitive function in COPD. *European Respiratory Journal 35*: 913–922.

Domino, G. (1968) A non-verbal measure of intelligence for totally blind adults. *Journal of Visual Impairment and Blindness 62* (8): 247–252.

Eastvold, A., Belanger, H. G., & Vanderploeg, R. D. (2012) Does a third party observer affect neuropsychological test performance? It depends. *The Clinical Neuropsychologist 26* (3): 520–541.

Eggermont, L., de Boer, K., Muller, M., Jaschke, A., Kamp, O., & Scherder, E. (2012) Cardiac disease and cognitive impairment: A systematic review. *Heart 98* (18): 1334–1340.

Elias, M., Dore G., & Davey, A. (2013) Kidney disease and cognitive function. *Contributions to Nephrology 179*: 42–57.

Fernandez, A. L., & Abe, J. (2018) Bias in cross-cultural neuropsychological testing: Problems and possible solutions. *Culture and Brain 6*: 1–35.

Fodor, J. A. (1983) *The Modularity of Mind.* Cambridge MA: MIT Press, 145pp.

Foundas, A. L., Macauley, B. L., Raymer, A. M., Maher, L. M., Heilman, K. M., & Rothi, L. J. G. (1995). Ecological implications of limb apraxia: Evidence from mealtime behavior. *Journal of the International Neuropsychological Society, 1*, 62–66.

Glen, T., Barisa, M., Ready, R., Peck, E., & Spencer, T R. (2021) Update on third party observers in neuropsychological evaluation: An interorganizational position paper. *The Clinical Neuropsychologist 19*: 1–10.

Goldenberg, G. (2013) *Apraxia. The cognitive side of motor control.* New York: Oxford University Press, 273pp.

Gregoire, J., Coalson, D., & Zhu., J. (2011) Analysis of WAIS-IV index score scatter using significant deviation from the mean index. *Assessment 18* (2): 168–177.

Greiffenstein M. (2009) Clinical myths of forensic neuropsychology. *The Clinical Neuropsychologist 23* (2): 286–296.

Guilmette, T. J., Sweet, J. J., Hebben, N., Koltai, D., Mahone, E. M., Spiegler, B. J., Stucky, K., Westerveld, M. & conference participants. (2020) American Academy of Clinical Neuropsychology consensus conference statement on uniform labelling of performance test scores. *The Clinical Neuropsychologist 34* (3): 437–453.

Halligan. P., & Marshall, J. (1996) (Eds) *Method in Madness. Case Studies in Cognitive Neuropsychiatry.* Hove: Psychology Press, 310pp.

Hill-Briggs, F., Dial, J. G., Morere, D. A., & Joyce, A. (2007) Neuropsychological assessment of persons with physical disability, visual impairment or blindness, hearing impairment or deafness. *Archives of Clinical Neuropsychology 22* (3): 389–404.

Howieson, D. (2019) Current limitations of neuropsychological tests and assessment procedures. *The Clinical Neuropsychologist, 33* (2): 200–208.

Karr, J., Garcia-Barrera, M., Holdnack, J., & Iverson, G. L. (2018) Advanced clinical interpretation of the Delis-Kaplan Executive Function System: multivariate base rates of low scores. *The Clinical Neuropsychologist 32* (1): 42–53.

Karr, J., Garcia-Barrera, M., Holdnack, J., & Iverson, G. L. (2020) The other side of the bell curve: Multivariate base rates of high scores on the Delis-Kaplan executive function system. *Journal of the International Neuropsychological Society 24* (4): 382–393.

Kay, T. (1999) Interpreting apparent neuropsychological deficits: What is really wrong? In: Sweet, J. U. (Ed) *Forensic Neuropsychology. Fundamentals and Practice.* Swets & Zeitlinger, Lisse, The Netherlands, 145–183.

Larrabee G. (2008) Flexible vs fixed batteries in forensic neuropsychological assessment: Reply to Bigler and Hom. *Archives of Clinical Neuropsychology 23*: 763–776.

Lee, H. Y., Park, J. H., Kim, A. R., Park, M., & Kim, T. (2020) Neurobehavioural recovery in patients who emerged from prolonged disorder of consciousness: A retrospective study. *BMC Neurology 20*: 198.

Levy, P. (1995). Charles Spearman's contributions to test theory. *British Journal of Mathematical and Statistical Psychology, 48* (2), 221–235.

Lewandowski, A., Baker, W. J., Sewick, B., Knippa, J., Axelrod, B. & McCaffrey, R. J. (2016) Policy statement of the American Board of Professional Neuropsychology regarding third party observation and the recording of psychological test administration in neuropsychological evaluations. *Applied Neuropsychology: Adult 23* (6): 391–398.

McCrimmon, R., Ryan, C., & Frier, B. (2012) Diabetes and cognitive dysfunction. *Lancet 379*: 2291–2299.

Nelson, P. A., Dial, J. G., & Joyce, A. (2002) Validation of the cognitive test for the blind as an assessment of intellectual functioning. *Rehabilitation Psychology 47* (2): 184–193.

Nisbett, R. E., & Miyamoto, Y. (2005) The influence of culture: Holistic versus analytic perception. *Trends in Cognitive Neurosciences 9* (10): 467–473.

Parker, Randall & Szymanski, E. M. (1992) Fishing and error rate problem. *Rehabilitation Counseling Bulletin*, 66–69.

Passingham, R. (1993) *The Frontal Lobes and Voluntary Action.* New York: Oxford University Press, 299pp.

Plaut, D. (1995) Double dissociation without modularity: Evidence from connectionist neuropsychology. *Journal of Clinical and Experimental Neuropsychology 17* (2): 291–321.

Priestley, N., Manchester, D., & Aram, R. (2013) Presenting evidence of executive functions deficit in court. *Journal of Personal Injury 4*: 240–247.

Russell, E. (1994) The cognitive-metric, fixed battery approach to neuropsychological assessment. In: Vanderploeg, R. (Ed) *Clinician's Guide to Neuropsychological Assessment.* Hillsdale, NJ. Lawrence Erlbaum, 211–258.

Russell, E. (2010) The 'obsolescence' of assessment procedures. *Applied Neuropsychology, 17* (1): 60–67.

Schretlen, D., Munro, C., Anthony, J., & Pearlson, G. (2003). Examining the range of normal intraindividual variability in neuropsychological test performance. *Journal of the International Neuropsychological Society, 9* (6), 864–870.

Seel., R. T., Sherer, M., Whyte, J., Katz D. I., Giacino, J. T., Rosenbaum, A. M., Hammond, F. M., Kalmar, K., Pape, T., Zafonte, R., Biester, R. C., Kaelin, D., Kean, J., & Zasler, N. (2010) Assessment scales for disorders of consciousness: Evidence based recommendations for clinical practice and research. *Archives of Physical Medicine and Rehabilitation 91*: 1795–1813.

Shallice, T. (1988) *From Neuropsychology to Mental Structure*. New York: Cambridge University Press, 462pp.

Shallice, T. & Burgess, P. (1991) Higher-order cognitive impairments and frontal lobe lesions in man. In: Levin, H., Eisenberg, H., & Benton, A. (Eds) *Frontal Lobe Function and Dysfunction*. New York: Oxford University Press, 125–138.

Shallice, T. & Cooper, R.P. (2011) *The Organisation of Mind*. New York: Oxford University Press.

Shiel, A., Horn, S.A., Wilson, B.A., Watson, M. J., Campbell, M. J., & McLellan, D. L. (2000) The Wessex Head Injury Matrix (WHIM) main scale: A preliminary report on a scale to assess and monitor patient recovery after severe head injury. *Clinical Rehabilitation 14*: 408–416.

Stuss, D., Murphy, K., Binns, M., & Alexander, M. (2003) Staying on the job: The frontal lobes control individual performance variability. *Brain 126*: 2363–2380.

Stuss, D. (2011) Functional of the frontal lobes: Relations to executive functions. *Journal of the International Neuropsychological Society 17*: 759–765.

Trahan, L. H., Stuebing, K. K., Fletcher, J. M., & Hiscock, M. (2014). The Flynn Effect: A meta-analysis. *Psychological Bulletin 140 (5)*: 1332–1360.

Wilson, S. L., Powell, G.E., Brock, D., & Thwaites, H. (1996) Behavioural differences between patients who emerged from vegetative state and those who did not. *Brain Injury 10 (7)*: 509–516.

Wood, J., & Grafman, J. (2003) Human prefrontal cortex: processing and representational perspectives. *Nature Reviews Neuroscience 4*: 139–147.

Wood, R. L., & Worthington, A. (2017) Neurobehavioural abnormalities associated with executive dysfunction after traumatic brain injury. *Frontiers in Behavioral Neuroscience 11*: 00195.

Worthington, A. (2019) Decision making and mental capacity: resolving the frontal paradox. *The Neuropsychologist 7*: 31–35.

Zasler, N. (2005) Forensic assessment issues in low level neurological states. *Neuropsychological Rehabilitation 15 (3/4)*: 251–256.

Appendix 4.1

Table A4.1 Psychometric Test Score Conversion Table

Standard Score	Percentile Rank	Scaled Score	T-Score	Z-Score	Descriptor
150	>99.9				Exceptionally high score
149	>99.9				Exceptionally high score
148	99.9				Exceptionally high score
147	99.9				Exceptionally high score
146	99.9				Exceptionally high score
145	99.9	19	80	3.0	Exceptionally high score
144	99.8				Exceptionally high score
143	99.8				Exceptionally high score
142	99.7		78	2.75	Exceptionally high score
141	99.7				Exceptionally high score
140	99.6	18	77	2.67	Exceptionally high score
139	99.5				Exceptionally high score
138	99				Exceptionally high score
137	99		75	2.50	Exceptionally high score
136	99				Exceptionally high score
135	99	17	73	2.33	Exceptionally high score
134	99				Exceptionally high score
133	99		72	2.25	Exceptionally high score
132	98				Exceptionally high score
131	98				Exceptionally high score
130	98	16	70	2.00	Exceptionally high score
129	97				Above average score
128	97		68	1.75	Above average score
127	96				Above average score
126	96				Above average score
125	95	15	67	1.67	Above average score
124	95				Above average score
123	94		5	1.50	Above average score
122	93				Above average score
121	92				Above average score

(*Continued*)

Standard Score	Percentile Rank	Scaled Score	T-Score	Z-Score	Descriptor
120	91	14	63	1.33	High Average score
119	90				High Average score
118	88		62	1.25	High Average score
117	87				High Average score
116	86				High Average score
115	84	13	60	1.00	High Average score
114	82				High Average score
113	81		58	0.75	High Average score
112	79				High Average score
111	77				High Average score
110	75	12	57	0.67	Average score
109	73				Average score
108	70		55	0.55	Average score
107	68				Average score
106	66				Average score
105	63	11	53	0.33	Average score
104	61				Average score
103	58				Average score
102	55		52	0.25	Average score
101	53				Average score
100	50	10	50	0.00	Average score
99	47				Average score
98	45		48	-0.25	Average score
97	42				Average score
96	40				Average score
95	37	9	47	-0.33	Average score
94	34				Average score
93	32		45	-0.50	Average score
92	30				Average score
91	27				Average score
90	25	8	43	-0.67	Average score
89	23				Low average score
88	21		42	-0.75	Low average score
87	19				Low average score
86	18				Low average score
85	16	7	40	-1.00	Low average score
84	14				Low average score
83	13		38	-1.25	Low average score
82	12				Low average score
81	10				Low average score
80	9	6	37	-1.33	Low average score
79	8				Below average score
78	7		35	-1.50	Below average score
77	6				Below average score
76	5				Below average score
75	5	5	33	-1.67	Below average score

74	4				Below average score
73	4		32	-1.75	Below average score
72	3				Below average score
71	3				Below average score
70	2	4	30	-2.00	Below average score
69	< 2				Exceptionally low score
68	< 2		28	-2.25	Exceptionally low score
67	1				Exceptionally low score
66	1				Exceptionally low score
65	1	3	27	-2.33	Exceptionally low score
64	1				Exceptionally low score
63	1		25	-2.50	Exceptionally low score
62	1				Exceptionally low score
61	0.5				Exceptionally low score
60	0.4	2	23	-2.67	Exceptionally low score
59	0.3				Exceptionally low score
58	0.2		22	-2.75	Exceptionally low score
57	0.1				Exceptionally low score
56	0.3				Exceptionally low score
55	0.3	1	20	-3.00	Exceptionally low score
54	0.3				Exceptionally low score
53	0.3				Exceptionally low score
52	0.3				Exceptionally low score
51	<0.1				Exceptionally low score
50	<0.1				Exceptionally low score

5 Paediatric outcomes after traumatic brain injury

Social and forensic risk management in multidisciplinary treatment approaches

Hope Kent, James Tonks and Huw Williams with Ian Brownhill

Introduction

Traumatic Brain Injury (TBI) is a leading global cause of death and disability in children and young people (Hyder, Wunderlich, Puvanachandra, Gururaj, & Kobunsingye 2007). TBI can have a devastating impact on social development in childhood, and can result in social, behavioural, and cognitive difficulties. TBI is a spectrum condition, with resultant symptoms ranging from mild concussion to severe disability depending on the 'dosage' of injury. Effects can also be cumulative, with multiple injuries often resulting in more complex and severe symptom profiles. Severe, longer-term consequences following a childhood TBI can endure with major behavioural changes associated with criminality and/or poor mental health. Rusnak (2013) describes paediatric TBI as a 'silent epidemic' among young forensic populations, with its diverse effects rarely recognised and accounted for in the criminal justice system. Injury in childhood can increase forensic risk in later life, and young people with TBI are significantly over-represented in youth justice settings (Williams et al., 2018). Working to avoid the criminalisation of this neuro-disability is crucial, and there are rehabilitative practices which can help to avoid a 'revolving door' justice system for those with TBI. This chapter will explore the sequelae resulting from paediatric TBI, and how these can lead to enduring social difficulties and increased risk of contact with the criminal justice system, as well as discussing protective factors and strategies for rehabilitation.

Normative development

Introduction to the brain

The brain is a hugely complex organ. It comprises some 80–100 billion neurons, each developing up to 30,000 connections during a lifetime. The brain can be considered to be organised into three primary structures – the cerebrum, midbrain, and cerebellum. These are divided by sulci (deep channels

DOI: 10.4324/9781003105763-6

or grooves) into two hemispheres, which are connected by a cluster of axons called the corpus callosum. The cerebrum, also known as the cerebral cortex, is divided into four lobes (frontal, parietal, occipital, and temporal), which are each responsible for numerous different aspects of cognition and behaviour, and the surface of the cerebrum is populated by sulci and gyri (folds). The frontal lobe is the largest lobe, and is associated with higher order functions such as planning, attention, reasoning, language, emotion, introspection, and self-regulation. The parietal lobe is responsible for complex sensory interpretation and integration, such as visuo-spatial processing. The occipital lobe pertains to visual processing, visual attention, and perception of visual gestures (e.g. body language), whilst the temporal lobe is associated with the perception and recognition of auditory stimuli, and with aspects of memory. The midbrain comprises structures which modulate emotional responses and the release of neurotransmitters (e.g. serotonin, dopamine). These structures include the hippocampus, amygdala, and tectum. The cerebellum is a smaller set of lobes located in the back of the skull, and these lobes are associated with motor co-ordination, balance, and postural control (Eagleman & Downar, 2015).

Developmental stages

The developing brain is highly plastic, and neurological maturation occurs in neither a linear nor a stepwise manner. Instead, there are varying 'growth spurts' and plateaus in development. Significant neurological changes occur during the first year of life, and peaks also occur at ages 3–4, 7–8, 11–13, and 15–17 years. Historically, the importance of neuromaturation during adolescence has been underestimated, but we now know it to be second only to infancy in terms of the maturation occurring in the cerebrum (Whittle et al., 2014; Decety, 2010). The frontal lobes are among the last structures to reach maturity during adolescence, and are frequently not fully developed until age 23–25 years (Johnson, Blum, & Giedd, 2009). Males typically reach peak white matter volume in the frontal lobes one–two years later than females, but there is substantial individual divergence in this general trend (Lenroot & Giedd, 2010). Neural connections are shaped behaviourally, cognitively, genetically, and epigenetically; rehearsed behaviours, thoughts, and responses form new neural pathways as neurons that 'fire together wire together' (Hebb, 1949). During periods of development, neuronal connections which have become redundant or unused are pruned away (Keysers & Perret, 2004).

These developmental changes map onto changes in functional ability and social cognition during childhood and adolescence. These changes are dynamic, and occur during development as a response to environmental changes and demands with maturity. Longitudinal development can be tracked using structural and functional MRI (Magnetic Resonance Imaging), and EEG (electroencephalogram) imaging (Poole, Santesso, Van Lieshout, & Schmit, 2018; DeLuca &

Leventer, 2008). Of particular relevance to social and forensic risk is the development of emotional cognition, empathy, impulse control, and responsivity. Most developmentally normal infants will recognise basic emotions including surprise, sadness, anger, and fear by six months (Heck, Chroust, White, Jubran, & Bhatt, 2018). Theory of Mind (ToM) is the ability to infer mental and affective states of others. It allows one to understand that others have different experiences, outlooks, and perspectives from our own, and develops around age three–five. It is a cornerstone of social cognition and interaction, and children with strongly developed ToM have more positive peer relationships (Slaughter, Imuta, Peterson, & Henry, 2015). Most 3-year-olds will fail a task which requires inferences about how a protagonist holding a false belief will behave, whereas most 6-year-olds can understand how the false belief will impact behaviour (Wellman, Cross, & Watson, 2001). More complex social-cognitive ToM (including recognising lies, sarcasm, figurative language, or multiple embeddings) typically develops between the ages of 8 and 12 years (Westby & Robinson, 2014). Recent evidence with large sample sizes aged 11–25 has found support for the theory that the development of ToM actually continues in adolescence, particularly in social-perceptual abilities which involve the inference of the mental states of others via non-verbal cues (Meinhardt-Injac, Daum, & Meinhardt, 2020). The adolescent frontal lobes constantly re-wire and develop to create convergence zones for social and affective cognition.

Neural plasticity

Neural plasticity underpins the key phases in brain development, and is an important adaptive feature of the brain. Plasticity describes the brain's ability to change functionally or structurally according to internal or external stimuli. It constitutes the reorganisation of connections between neurons to reshape neural pathways, and is necessary not only for the acquisition of new functional properties, but for acquired functions to remain robust and stable in changing environments (Bernhardi, Bernhardi, & Eugenin, 2017). The brain is most plastic during phases of rapid development during infancy and early childhood. Plasticity generally decreases after age 25, but our ability to learn new skills in adulthood persists as long as the brain is healthy (Pauwels, Chalavi, & Swinnen, 2018). Plasticity underpins all learned behaviour and responses, allowing humans to quickly adapt to changing environments, social pressures, and threats. Our decision making and behaviours can change in different environments (for example, in the presence of peers vs in the presence of authority figures), and neural plasticity allows for adaptation to changing social pressures. It is particularly important during turbulent social times such as the threshold between childhood and adolescence.

Paediatric TBI

TBI occurs following a blunt or penetrating trauma to the head, leading to lacerations and contusions (bruising) of brain structures, and in more severe cases internal swelling and bleeding. The brain can also move in the skull, which can lead to shearing and tearing of white matter tracts, particularly in rotational injuries (e.g. a punch to the side of the head). Movement can also cause contusions on the opposite side of the brain to the direct impact. The inside of the skull is not smooth, and rough bone can also cause lacerations and contusions where the brain moves or swells against it. Milder injuries often lead to disruption of axonal connectivity (Caeyenberghs et al., 2014). The primary causes of paediatric TBI vary by age. Adolescents aged 15–24 years are in the highest risk population for TBI, and are most vulnerable to car, bicycle, and motor-cycle related accidents, injuries sustained during fights, and sports-related injuries (Araki, Yokota, & Morita, 2017). A secondary peak in incidence occurs in those under five years old, where children are most likely to be injured due to falls or abusive home environments, whilst road traffic accidents or other transportation accidents (e.g. bicycle accidents) become a more prominent risk in children aged four to eight. In infants and children under two years old, abusive home environments are the biggest cause of TBI, and approximately 30 in 100,000 infants are hospitalised for injury caused by abuse (Keenan et al., 2003). Annually, paediatric TBI in the USA is responsible for 300,000–400,000 hospitalisations, 6,000–7,000 deaths, and an estimated $10 billion in direct care costs (Ommaya, Goldsmith, & Thibault, 2002). In the UK, the long-term cost of a TBI at age 15 is estimated to be £155,000 per case, rising to £345,000 per case for those who come into contact with the law (Parsonage, 2016). This is a huge cost, financially, emotionally, and socially.

Paediatric vulnerability

There are unique impacts of paediatric brain injury, and particularly brain injury during infancy and early childhood, due in part to extremely high levels of neural plasticity, and less rigid skulls. This leads to external forces being absorbed in different ways to add trauma to the adult brain (Araki et al., 2017). Additionally, myelination (increases in the volume of the fatty 'sheath' surrounding neurons) occurs with development, and increases brain density, altering the absorption of traumatic forces. Myelination occurs at different rates in different brain areas, resulting in increased susceptibility to TBI in unmyelinated regions during development, and in the whole brain in infants who have not begun the myelination process (Goldsmith & Plunkett, 2004).

Neural plasticity is an important mechanism in recovery from paediatric TBI. Whilst profoundly damaged neural structures cannot regenerate, plasticity can facilitate the reorganisation of functions, essentially 'rerouting' them away from damaged areas and allocating some neural capability to these functions in other brain structures. This is a crucial component of long-term recovery of function. Following moderate or severe TBI, a sterile immune response can trigger a cascading neuroinflammatory response. Acutely, this immune response promotes tissue repair and recovery in response to trauma. However, when prolonged, it can lead to emotional and behavioural dysregulation due to dysregulation in the release of hormones and neurotransmitters, and can interfere with neural regeneration and plasticity (Russo & McGavern, 2016). Neuroinflammation is a complex mechanism impacting a variety of inflammatory networks, interfering with the central nervous system's response to stress, and disrupting the blood brain barrier (Skaper et al., 2018). Where neuroinflammation is unmanaged and unmonitored, it can contribute to ongoing problems and impair recovery.

Social issues following paediatric TBI

Our ability to interact socially is at the core of our human experience, and a crucial part of a child's ability to function in school and form positive relationships. The ability to relate appropriately to those around us is developmentally critical (Zamani et al., 2019). Paediatric TBI peaks in recovery of social function after 6–12 months are often reported, but longer-term effects of early-life TBI often do not become apparent until later developmental stages when more complex social and academic demands are placed on the individual. Difficulties often become more evident at the threshold between childhood and adolescence, when complex social demands are increased. Deficits in social skills such as ToM, or problems with emotional and behavioural dysregulation, may not be immediately obvious as stemming from the childhood TBI, due to the long periods of time which can pass between injury and the presentation of difficulties – a phenomenon termed 'neurocognitive stall' (Chapman, 2007). Plasticity is a crucial element in the recovery and development of social skills. Injury in both hemispheres generally leads to more limited ability to reorganise functions away from injured areas. Frontal injuries typically lead to more severe deficits, particularly when attained before the age of 11 (Verger et al., 2009). Deficits in social abilities following paediatric TBI have been linked to declines in quality of life and psychological wellbeing (Battista, Soo, Catroppa, & Anderson, 2012).

Issues with social competence are widely documented following paediatric TBI (Rosema, Crowe, & Anderson, 2012). TBI disrupts neural circuits which modulate social functioning (Ryan et al., 2015). Children with severe TBI have generally fewer close friendships and lower levels of social participation than those with mild TBI (Prigatano and Gupta, 2006). Key neurocognitive social skills include executive functions, pragmatic language, and social problem-solving. Deficits in these areas are likely to reflect injury in a network of brain regions implicated in social cognition. Problems with executive function and attentional control are closely linked to poor social outcomes, and children whose ability to self-regulate emotional responses have the poorest outcomes (Ganesalingam, Sanson, Anderson, & Yeates, 2007). Poor communication skills and language deficits following more severe injury also predict poorer social functioning (Anderson et al., 2013). Children with TBI have been found to have poorer emotion perception (an underlying skill in enabling ToM-based inferences about the affective states of others) skills than uninjured children (Tonks et al., 2006). Adolescents with high levels of peer relationship stress and low levels of school resources are at greatest risk of difficulties with adjustment following TBI, and these risk factors are associated with greater levels of internalising and externalising symptoms (Lantagne et al., 2018). These deficits in social functioning have been shown to persist among young adult survivors of paediatric TBI (McLellan & McKinley, 2013).

Other wider social issues following paediatric TBI include poor academic attainment, school exclusion, and poor community integration. Children with TBI are vastly under-identified in schools and education services. A study conducted in the USA in 2019 identified that an estimated 145,000 children and adolescents in the United States are living with long-lasting and significant difficulties with behavioural, physical, social, and cognitive functioning following a TBI. However, only 26,371 students receive special education services for TBI currently. Therefore, a significant number of children and adolescents with ongoing disability resulting from TBI are unidentified in the education system, and not receiving proper support (Nagele et al., 2019). Many young adults with ongoing TBI symptoms are also at risk of complex needs including alcohol and drug misuse problems, self-harm, suicidality, and homelessness. Interpersonal problems could also mean that family support networks are precarious, furthering the risk of poor support with these issues (Topolovec-Vranic et al., 2013).

Paediatric TBI and forensic risk

Pathways linking TBI and offending behaviour are complex. A range of risk factors for criminal behaviour are also risk factors for, or exacerbated by, TBI including male sex, low socioeconomic status, and risk-raking tendencies (Williams et al., 2018). Young people with TBI are significantly over-represented in the criminal justice system. Estimates of the prevalence of TBI leading to a loss of consciousness in the general population range from 8%–12% (Silver, Kramer, Greenwald, & Weissman, 2001; Frost, Farrer, Primosch, & Hedges, 2013). In studies of young offenders, prevalence estimates of TBI are far higher. Williams and colleagues (2010) found that 65% of young offenders reported a TBI that left them feeling 'dazed and confused', 46% suffered a TBI with loss of consciousness, and 32% reported a history of more than one TBI. This high incidence rates were corroborated by Davies and colleagues (2012) and Kent and colleagues (2020) who found that 41% and 46% of young offenders respectively had experienced a TBI leading to a loss of consciousness. TBI has been linked to both more violent offending, and persistent re-offending (Williams et al., 2018).

Criminal behaviour peaks in adolescence, for several reasons. In general, adolescents are less 'harm avoidant' than adults, favouring instant gratification over future rewards – a phenomena known as 'temporal discounting' which devalues a reward the further away in time it is (Frost & McNaughton, 2017). In the adolescent brain, hedonism is not yet properly regulated by the frontal lobes which are still developing. This leads to short-term decision making (favouring social acceptance, substance use 'highs', or peer status) with less regard for long-term consequences such as a criminal record (White et al., 2014). An adolescent generally has a similar capability to an adult to cognitively reason out and understand the consequences of an action, but will be more prone to 'in the moment' emotional or reward-driven decision making, particularly in the presence of peers. TBI affecting the frontal lobes can disrupt the development of inhibitory control, contributing to behavioural problems and a lack of harm-avoidance. Frontal lobe dysfunction also leads to increased agitation and reactive aggression in response to perceived threats (Edward, 2002). Dysfunction in the medial prefrontal cortex is linked to poorer emotion regulation and resilience (Van der Horn, Liemburg, Aleman, Spikman, & Van der Naalt, 2016). TBI can also exacerbate existing neuro-diverse conditions including ADHD (Attention Deficit Hyperactivity Disorder). An estimated 36% of children with injury to the dorsal prefrontal cortex develop subsequent psychiatric disorders, with ADHD and oppositional defiance disorder being the most common of these (Max et al., 2005). The cumulative impact of this is that young people with TBI often struggle with inattention, impulse control, and making rational decisions in emotionally pressured situations, leading to greater propensity for reactive, frequently violent, behaviour.

Paediatric TBI has been associated with increased levels of violent behaviour, externalising behaviour, poor pragmatic communication, and contact with the law (Stoddard & Zimmerman, 2011). In a 35-year total population study in Sweden, 2.3% of population controls committed violent crime, compared to 8.8% of those who had a history of TBI (Fazel, Lichtenstein, Grann, & Langstrom, 2011). In a study in northern Finland, adolescents with a history of TBI who were admitted to psychiatric care were at increased risk of criminality compared to controls with no TBI (Luukkainen, Riala, Laukkanen, Hakko, & Rasanen, 2012). The existing range of evidence indicates that TBI is an independent risk factor for criminal behaviour, and also adds to established criminogenic risk factors. TBI can be considered to sit at the centre of a 'melting pot' of multiplicative risk factors for crime including school exclusion, peer rejection, and reduced resilience. The internalising and externalising sequelae of TBI can lead to problems in school, and difficulties with classroom behaviour. TBI contributes to both problematic classroom behaviours, social issues, and attentional problems, leading to disruptive behaviours and poor social integration. Resultant exclusions, poor educational achievement, and peer rejection can further impact developmental trajectories. The presence of paediatric TBI is a pervasive factor in pathways from poor educational attainment to perseverative criminal behaviour in young offenders (Clasby et al., 2020).

As well as increasing risk of criminal behaviour, young people with TBI may struggle to understand and engage with legal processes. They may be more prone to erratic and emotional behaviour in custody, resulting in violent altercations or in harsh punishments. Young people with TBI may also be more vulnerable to extortion and manipulation. Difficulties with language and communication, memory, and information processing could make legal processes confusing and hard to engage with for young people with ongoing TBI sequelae. The pilot introduction of linkworkers (key workers with specific training in TBI) has been shown to improve engagement with rehabilitation services in young people with TBI in prisons, and can help adapt services to be more appropriate for the complex profiles of needs of young people with TBI (Williams et al., 2018; Ramos, Oddy, Liddemont, & Fortescue, 2018).

Assessment of paediatric TBI

The clinical presentation of paediatric TBI is diverse and variable, depending on the locality, mechanism, and severity of injury. Assessment of TBI relies on gaining perspective on the 'dosage' of injury. These dosages are additive, and multiple injuries result in more serious and complex symptom profiles. Poorer outcomes of TBI in adolescents are associated with both more severe injuries, and delay in assessment and intervention. The closer the assessment to the time of injury, the better the outcomes (Battista et al., 2012). Measures which do not truly capture the 'dosage' of the injury, and do not account for the cumulative effects of multiple TBIs, can risk underestimating what the ongoing effects of the injury will be and what support will be required. It is also key to understand the pre-morbid ability of children and young people with TBI, as much of the prognosis depends on when in development the TBI was sustained. This can help in determining the impact of neurocognitive stall, and allows the change in development post-injury to be understood more completely. See Appendix 5.1 for more discussion of understanding pre-morbid function in children and young people. Those with paediatric TBI frequently have co-morbid diagnoses, further adding to the myriad of neuropsychological symptoms to be disentangled. Currently clinicians do not routinely assess for deficits in emotion and empathy, but identifying those with these deficits would provide a more holistic view of target areas for intervention (Tonks et al., 2008).

One widely used measure of capturing TBI dosage is the BISI (Brain Injury Screening Index) (Disabilities Trust, 2019). This is a well-validated self-report measure used to assess history of TBI (Da Silva Ramos, Liddement, Addicott, Fortescue, & Oddy, 2020). Semi-structured interviews provide more rich history and detail. An example of this is the TBI section of the CHAT (Comprehensive Health Assessment Tool), which is a sensitive and specific interview identifying the severity, nature, causes, and ongoing symptoms from lifelong TBIs (Chitsabesan, Lennox, Williams, Tariq, & Shaw, 2015).

Familial factors in recovery and minimising risk

TBI does not occur in a vacuum, and risk of injury, severity of injury, and prognosis following TBI are directly determined by a myriad of multiplicative risk factors which can be difficult to disentangle. Psychologically traumatic experiences can trigger neuroinflammatory responses in a similar way to physical brain trauma, and so where TBI occurs in a traumatic environment (e.g. an abusive home) risk of a severe neuroinflammatory response can be magnified (Lisieski, Eagle, Conti, Liberzon, & Perrine, 2018). Environment is therefore a key protective factor against injury, and recovery from TBI may be compromised in stressful environments which are not conducive to health immune responses. The family environment, parental responsiveness, and socioeconomic status impact longevity and severity of symptoms. As previously discussed, age predisposes children to TBI from different causes and contributes to level of risk. Socioeconomic status is also a risk factor for paediatric TBI, and those in the poorest 5% of the population are at higher risk. Deprivation is closely linked to chaotic and abusive family environments, with increased risk of TBI through physical abuse (Fontes, Conceicao, & Machado, 2017). Often, violence towards a child will have occurred over an extended period. This time will span several critical phases of brain development.

Children from families with low socioeconomic status are also less likely to receive long-term comprehensive rehabilitation and educational support, furthering their risk of poorer long-term outcomes (Haines et al., 2019). Fewer family resources are associated with more severe deficits in executive function, regardless of the type of injury (Potter et al., 2011). Parental behaviours modify risk of, and outcomes following, paediatric TBI. One of the leading causes of TBI in young children is falls. Attentive and responsive parenting practices can modify this risk, by closely monitoring the child's activity and modifying the environment to be safe for a child of that age, therefore reducing risk of accidents leading to TBI. There is some emerging evidence that poor parental supervision or lack of parental involvement is associated with more severe lifetime TBI and increased levels of reactive aggression in young offenders (Kent et al., 2021). Likewise in adolescents, those with uninvolved parents are twice as likely to drive when intoxicated, and more likely to use a mobile phone whilst driving, placing them at higher risk of accidents leading to TBI (Ginsburg, Durbin, Garcia-Espana, Kalika, & Winston, 2009). By contrast, children with authoritative (high warmth, high demand) parents have generally better social competence and executive functioning following severe TBI (Schorr et al., 2020). Parenting interventions have been evidenced as a way to improve outcomes in children with moderate-severe TBI, particularly in families with low socioeconomic status (Antonini et al., 2014).

We note that many issues arising from paediatric brain injury often become critical as young people reach transition into adulthood. We provide the case treatment of a litiganty below to demonstrate issues of risk and how to assess it, understanding of the role of resources (family and environment) drawing on the above discussion.

Case study: Client A

Client A is now 16 years and has hemiplegia (weakness on one side of the body). She has a mild learning disability and a degree of difficulties with executive function following brain injury at birth. She has a long-standing history of damaging property and other objects, and occasionally lashes out at parents, teachers and other staff who work with her. She can also be verbally aggressive and inappropriate. She will regularly damage property in her own home, including items of personal value such as her new phone. The damage she causes can be extremely expensive and she recently climbed onto the roof of a car. Her family are at breaking point with her and are concerned about the negative impact of her behaviour on her younger siblings. The family feel they should no longer accommodate her. She is involved in a personal injury claim and the defendant's expert in her legal case is suggesting that all of her problems are nothing to do with her brain injury but are instead as a result of poor boundaries in the home. Client A feels out of control, she is saddened by the negative effect of her behaviour on her relationships, she is anxious and displays rigid and inflexible thinking. Triggers for her behaviour are in part related to her over-dependence upon structure and routine, and her inability to cope with unexpected events or changes.

In a case of this kind a multifactorial approach involving interdisciplinary approaches and objective assessments of Client A's presentation are essential. Everything should start with an initial, comprehensive assessment of risk. This should document the agencies involved, who were consulted in gathering information and the person's legal status. It is important to consider both historic and current factors in understanding the risks. What are the behavioural issues? What personal, clinical, and care-related issues are evident, both at present and in the young person's past? Who is most at risk? There is clearly potential of risk of harm to others, but the young person is also at risk of coming into contact with criminal justice systems and they are potentially vulnerable in these systems. Does the young person have any insight and what do they think might help to reduce risk? What protective, personal, family, and wider systemic factors could be mobilised or increased to reduce risk, and what has been tried before?

This will enable a formulation to seek to reduce risk and prevalence of problematic behaviour. Whilst it may be tempting to lean towards a single approach (such as Cognitive Behavioural approaches with the individual, or family support), we would advocate most strongly against this. This is because such a unitary approach may increase the propensity of risk, particularly if the multifactorial features of this complex picture are not addressed simultaneously. It will invariably be the case that the neuro-cognitive effects of injury are worthy of consideration. Individual approaches with Client A will likely require her to recall accurately when problems have arisen, discuss and learn from these in therapy, then apply learning in the 'heat of the moment' later, when the next challenge arises. These are not necessarily skills that Client A may have. Equally, it would be quite inappropriate to advise the family that if they can only function better, the problems will resolve, given the potential for a neurologically driven nature to Client A's difficulties. We advocate for a dynamic approach that seeks to understand whether Client A, and the family can engage with any kind of intervention, whether changing the demands of the environment around Client A may be a factor, and whether wider practical changes may also help. Does Client A have a sense of purpose? Does she have liberty to make situated, or age-appropriate choices and does having greater agency improve her, or does it increase the demands upon her leading to increased problematic behaviour? What is happening before during and after an outburst? How do others respond? Is there any functional gain from the behaviour? Only after months of work will the patterns emerge that are dictating this person's complex needs. Interventions often involve speech therapy to consider social function and communication issues, occupational therapy to understand sensory needs and maximising independence, and neuropsychology to consider everything including sleep and all other aspects of intervention. This would need monitoring in highly structured intervention plans that can change as the information about Client A evolves. Here Neuropsychiatric advice should also be carefully considered. It would be remiss to find that after months of rehabilitation that the issue was solved quite quickly with medical management. We suspect from experience that a mix of medical management and rehabilitative approaches may yield maximal success.

Conclusion

Improved linkage between healthcare services, schools, and social services could aid the earlier identification and management of paediatric TBI, particularly in families with low socioeconomic status. This approach could help to reduce risks associated with school exclusion and social isolation. Paediatric brain injury gives rise to dynamic and complex deficits which contribute to an increased risk of social isolation and ultimately contact with the criminal justice system. Multiplicative risk factors including low socioeconomic status, low levels of parental involvement, and comorbidities lead to additive risk of poor outcomes. Paediatric brain injury is beginning to be considered by professionals when assessing the rehabilitative needs of these individuals, or when writing policy documents, but we advocate that more is needed if we are to understand the impact of brain injury and mediate its devastating effects upon individuals and communities. This is a key area, which has recently gained attention in the United Nations global study on children deprived of liberty, and support for young people in the justice system with TBI must be considered a global priority moving forwards (Nowak, 2019). Assessment is complex, with diverse symptoms to be disentangled, but is crucial for implementing intervention. Optimal care for those affected by paediatric TBI requires a multidisciplinary approach during each phase of management to create ecology of collaborative support from education, healthcare, and justice professionals.

The legal framework in managing the risk posed by patients who have sustained a brain injury

Ian P. Brownhill, Lincoln's Inn. Barrister at 39 Essex Chambers and Her Majesty's Assistant Coroner for Kent.

Introduction

There remains a concerning lack of understanding of the prevalence of offenders who have suffered brain injuries and how this may impact on their behaviours. Whilst there is a greater awareness of how an offender's mental health may impact their risk, it is apparent that those who have sustained a brain injury may, sometimes, simply fall through the net.[1]

However, the management of the risk posed by persons who have sustained brain injuries is becoming an issue grappled with more frequently by the criminal Courts[2] and the Court of Protection.[3]

This commentary sets out briefly how the risks posed by a person with a brain injury are managed by the legal frameworks available. From the outset it is important to note that there is not a single framework which applies in these circumstances, in some cases there may be multiple different frameworks which apply to a single person.

Compulsion versus consent

Broadly, risk management measures are imposed on a person with a brain injury, or, they are something to which the person consents. The

---

1 See the discussion of May J at paragraphs 72 and 73 of the judgment in *EG, R (On the Application Of) v The Parole Board of England and Wales* [2020] EWHC 1457 (Admin) (09 June 2020)
2 See *PS, Abdi Dahir, CF v The Queen* [2019] EWCA Crim 2286
3 See *X Council v BB, CB, AB (by her litigation friend, The Official Solicitor), The NHS Trust* [2021] EWCOP 21 as a recent example.

latter category is straight forward, for example, a person with a brain injury consents to live in a residential setting where they cannot consume alcohol, or where they agree to particular restrictions on their internet access. In those circumstances, the issue is whether the person is able to consent to the particular restrictions, i.e whether they have the mental capacity to do so.

Where the person lacks the mental capacity to consent to the restrictions

In circumstances where the person poses a risk of harm to others, the relevant decisions in respect of capacity are usually linked to: (i) contact with others; (ii) care and support; (iii) access to the internet or use of social media. To illustrate:

If the issue is that a person with a brain injury poses a risk of contact sexual offending, then the relevant decision is whether the person has the mental capacity to make decisions in respect of contact with others.[4]

In cases where the person poses a risk of the destruction of property or fire starting, the relevant decision is whether the person has the mental capacity to make decisions as to their care and support (that care and support evidently avoided this risk).

The Court of Protection is increasingly familiar with cases where a person's disorder of the functioning of mind or brain causes sexual dysfunction or disinhibition. That dysfunction or disinhibition may manifest in the way in which that person uses the internet or social media. In those cases, the relevant decision is whether the person has capacity to access the internet and social media.[5]

The more difficult issue is the decision as to any restrictions which follows a finding that a person lacks capacity. Decisions made under the Mental Capacity Act 2005 are made in a person's best interests. The protection of the public is not a factor which appears in the best interests checklist in section 4 of the Mental Capacity Act 2005. It follows that the Mental Capacity Act 2005 cannot be used to impose restrictions on a person in order to protect the public.

---

4 There may be, in certain circumstances, a consideration as to whether the relevant question is if P has capacity to make decisions as to contact with people to whom they are attracted. However, this has tended to be used in the context of where P is at risk of sexual harm from other people rather than where P poses a risk. For greater discussion on this point see the judgment of Baker LJ in *A Local Authority v JB (by his litigation friend, the Official Solicitor)* [2020] EWCA Civ 735.

5 See *B v A Local Authority* [2019] EWCA Civ 913.

However, in practice, restrictions continue to be imposed with a view to stopping a person who lacks capacity to make particular decisions from committing offences. The judgment which is oft quoted is *Y County Council and ZZ*,[6] where Moor J stated:

> I have come to the clear conclusion, for all the reasons given by the various doctors, that it is lawful as in Mr ZZ's best interests to deprive him of his liberty in accordance with the local authority care plan, pursuant to schedule A1 of the Mental Capacity Act 2005. I make that declaration. In doing so, I am following the advice of the expert professionals who know Mr ZZ so well. Indeed, the Official Solicitor accepts, on his behalf, that I should do so. I make it clear to Mr ZZ that I have no doubt that the restrictions upon him are in his best interests. They are designed to keep him out of mischief, to keep him safe and healthy, to keep others safe, to prevent the sort of situation where the relative of a child wanted to do him serious harm, which I have no doubt was very frightening for him, and they are there to prevent him from getting into serious trouble with the police.

Almost a decade on, it is unclear whether the court would couch its judgment in the same language if it were to decide the case now. However, the accepted approach is now that restrictions can be imposed on a person who lacks capacity if they are in their best interests. That analysis of best interests may conclude restrictions should be imposed to protect a person from entering the criminal justice system or being the victim of community reprisals due to their behaviour.

Other, coercive, legal frameworks do not rely on a person's consent or involve an analysis of that person's best interests at all.

Restrictions imposed by legal frameworks despite brain injury

Other legal frameworks may be used to manage the risk that a person with a brain injury poses. Those frameworks are often reactive rather than proactive and, in some cases, may be punitive.

Persons with brain injuries are over-represented in the criminal justice but despite this a specific guideline for these offenders[7] was only produced in 2020. The brain injury is not a shield rather instead culpability (and the sentence which follows) will only be reduced if there

---

6 [2012] EWCOP B34.
7 Sentencing offenders with mental disorders, developmental disorders, or neurological impairments. Effective from: 1 October 2020.

is sufficient connection between the offender's impairment or disorder and the offending behaviour.

Surprisingly, other pieces of core statutory guidance do not mention persons with brain injuries at all. Most startling is the statutory guidance[8] which accompanies the Anti-social Behaviour, Crime and Policing Act 2014. Despite the established link between brain injury and greater propensity for what would, legally, be described as anti-social behaviour there is little allowance made. A person with brain injury could find themselves subject to a huge raft of restriction which, if breached, could lead to financial penalties or even imprisonment.

Finally, it ought not be forgotten that injury to the brain can lead to the development of a mental disorder. The corollary being that the Mental Health Act 1983 may be used to detain a person for assessment or treatment.

Conclusion

The relationship between brain injury and the risk of offending are established by research. Despite this, there is not a universal response to how those risks are managed. Proactive management of those risks can lead to restrictive care practices which are difficult to reconcile with the Mental Capacity Act. Reactive management of those risks can expose vulnerable adults to serious criminal sanction, including imprisonment.

Those lawyers representing persons with brain injuries must always be clear: what is the risk, how likely the risk to eventuate and what is the impact if so? Hugely restrictive care packages are unlikely to be sustainable in the long term and are legally difficult to justify.

8 Anti-social behaviour powers statutory guidance for frontline professionals Revised in January 2021.

References

Anderson, V., Beauchamp, M. H., Yeates, K. O., Crossley, L., Hearps, S. J. C. Hearps & Catroppa, C. (2013). Social competence at 6 months following childhood traumatic brain injury. *J. Int Neuropsych Soc, 19*, 539–550.

Antonini, T. N., Raj, S. P., Oberjohn, K. S., Cassedy, A., Makoroff, K. L., Fouladi, M., & Wade, S. L. (2014). A pilot randomised trial of an online parenting skills program for paediatric traumatic brain injury: Improvements in parenting and child behaviour. *Behavioural Therapy, 45*, 455–468.

Araki, T., Yokota, H., & Morita, A. (2017). Paediatric traumatic brain injury: Characteristic features, diagnosis, and management. *Neurologia medico-chirurgica, 57*, 82–93.

Battista, A. D., Soo, C., Catroppa, C., & Anderson, V. (2012). Quality of life in children and adolescents post-TBI: A systematic review and meta-analysis. *J. Neurotrauma*, 29, 1717–1727.

Bernhardi, R., Bernhardi, L. E., & Eugenin, J. (2017). What is neural plasticity? *Adv Exp Med Biol*, 1015, 10–15.

Caeyenberghs, K., Leemans, A., Leunissen, I., Gooijers, J., Michiels, K., Sunaert, S., & Swinnen, S. P. (2014). Altered structural networks and executive deficits in traumatic brain injury patients. *Brain Structure & Function*, 219, 193–209.

Chapman, S. B. (2007). Neurocognitive stall: A paradox in long-term recovery from paediatric brain injury. *Brain Inj Prof*, 3, 10–13.

Chitsabesan, P., Lennox, C., Williams, W. H., Tariq, O., & Shaw, J. (2015). Traumatic brain injury in juvenile offenders: Findings from the comprehensive health assessment tool study and the development of a specialist linkworker service. *The Journal of Head Trauma Rehabilitation*, 30, 106–115.

Clasby, B., Bennett, M., Hughes, N., Hodges, E., Meadham, H., Hinder, D., Williams, W. H., & Mewse, A. J. (2020). The consequences of traumatic brain injury from the classroom to the courtroom: Understanding pathways through structural equation modelling. *Disability Rehabilitation*, 42, 2412–2421.

Da Silva Ramos, S., Liddement, J., Addicott, C., Fortescue, D., & Oddy, M. (2020). The development of the Brain Injury Screening Index (BISI): A self-report measure. *Neuropsychological Rehabilitation*, 30, 948–960.

Davies, R. C., Williams, W. H., Hinder, D., Burgess, C., & Mounce, L. (2012). Self-reported traumatic brain injury and postconcussion symptoms in incarcerated youth. *Journal of Head Trauma Rehabilitation*, 27, 21–27.

Decety, J. (2010). The neurodevelopment of empathy in humans. *Developmental Neuroscience*, 32, 257–267.

DeLuca, C. R., & Leventer, R. J. (2008). *Developmental trajectories of executive functions across the lifespan*. In: Anderson, V., Jacobs, R., & Anderson, P. J. (Eds.). *Executive Functions and the Frontal Lobes*. Taylor & Francis: London.

Disabilities Trust. (2019). *Brain Injury Screening Index (BISI)*. Available from: https://www.thedtgroup.org/foundation/brain-injury-screening-index.

Eagleman, D., & Downar, J. (2015). *Brain and behaviour: A cognitive neuroscience perspective*. Oxford University Press: Oxford.

Edward, K. (2002). Agitation, aggression, and disinhibition syndromes after traumatic brain injury. *Neurorehabilitation*, 17, 297–310.

Fazel, S., Lichtenstein, P., Grann, M., & Langstrom, N. (2011). Risk of violent crime in individuals with epilepsy and traumatic brain injury: A 35-year Swedish population study. *PLoS Med*, 8, e1001150.

Fontes, L. F. C., Conceicao, O. C., & Machado, S. (2017). Childhood and adolescent sexual abuse, victim profile, and its impact on mental health. *Ciencia & Saude Coletiva*, 22, 2919–2928.

Frost, R., & McNaughton, N. (2017). The neural basis of delay discounting: A review and preliminary model. *Neuroscience & Bio-behavioural Reviews*, 79, 48–65.

Frost, R., Farrer, T. J., Primosch, M., & Hedges, D. W. (2013). Prevalence of traumatic brain injury in the general adult population: A meta-analysis. *Neuroepidemiology*, 40, 154–159.

Ganesalingam, K., Sanson, A., Anderson, V., Yeates, K.O. (2007). Self-regulation as a mediator of the effects of childhood traumatic brain injury on social and behavioral functioning. *Journal of the International Neuropsychological Society*, 13, 298–311.

Ginsburg, K. R., Durbin, D. R., Garcia-Espana, J. F., Kalika, E. A., & Winston, F. K. (2009). Associations between parenting styles and teen driving, safety-related behaviours and attitudes. *Pediatrics, 124*, 1040–1051.

Goldsmith, W., & Plunkett, J. (2004). A biomechanical analysis of the causes of traumatic brain injury in infants and children. *Am J Forensic Med Pathol, 25*, 89–100.

Haines, K. L., Nguyen, B. P., Vatsaas, C., Alger, A., Brooks, K., & Agarwal, S. K. (2019). Socioeconomic status affects outcomes after severity-stratified traumatic brain injury. *Journal of Surgical Research, 235*, 131–140.

Heck, A., Chroust, A., White, H., Jubran, R., & Bhatt, R. S. (2018). Development of body emotion perception in infancy: From discrimination to recognition. *Infant Behaviour and Development, 50*, 42–51.

Hebb, D. 1949. *The organisation of behaviour*. New York, NY: John Wiley and Sons.

Hyder, A. A., Wunderlich, C. A., Puvanachandra, P., Gururaj, G., & Kobunsingye, O. C. (2007). The impact of traumatic brain injuries: A global perspective. *Neurorehabilitation, 22*, 341–353.

Johnson, S., Blum, R. W., & Giedd, J. N. (2009). Adolescent maturity and the brain: The promise and pitfalls of neuroscience research in adolescent health policy. *Journal of Adolescent Health, 45*, 216–221.

Keenan, H. T., Runyan, D. K., Marshall, S. W., Nocera, M. A., Merten, D. F., & Sinal, S. H. (2003). A population-based study of inflicted traumatic brain injury in young children. *JAMA, 290*, 621–626.

Keysers, C., & Perret, D. I. (2004). Demystifying social cognition: A Hebbian perspective. *Trends in Cognitive Sciences, 8*, 501–507.

Kent, H., Williams, W. H., Hinder, D., Meadham, H., Hodges, E., Agarwalla, V., Hogarth, L., & Mewse, A. J. (2021). Poor parental supervision is associated with traumatic brain injury and reactive aggression in young offenders. *Journal of Head Trauma Rehabilitation. [ePub ahead of print]*. Doi:10.1097/HTR.0000000000000678.

Lantagne, A., Peterson, R. L., Kirkwood, M. W., Taylor, G. H., Stancin, T., Yeates, K. O., & Wade, S. (2018). Interpersonal stressors and resources as predictors of adolescent adjustment following traumatic brain injury. *J Pediatr Psychol, 43*, 703–712.

Lenroot, R. K., & Giedd, J. (2010). Sex differences in the adolescent brain. *Brain & Cognition, 72*, 46–55.

Lisieski, M. J., Eagle, A. L., Conti, A. C., Liberzon, I., & Perrine, S. A. (2018). Single-prolonged stress: A review of two decades of progress in a rodent model of post-traumatic stress disorder. *Frontiers in Psychiatry, 9*, 1–22.

Luukkainen, S., Riala, K., Laukkanen, M., Hakko, H., & Rasanen, P. (2012). Association of traumatic brain injury with criminality in adolescent psychiatric inpatients from Northern Finland. *Psychiatry Research, 200*, 767–772.

Max, J. E., Levin, H. S., Landis, J., Schacher, R., Saunders, A., Ewing-Cobbs, L., Chapman, S. B., & Dennis, M. (2005). Predictors of personality change due to traumatic brain injury in children and adolescents in the first six months after injury. *J Am Acad Child Adolesc Psychiatry, 44*, 434–442.

McLellan, T., & McKinley, A. (2013). Sensitivity to emotion, empathy and theory of mind: Adult performance following childhood TBI. *Brain Inj, 27*, 1032–1037.

Meinhardt-Injac, B., Daum, M. M., & Meinhardt, G. (2020). Theory of mind development from adolescence to adulthood: Testing the two-component model. *British Journal of Developmental Psychology, 38*, 289–303.

Nagele, D. A., Hooper, S. R., Hildebrant, K., McCart, M., Dettmer, J., & Glang, A. (2019). Under-identification of students with long term disability from moderate to severe TBI. *Physical Disabilities, 38*, 10–25.

Nowak, M. (2019). *The United Nations global study on children deprived of liberty*. Accessed January 2020. Available from: https://childrendeprivedofliberty.info/.

Ommaya, A. K., Goldsmith, W., & Thibault, L. (2002). Biomechanics and neuropathology of adult and paediatric head injury. *British Journal of Neurosurgery, 16*, 220–242.

Parsonage, M. (2016). *Traumatic brain injury and offending: An economic analysis*. Centre for Mental Health Report. Barrow Cadbury Trust: UK.

Pauwels, L., Chalavi, S., & Swinnen, S. P. (2018). Aging and brain plasticity. *Aging, 10*, 1789–1790.

Poole, K. L., Santesso, D. L., Van Lieshout, R. J., & Schmidt, L. A. (2018). Trajectories of frontal brain activity and socio-emotional development in children. *Developmental Psychobiology, 60*, 353–363.

Potter, J. L., Wade, S. L., Walz, N. C., Cassedy, A., Stevens, M. H., Yeates, K. O., & Taylor, H. G. (2011). Parenting style is related to executive dysfunction after brain injury in children. *Rehabilitation Psychology, 56*, 351–358.

Prigatano, G.P., & Gupta, S. (2006). Friends after traumatic brain injury in children. *Journal of Head Trauma Rehabilitation, 21*, 505–513.

Ramos, S. D., Oddy, M., Liddemont, J., & Fortescue, D. (2018). Brain injury and offending: The development and field testing of a linkworker intervention. *Int J Offender Ther Comp criminol, 62*, 1854–1868.

Rosema, S., Crowe, L., Anderson, V. (2012). Social function in children and adolescents after traumatic brain injury: A systematic review 1989–2011. *Journal of Neurotrauma, 29*, 1277–1291.

Rusnak M. (2013). Traumatic brain injury: giving voice to a silent epidemic. *Nat Rev Neurol, 9*, 186–187.

Russo, M. V., & McGavern, D. B. (2016). Inflammatory neuroprotection following traumatic brain injury. *Science, 19*, 783–785.

Ryan, N. P., Hughes, N., Godfrey, C., Rosema, S., Catroppa, C., & Anderson, V. A. (2015). Prevalence and predictors of externalising behaviour in young adult survivors of paediatric traumatic brain injury. *J. Head Trauma Rehabilitation, 30*, 75–85.

Schorr, E., Wade, S. L., Taylor, H. G., Stancin, T., & Yeates, K. O. (2020). Parenting styles as a predictor of long-term psychosocial outcomes after traumatic brain injury (TBI) in early childhood. *Disability Rehabilitation, 42*, 2437–2443.

Silver, J. M., Kramer, R., Greenwald, S., & Weissman, M. (2001). The association between head injuries and psychiatric disorders: Findings from the New Haven NIMH Epidemiologic catchment area study. *Brain Injury, 15*, 935–945.

Skaper, S. D., Facci, L., Zusso, M., & Guisti, P. (2018). An inflammation-centric view of neurological disease: Beyond the neuron. *Frontiers in Cellular Neuroscience, 12*, 1–26.

Slaughter, V., Imuta, K., Peterson, C. C., & Henry, J. D. (2015). Meta-analysis of theory of mind and peer popularity in the preschool and early school years. *Child Development, 86, 4*, 1159–1174.

Stoddard, S. A., & Zimmerman, M. A. (2011). Association of interpersonal violence with self-reported history of head injury. *Paediatrics, 127*, 1074–1080.

Tonks, J., Slater, A., Frampton, I., Wall, S. E., Yates, P., & Williams, W. H. (2008). The development of emotion and empathy skills after childhood brain injury. *Developmental Medicine and Child Neurology, 51*, 8–16.

Tonks, J., Williams, W. H., Frampton, I., Yates, P., & Slater, A. (2006). Reading emotions after child brain injury: A comparison between children with brain injury and non-injured controls. *Brain Injury, 21*, 731–739.

Topolovec-Vranic, J., Ennis, N., Ouchterlony, D., Cusimano, M. D., Colantonio, A., Hwang, S. W., Kontos, P., Stergiopoulos, V., & Brenner, L. (2013). Clarifying the link between traumatic brain injury and homelessness: Workshop proceedings. *Brain Injury*, 27, 1600–1605.

Van der Horn, H. J., Liemburg, E. J., Aleman, A., Spikman, J. M., & Van der Naalt, J. (2016). Brain networks subserving emotion regulation and adaptation after mild traumatic brain injury. *J Neurotrauma*, 33, 1–9.

Verger, K., Junque, C., Jurado, M. A., Tresserras, P., Bartumeus, F., Nogues, P., Poch, J. M. (2009). Age effects on long-term neuropsychological outcome in paediatric traumatic brain injury. *Brain Injury*, 14, 495–503.

Wellman, H. M., Cross, D., & Watson, J. (2001). Meta-analysis of theory-of-mind development: the truth about false belief. *Child Development*, 72, 655–684.

Westby, C., & Robinson, L. (2014). A developmental perspective for promoting theory of mind. *Top Lang Disorders*, 34, 362–382.

White, S. F., Clanton, R., Brislin, S. J., Meffert, H., Hwang, S., Sinclair, S., & Blair, J. R. (2014). Reward: Empirical contribution. Temporal discounting and conduct disorder in adolescents. *Journal of Personality Disorders*, 28, 5–18.

Whittle, S., Lichter, R., Dennison, M., Vijayakumar, N., Schwartz, O., Byrne, M. L.... & Allen, N. B. (2014). Structural brain development and depression onset during adolescence: A prospective longitudinal study. *American Journal of Psychiatry*, 171, 564–571.

Williams, W. H., Chitsabesan, P., Fazel, S., McMillan, T., Hughes, N., Parsonage, M., & Tonks, J. (2018). Traumatic brain injury: A potential cause of violent crime? *Lancet Psychiatry*, 5, 836–844.

Williams, W. H., Giray, C., Mewse, A. J., Tonks, J., & Burgess, C. (2010). Self-reported traumatic brain injury in male young offenders: A risk factor for re-offending, poor mental health, and violence? *Neuropschological Rehabilitation*, 20, 801–812.

Zamani, A., Mychasiuk, R., & Semple, B. D. (2019). Determinants of social behaviour deficits and recovery after paediatric traumatic brain injury. *Experimental Neurology*, 314, 34–45.

Appendix 5.1

Understanding pre-morbid function in children and young people under the age of 16

When it comes to understanding pre-injury status in younger populations, all the information a practitioner may require probably exists, but much depends upon when in development an injury-event occurred. Tracking a young person's development and learning with ongoing descriptive records and with standardised tests, is an integral component of school-based, 'healthy' educational experience. Further, school-records accumulate as a significant and increasingly reliable indicator of 'ability' over-time. This is true for all children in school.

It is first helpful to consider some of the difficulties with this approach. Foremost among these is the scenario of birth, or early-life injury. Here there will be no record of pre-injury status, and it follows that until the infant begins their education, no such records will be accumulated. One is then in a best estimate scenario, based upon the achievements of siblings or parents in terms of their academic achievements and occupational status. In relying upon such information, one must carefully consider a range of other variables, such as presence of Attention Deficit Disorder, learning difficulties of other kinds, mental health history, or history of Autism in other family members. If everyone else in the family is a rocket-scientist, there are more compelling arguments for positive pre-injury status than if everyone else in the family has a poorly understood genetic disorder that might be associated with challenges with learning.

There are also paradoxes that are opposite to the 'ground-rules' that can apply in understanding pre-injury status in adults. If we set-aside some of the rare acquired-dyslexias, reading ability is usually quite robust against injury effects and so is a favoured measure of pre-injury status. Administering any test that would rely upon reading as a pre-injury estimate (such as the WTAR - Wechsler Test of Adult Reading), would be an awfully bad idea if administered with a child, or young person who is still learning to read. The WTAR can be used reliably only in testing an individual aged 16 or over ('A' is for Adult in WTAR), but one must be satisfied that this individual has learned to read.

Setting aside the difficulties, it is first possible to access records from pre-school. These provide level-descriptors from the Early Years Foundation Curriculum (3-to-4 years). These will give an indication of whether social, emotional, behavioural, and learning targets are 'on-time' or in-line with expectation. They are comprehensive and involve the teacher recording actual evidence of an achieved goal. Pre-Curriculum Level Descriptors are useful here, that are recorded from P-Level 1 to 8. At the end of the reception year, an average child about to transition into Year 1 should achieve a P-Level of 5-or-6.

The descriptors then become more structured with age (from 5-to-6 years). These set out specific targets for acquiring literacy and numeracy, which the teacher must again evidence as achieved from records ('can demonstrate number bonds to 10 using blocks' etc.). Teaching of reading and writing has been enhanced through schools adopting a phonics learning scheme with records demonstrating which phonics are evidenced within work (phonics are letter sounds – e.g. word openings thr, wh, then later, complex blends at the end of words 'ought' – for thought, bought, etc.). By 7 years, lots of children will then take their first standardised tests. These can include reading tests National Foundation for Educational Research (NFER), the Salford, The Neile etc), and/ or Key-stage 1 SATs Statutory Attainment Tests (lots of schools now only use teacher assessments at 7 years). With the tracking of learning in place, if a child's pre-injury status is one where there is already problems with learning, the greater their difficulties, the more likely it will be that they will be more closely scrutinised. They commonly generate more standardised assessment and monitoring that might be usual.

The next big benchmark then is end of Key-stage 2 SATs which all children will take upon completion of Primary School. These are self-standardising tests that utilise normative data from all children who take that test during that year (the entire population – with a mean of 100 and an SD of 15). Scores are for literacy numeracy and science only, but as an indicator of pre-injury status, there is little that can be better. There are some issues with this data. Children with learning difficulties can be 'dis-applied' from SATs tests (schools can make an application to mean that certain children do not have to sit/suffer these tests unnecessarily if it is inappropriate to subject them to this – this can be children with behavioural, mental health related or learning issues). That is, the normative population who generate the data, will, exclude any children with significant impairment. This means that one can only plot an individual's score on a continuum derived from assessment of healthy children (the sample is not representative of the whole population – which would naturally include individuals with some disability – which tests like the Wechsler Preschool and Primary Scale of Intelligence (WPPSI), Wechsler Intelligence Scale for Children (WISC) and WAIS would do). One can however be reasonably satisfied that if a child scores within the average range in their SATS this is reasonably reliable and valid.

The next great landmark in the quest for a decent indicator of pre-injury status arises in the first term of secondary school. The CATs – Cognitive Ability Test. These tests (typically taken at 11-to-12 years) offer a non-verbal IQ estimate, a verbal IQ estimate, quantitative reasoning and a mean-average.

They often generate a score that is within the predicted confidence intervals seen on the WISC-V, and whilst administered differently (online, rather than face-to-face) they do provide comparable constructs – one can look at the quantitative reasoning index from the WISC and compare to the CAT quantitative score etc.

The tracking and assessments continue, up until the end of Key-stage 3 (13-to-14 years), where again tests are used. By this point most schools have moved to a 'flight-path system'. This involves predicting the child's expected GCSE grade, and their grades each term for the remaining school years. If they dip below the 'flight-path' this is flagged-up and reasons for this may be explored with the child and family (reasons can include 'attitude to learning', behaviour, absence, and disruption to home life etc). This takes us up until GCSEs and school leaving.

If the circumstances of injury fall during the developmental course it is possible to literally plot the change in a child's developmental trajectory from the point of injury, using these tests. Not only can one quickly identify pre-injury status, it is also possible to comment upon the extent and uniformity of change in development post-injury.

One must end with a final note of caution in the medico-legal arena. There are lots of routes to training in Paediatric Neuropsychology and Clinical Psychology. Each practitioner must be satisfied that their route has included some form of training to support the view that they are qualified to interpret educational records and provide an opinion for the court. Lots of Clinical Neuropsychologists will have trained via the Educational Psychology route, whilst others may have qualified and worked as teachers before training in Clinical Psychology. If the practitioner does not have a background to support the view that they have qualification and competence in interpretation of educational records the simple solution is to seek the view of an expert Educational Psychologist to provide a view on pre-injury status based upon the records to hand.

Part 2
Current condition

6 Effort testing, performance validity, and the importance of context and consistency

Simon Gerhand, Chris A. Jones and David Hacker

Assessment of effort will be considered in terms of different approaches, such as stand-alone tests and embedded measures. The rationale underpinning effort testing will be reviewed, alongside professional guidelines for how this is accomplished. Interpretation of effort test results will next be considered. Different scenarios will be considered which may underlie effort test failure, in addition to a review of the updated criteria for malingering (Sherman, Slick & Iverson, 2020). Case studies will be used to illustrate why interpretation of failed effort tests is rarely straightforward, and why more information than scoring below cut-off is required. This section will emphasise the importance of consistency, and consideration of effort test results within the context of the patient's cognitive profile and functional presentation.

Introduction

The assessment of response validity is now considered routine practice within neuropsychology (Bigler, 2012, 2014; Brooks, Ploetz, & Kirkwood, 2015; Dandachi-Fitzgerald, Ponds & Merten, 2013). Within the medico-legal context the principal use of response validity tasks has been to assess the validity, veracity and honesty of the self-report symptoms and the legitimacy of performance-based measures of cognitive ability. Bigler (2014) and Larrabee (2012) suggest that the term "Performance Validity Tests (PVTs)" should be used when describing tests designed to detect non-credible underperformance on neurocognitive tests whilst "Symptom Validity Tests (SVTs)" should be used to describe the non-credible reporting of symptoms that are in excess of that which would be expected.

Terminology

Such response validity or performance validity tasks have been variously referred to as "effort tests" (particularly in the United Kingdom), as tests designed to detect Malingered Cognitive Dysfunction (Sherman et al., 2020); particularly in the United States of America, SVTs and PVTs. Unfortunately, the correct interpretation of such validity tests has arguably been hampered

DOI: 10.4324/9781003105763-8

90 *Current condition*

by the use of such labels. Firstly, tasks designed to detect potential dissimulation do not, and cannot, in themselves, measure "malingering" (although may contribute to an overall formulation of such). This is because the diagnosis of malingering requires that the respondent *intentionally* underperforms or exaggerates symptomatology in order to gain an external reward, such as a more beneficial settlement to person injury litigation. However, no dissimulation task to date can claim to be able to empirically demonstrate the motivational basis for underperformance. Secondly, tests designed to identify dissimulation, or poor response validity, intentionally use areas of cognitive ability (e.g. semantic priming) that do not require the respondent to engage in extensive cognitive processing. Indeed, if extensive cognitive processing were required to complete the task then the validity test would become sensitive to cognitive impairment and not fit for its intended purpose. In essence therefore "effort" tests are designed to be as close to "effortless" as possible. As Frederick and Crosby (2000) discussed effort and motivation can, in fact, be viewed as orthogonal dimensions.

Classifying invalid responses

Frederick and Crosby (2000) usefully provided a classification of invalid responses based on the cross-tabulation of motivation and effort (see Figure 6.1).

Compliant respondents have a high motivation to perform well and present effortful engagement with the test stimuli and procedures, meaning that their performance on the neuropsychological tests can be considered to accurately

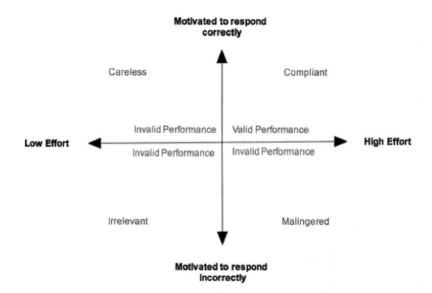

Figure 6.1 Classification of invalid responses
Source: Adapted from Frederick and Crosby (2000).

represent their cognitive abilities. Alternatively, careless responders also have a high motivation to perform well, however, their responding is invalidated by incomplete effort to engage with the test stimuli and procedures. Such careless test-taking may result from inattention, distraction, or fatigue. For example, someone with severe and acute psychotic symptoms might be unable to pay attention to the test stimuli for genuine reasons despite motivation to do well. Irrelevant responders present only token engagement with test stimulating procedures and are not motivated to perform well. Such responders may be disinterested in responding to the task correctly, perhaps perceive the outcome of the assessment as irrelevant to them and produce a profile with inconsistent, possibly random, and certainly inaccurate results. Finally, effortful engagement when motivated by the desire to perform poorly can be observed in situations where the test taker attempts to fabricate or exaggerate cognitive deficits in a convincing manner. When this occurs to obtain external rewards (such as obtaining benefits or to obtain a more beneficial settlement to person injury litigation) then the respondent may be considered to be malingering.

Malingering and factitious disorder

Resnick (1997) described three types of malingering, labelled "*pure malingering*", "*partial malingering*", and "*false imputation*". 1) Pure malingering is characterised by a complete fabrication of symptoms. 2) Partial malingering is defined by exaggerating actual symptoms or by reporting past symptoms as if they are continuing. 3) False imputation refers to the deliberate misattribution of actual symptoms to the compensable event. Therefore, malingered and exaggerated disabilities can occur in persons with legitimate and authentic symptomatology. The presence of invalid responding does not therefore lead automatically to the conclusion of absence of impairment, but one must rely on other nomothetic sources of information (for example the expected outcome given the severity and mechanism of injury) as well as non-self-report data to draw conclusions about the likelihood of deficits in such cases. Sreenivasan, Eth, Kirkish, and Garrick (2003) proposed a model for classifying assessment results, which consisted of four outcomes:

1. Genuine disorder with no symptom exaggeration.
2. Genuine disorder with atypical symptoms related to non-neurological or other factors.
3. Atypical presentation – "amplification", characterised by deficits and symptoms not consistent with a medical/neurological disorder, and a level of severity disproportionate to the degree of trauma. This would be associated with a non-financial incentive such as conversion disorder, or factitious disorder.
4. Atypical presentation – malingering. Intentionally produced deficits, with a discernible external incentive.

Intentional underperformance may also occur in respondents who present with motivations other than the desire to obtain external financial reward. For example, the respondent may be motivated to perform poorly to emphasise their distress and disability, and to obtain access to what they might perceive as appropriate treatment. Such a "cry for help" may be seen in persons with legitimate serious psychological or psychiatric problems who are desperately seeking the recognition of, and attention for, these difficulties. Also, a person might deliberately exaggerate because he or she desires to be perceived as sick and disabled and to consequently receive care from significant others. Under these circumstances, the person might receive a diagnosis of factitious disorder (DSM 5, APA, 2013). A diagnosis of factitious disorder is appropriate where the motivation to exaggerate symptoms is due to an internal factor such as a psychological drive whereas malingering, which is not listed as a medical disorder in DSM-5 arises when there is some form of external incentive. This distinction has received criticism, not least because it has changed little since the introduction of DSM-III in 1980 and does not take into account the considerable amount of literature published on the subject in the intervening years (Bass & Halligan, 2014; Bass & Wade, 2018). As tests measure behaviour, anything else has to be inferred. The need for an external incentive is central to definitions of malingering although the presence of an external incentive in healthcare settings may not always be either obvious or admitted (Sherman et al., 2020). Factitious disorder requires the "absence of obvious rewards" (DSM 5), which is usually taken to mean you cannot diagnose factitious disorder in the context of litigation, even though there may be incentives other than the litigation driving the factitious disorder.

Therefore, when faced with either underperformance on neurocognitive testing or over-reporting of symptoms, one should consider the 1) range of information available, 2) the possible motivational scenarios and 3) highlight the evidence that is consistent for and against each of the different formulations in order to assist the Court. Although the expert may express an opinion regarding why a person might respond sub-optimally and may highlight other evidence that is consistent which such an opinion, it is ultimately the responsibility of the Court to make a determination regarding causation including the credibility of the Claimant and the possibility of malingering. In cases where there is considered to be deliberate symptom exaggeration, it is possible that the concept of fundamental dishonesty may be evoked (*Howlett v Davies* [2017] EWHC Civ 1696). A test for this was set out in *Ivey v Genting Casinos (UK) Ltd* [2017] UKSC 67, which requires the Court to consider the individual's beliefs or knowledge, and if the person was considered to have been dishonest, whether this was in line with the standards of "ordinary decent people". An example of a case considered to represent fundamental dishonesty was that of *Tess Garraway v Holland & Barrett Ltd* where there was considered to be a considerable discrepancy between claimed injuries and documentary evidence and the views of the expert witnesses. The consequence of a finding of fundamental dishonesty would be that the person will not only lose the claim, but be liable for the defendants' legal costs. In cases where there is evidence of an invalid neuropsychological test profile, it is possible that the Court may decide the case constitutes fundamental dishonesty. However, whilst neuropsychological assessment may assist the Court determination of "fundamental dishonesty" cannot be logically derived from performance validity testing alone, in that "fundamental dishonesty" requires that the patient has been wilfully and intentionally modifying performance or falsely reporting symptoms to gain an advantage over the claim. The motivation basis for this cannot be established from performance validity tests alone and must include a consideration of other, additional evidence (e.g. surveillance footage) which will be available to the Court.

Performance validity and symptom validity

SVTs focus on the validity of *self-reported symptoms* in relation to known groups. For example, the person with mild traumatic brain injury (TBI) and a minor whiplash injury might report cognitive symptoms in excess of those for even severe TBI with imaging abnormalities and report pain symptoms in excess of spinal surgery candidates or acute spinal trauma patients. PVTs by contrast focus on the validity of performance on *tasks of cognitive ability*. In a similar vein, comparison is made to known groups. For example, the person with unequivocally mild TBI who performs worse than patients with severe TBI or dementia would likely be responding in an invalid manner. The differentiation between SVTs and PVTs is important and clearly exemplified by Van Dyke, Millis, Axelrod and Hanks (2013). Confirmatory factor analysis was used to determine the factor model best describing the relationship between cognitive performance, symptom self-report, performance validity and symptom validity. The authors concluded that the strongest and simplest model was a three-factor model in which cognitive performance, performance validity and self-reported symptoms (including both standard and symptom validity measures) were separate factors. The findings indicated that a) PVTs do not measure cognitive ability and b) failure in one validity domain does not necessarily invalidate the other domain. Thus, performance validity and symptom validity should be evaluated separately (p. 1234) and may dissociate in the individual case. For example, someone may pass PVTs and indeed display intact cognition on testing but reporting significant day-to-day cognitive symptoms that are being genuinely misattributed to brain injury but are in fact due to mood disorder. Alternatively, a Claimant might choose to exaggerate psychiatric disorder, but not cognitive disorder and the former would not necessarily be detected on PVTs. In other cases, there may be genuine reporting of psychiatric and pain symptoms yet exaggeration of cognitive deficits on formal testing. Non-credible performance is a term which is becoming more popular to describe inconsistent results, although the results may still be credible in terms of mechanisms other than brain injury.

We have addressed the notion that no measure of over-reporting (SVT) or underperformance (PVT) can itself establish the motivational basis for the behaviour. Even where there is clear and deliberate underperformance the intent behind such behaviour remains ultimately a matter for the Court. Nonetheless, from a neuropsychological perspective failure on PVTs can clearly be seen to indicate the presence of invalid performance irrespective of the client's motivation to respond. It is for this reason that our preferred term is "validity measures". PVTs are now central to the interpretation of neuropsychological data given that it has been demonstrated that failure on PVTs has a greater effect on scores of tests of cognitive ability than do other factors such as the severity of the brain injury (Green, Rohling, Lees-Haley & Allen, 2001).

Within the field of neuropsychology and in particular forensic neuropsychology (the USA term for medico-legal neuropsychology as well as the UK version of the term applying to criminal rather than civil cases) there has been an increasing expansion in the development of well-validated SVTs and PVTs. SVTs share a common theme of comparison of subjective complaints to known clinical groups as well as the normative population. Within these SVTs various measures have been developed that are differentially sensitive to cognitive, psychiatric and somatic (e.g. pain, fatigue) symptom over-reporting. Examples include the inventories designed to measure a broad range of symptomatology such as the Minnesota Multiphasic Personality Inventory (Ben-Porath & Tellegen, 2020), Personality Assessment Inventory (Morey, 2007) or Millon Clinical Multi-Axial Inventory (Millon, Grossman & Millon, 2015) or SVT's focussed on more discrete symptoms such as the Memory Complaints Inventory (Green, 2004), Pain (Modified Somatic Perceptions Questionnaire, Main, Wood & Hillis, 1992) or Post-Traumatic Stress (DAPS; Briere, 2001). Such inventories may produce profiles indicating that the Claimant has responded randomly or inconsistently, has endorsed unusual items rarely seen in clinical populations or has reported a level of symptoms that would be highly unusual considering the features of their clinical condition.

The development of PVTs has, if anything gathered even greater pace. It is beyond the remit to review specific measures here but the methods and procedures that are typically used to assess validity are presented in Table 6.1.

Cut-off scores: The basics

PVTs can be thought of as screening instruments, the purpose of which is to alert the assessor to the possibility that the test profile may not be a true representation of an individual's cognitive ability. They may be stand-alone instruments or may be "embedded measures" derived from responses within a larger battery measuring cognitive ability. The key feature of people requested to feign cognitive impairment is a tendency to overestimate the extent to which brain injury or illness impairs cognition, and consequently

Table 6.1 Methods and procedures used to assess symptom and performance validity

Procedure	Description
Hold tests	Measures performance an area of cognitive functioning known to be resistant to the effects of TBI (e.g. priming) but which appears to the naïve respondent to measure an area of cognition associated with legitimate symptoms.
Forced-choice tests	Use of a forced-choice test with a fixed number of alternative responses. The examinee's performance is compared to that expected by chance (i.e. random responding).
Floor effect tasks	Tasks or problems that concern overlearned material (e.g. reciting the alphabet) or easily accomplished tasks (e.g. Rey 15-Item Memory Test; Portland Digit Recognition Test of Memory Malingering [TOMM; Tombaugh, 1997]). They typically rely upon a comparison of performance that is not worse than chance.
Atypical performance	(1) Evaluates consistency by comparing the test results with those of genuine patients or normal individual. (2) Measures consistency of performance across two administrations of the same tests.
Magnitude of error	Involves a quantitative and qualitative analysis of performance failures e.g. "Near miss" responses (e.g. 2 + 2 = 5).
Performance curve analysis	Analysis of performance on test items across a broad range of difficulty. Examinee's average performance on test items is compared against average item difficulty with the expectation that response accuracy will decrease as item difficulty increases.

perform at a level lower than that seen in patients with genuine cognitive impairment. Like other screening instruments, PVTs make use of cut-off scores, but in the case of PVTs the cut-off scores are set at a level where sub-cut-off performance is highly unlikely in people with impairment who are responding to the best of their ability. This relatively simple logic is complicated somewhat by the fact that the threshold for normal/abnormal responding can differ according to the clinical population, and some PVTs have different cut-offs reported for different populations e.g. the Dot Counting Test (Boone et al., 2002). Adjusting the cut-off scores up or down slightly will affect the sensitivity and specificity of the test, which could create a potential for two psychologists to interpret the same score differently as a pass or fail by using different criteria.

Typically, cut-offs are derived in two ways. Firstly, by examining their sensitivity to feigned or exaggerated cognitive impairment by comparing scores from a sample of people instructed to complete the tests to the best of their ability, with scores from a sample of people who have been instructed to complete the tests according to how they believe someone with a brain injury might perform. The general finding is that people trying to simulate the performance of someone with a brain injury overestimate the severity of impairment and perform worse than somebody with a confirmed brain injury

(Green et al., 2001; Carone, 2008; Goodrich-Hunsaker & Hopkins, 2009). A cut-off score is selected which provides the best combination of sensitivity (in this case the ability to detect people who are underperforming – true positives) with specificity (the ability to not misclassify people with genuinely severe impairment – false positives). The second aspect of cut-off development is the establishment of the test's specificity by ensuring that the vast majority of people (typically >90%) of people with neurological/ psychiatric diagnoses which are associated with cognitive impairment, are able to score above cut-off. In medical investigations, screening instruments emphasise sensitivity, identifying as many potential cases as possible. Diagnostic tests place more emphasis on specificity, as their role is to confirm the diagnosis. As with any other screening instrument, a positive result requires further investigation/consideration to confirm. A number of reviews of sensitivity and specificity in performance validity measures have been published (e.g. Boone, 2007; Larrabee, 2007). Scoring above cut-off on a set of PVTs does not necessarily mean the obtained cognitive test profile is valid. It simply means that the PVTs did not provide evidence to doubt the validity. Absence of evidence does not constitute evidence of absence. As Heilbronner, Sweet, Morgan, Larrabee, Millis and Conference Attendees (2009) state "a positive finding tends to 'rule in' insufficient effort, whereas a negative finding may or may not 'rule out' insufficient effort". Thus, it can never be concluded with absolute certainty that full effort was applied – it can however be stated that there is no evidence of underperformance. It is possible to view a set of tests scores where someone has passed all the PVTs yet still conclude the test profile is likely to be invalid based upon the overall presentation and pattern of results. It is also possible for someone to fail a PVT, but conclude the test profile is valid as performance is largely in accordance with expectations on other tests.

How many PVTs should be utilised?

Whilst the cut-offs for any PVT are developed to be very conservative and to avoid the misclassification of genuinely responding but nevertheless impaired patients, it is typically the case that performance on a single PVT is not interpreted in isolation (an exception to this may be the presence of below-chance responding which whilst relatively rare, indicates that the person knew the correct answers and deliberately gave the wrong ones. In this respect such a response pattern is the sine qua non of deliberate underperformance). Over-interpreting the results of a single test can be problematic, as all manner of factors can produce an aberrant result. Consequently, neuropsychologists often focus on index scores made up of two or more individual tests which are thought to tap into related underlying cognitive constructs. A similar approach has also been adopted when approaching assessment of performance validity, as most assessments will feature a mixture of stand-alone and embedded measures to adequately assess engagement throughout the assessment and to minimise the possibility of false positive findings. Boone (2009) recommends the use of multiple PVTs administered throughout the assessment, and also that they cover a range of domains rather than just memory.

The British Psychological Society (BPS) recommended using at least one stand-alone and one embedded measure (McMillan, Anderson, Baker, Berger, Powell & Knight 2009). The American Academy of Clinical Neuropsychology recommend using multiple symptom validity measures administered throughout the evaluation (Heilbronner et al., 2009). The chance of false positive findings may be reduced with the use of multiple measures (Sherman et al., 2020) but consideration should be given to the number of fails and passes on PVTs in light of the number of PVTs administered and their individual psychometric properties. Sherman et al.'s criteria for concluding there is invalid cognitive test performance includes at least two or more failures on PVTS. The only instance whereby invalid test performance can be concluded on the basis of a single PVT is when there is significantly below-chance performance.

With conventional tests of cognitive ability, increasing the number of tests administered increases the likelihood of a few low scores being obtained by chance. This should not occur with PVTs, because very little cognitive ability is required to pass them. So administering multiple PVTs will increase the sensitivity, but should not significantly raise the likelihood of false positive errors.

How to interpret effort test performance

When interpreting any neuropsychological assessment data, there are two things which should always be borne in mind: *Context* and *Consistency*. In the case of '*context*' one needs to consider the person's premorbid abilities because some PVTs, but not all, may be failed by people with learning disabilities (Dean, Victor, Boone & Arnold, 2008) and low scores on tests of ability are common in people with low levels of premorbid intellect with no brain injury (Holdnack, Drozdick, Weiss & Iverson, 2013). One also needs to consider the 'Context' of the literature on the clinical diagnosis in question. What is the purported mechanism by which the person might have developed cognitive impairment; what is the expected pattern and severity of impairment based on that mechanism/their diagnosis? The *context* of any premorbid disability or diagnoses as well as any concurrent problems such as pain, medication, or psychiatric disorder will also need to be considered.

In the case of 'consistency', one needs to consider whether the test scores are consistent with other test scores, an organic presentation, and the person's overall level of function.

The consideration of both 'context' and 'consistency' guards against simplistic interpretations of PVT and SVT scores as being indicative of 'malingering' or 'not malingering'. In particular there may be genuine reasons for PVT failure, such as severe cognitive impairment as seen with dementia (McGuire, Crawford & Evans, 2019; Tombaugh, 1997; Rudman, Oyebode,

Jones & Bentham, 2011) where the PVT fail reflects the patient's severe impairment. Alternatively, severe mental illness such as schizophrenia, particularly with acute symptoms, (Hunt, Root & Bascetta, 2015) can cause failure depending on the test used and in which case the results may not a 'valid' indication of the level of cognitive impairment but may equally reflect genuine clinical problems. However, for reasons discussed, later it would be equally misleading to suggest that less severe pathologies (e.g. depression) necessarily cause failure as this is inconsistent with the PVT literature.

Validity: PVTs, context and consistency

We have earlier argued that the key interpretation for neuropsychologists is one of 'validity' rather than 'malingering'. It is important to note that 'validity' is not a dichotomous dimension in the same way that a diagnosis of 'malingering' might be. However, whilst failure on a single or indeed multiple PVTs does not always imply malingering it certainly raises doubt over the interpretation of the other data obtained on tests of cognitive ability. Failure on a single PVT causes a degree of suppression across a battery of cognitive tests reducing the confidence in any interpretation of the data offered. This is unsurprising given the lengths that test developers go to in order to maximise the specificity of the tests. However, the extent of suppression on tests of ability is itself on a continuum with the degree of deviation of the person's score below the PVT cut-offs and the number of PVTs failed causing increasing levels of suppression of the test profile (Sherman et al., 2020). If invalid data are produced one is forced to an extent to rely upon other sources of information. For example, in the case of mild TBI there are studies which demonstrate no impairment 1–3 months post-injury for the majority (Schretlen & Shapiro, 2003; Frencham, Fox & Maybery, 2005; Rohling, Green, Allen & Iverson, 2002; Larrabee, Binder, Rohling & Ploetz, 2013). Therefore, if a claimant with a mild TBI and normal brain imaging fails to produce valid data it would be more reasonable than not to assume that there is unlikely to be any enduring cognitive impairment.

Whilst validity, rather than malingering, remains the focus of neuropsychological interpretation a useful diagnostic algorithm has been developed for the detection of Malingered Neurocognitive Dysfunction (MND) (Sherman et al., 2020) which provides a framework for examining the validity of neuropsychological tests data.

Within the MND criteria four criteria were identified which must be met in order to arrive at a conclusion of MND:

A. Presence of an external incentive.
B. Invalid presentation on examination indicative of feigning or exaggeration.
C. Marked discrepancies between test data/symptom reports and other available forms of evidence (e.g. natural history and pathogenesis of the condition, records and other media, collateral informant reports).

Effort testing and performance validity 99

D. The invalid presentation cannot be accounted for by another developmental, medical, or psychiatric condition. Examples cited of such conditions are: Moderate/severe dementia, intellectual disability with IQ < 60, severe psychiatric, neurological, or other medical disorders associated with sufficient cognitive impairment sufficient to prevent independent daily living.

The MMD model defines four types of malingering which can be identified using the above criteria: (a) Malingering of Neurocognitive Dysfunction, (b) Malingering of Somatic Symptoms, (c) Malingering of Psychiatric Symptoms, and (d) Malingering with Mixed Presentation.

It should be noted that the way the term 'malingering' is used by Slick et al. (2020) may not overlap perfectly with the way it is used in Figure 6.1, which confines malingering to a single quadrant, and cases of low effort to another. Our understanding of the Slick et al. (2020) usage of the term is that it is more inclusive and includes cases of low effort.

As the focus of this chapter is the use of effort testing, or PVTs, malingering of neurocognitive dysfunction is where we will focus our attention.

Mittenberg, Patton, Canyock and Condit (2002) and Heilbronner et al (2009) all suggested a number of factors to consider when finding the reason for PVT scores below cut-off. Rather than attempting to compile an exhaustive list of factors, we propose examining the following issues of context and consistency:

1. **Internal Test Consistency:** Are the PVT results internally consistent (e.g. does the person perform relatively worse on harder aspects)? Are the results obtained consistent with other PVTs administered? Are the results obtained on measures of ability consistent with failure on the PVT (e.g. the person's general profile is indicative of very severe impairment)? Do scores for tests which are thought to tap into similar underlying cognitive abilities align? Does the person appear to have an impairment in one aspect of cognitive function, which would be required in order to achieve a higher score they on another test e.g. scoring within the Extremely Low range (<2nd percentile) for digit span, whilst simultaneously scoring within the Average range for arithmetic? Are scores consistent across different assessments? For example, if someone with a TBI showed a pattern of declining scores across a series of assessments, for which there would be no valid medical reason.
2. **Consistency of Tests with Functioning:** Are the scores consistent with the person's level of everyday function and clinical presentation? For example, is someone impaired visual-spatial ability able to navigate their way to different locations without getting lost? Is the person who has apparently profound amnesia able to manage their day-to-day affairs without assistance?
3. **Injury Context:** Are the scores in keeping with the person's diagnosis in terms of the pattern and severity? For example, does someone with

a mild TBI demonstrate a defect in general intellect? Is the pattern of scores consistent with the known mechanism of injury, e.g. is there relative impairment on tests more susceptible to organic insult.
4. **Premorbid Context:** Are the person's scores consistent with their premorbid level of function? Is there a developmental disorder or level of dyslexia that has been shown to affect performance on the tests or PVTs in question? Is there any possible effect of acculturation/language on the PVTs? Can low scores on measures of ability be reasonably accounted for solely by low premorbid abilities. Conversely, is the person's IQ (which is less affected by TBI) in the learning disability range in someone with a high-powered and responsible job role previously.
5. **Comorbid Context:** Is there any other condition that might cause PVT failure present and/or account for low scores on measures of ability. There are few conditions that have been demonstrated to cause failure on PVTs. Severe cognitive impairment, such as that seen with dementia, can result in failure of PVTs (McGuire, Crawford & Evans, 2018). For example, Green, Montijo & Brockhaus (2011) reported failure rates of 71% and 43% on two PVTs in patients with clinically defined dementia. However, there is usually a distinctive pattern of performance in such cases. Studies of patients with severe psychiatric disorders such as schizophrenia have reported failure rates of up to 72% (Gorissen, Sanz & Schmand, 2006). It is commonly suggested in litigation cases that less severe psychopathology such as PTSD or Depression might cause PVT failure and we brief address this below.

Depression as a cause of cognitive impairment and PVT failure

In order to suggest that depression causes PVT failure one would have to assume that the patient's depression reduces their cognitive functioning to a level lower than severe TBI. It is of course possible that severe depression (for example requiring inpatient admission with marked lack of engagement in activities and psychomotor retardation) could affect motivation to a degree that the person does not engage with testing. It could also be argued that the mechanism whereby depression reduces cognitive scores is via its effect on motivation. In this case there would an explanation for PVT failure other than 'malingering' but this would still mean that the results are invalid and not interpretable and such a level of motivational problems would be all too apparent.

The effect of depression on cognitive scores is controversial. There is a significant evidence base to indicate major depressive disorder is associated with lower scores on cognitive testing (Burt, Zembar & Niederehe, 1995; Christensen, Griffiths, MacKinnon & Jacomb, 1997; Zakzanis, Leach & Kaplan, 1998), and also evidence suggesting greater severity of depression corresponds with lower cognitive scores (Christensen et al., 1997; McDermott & Ebmeier, 2009). However, it should be noted that depression-related reduction in cognitive function is typically not of a level of severity comparable to that seen in Alzheimer's disease (Burt et al., 1995; Christensen et al., 1997), except possibly in the extreme examples of depressive pseudodementia or psychotic depression. However, the presumption that depression causes a reduction in cognitive function was challenged by Rohling et al. (2002). They compared cognitive scores in a mixed sample of patients with acquired brain injury and neurological disorders, dividing them into depressed and non-depressed groups on the basis of scores on three measures of depression. When considering only patients who scored above cut-off on PVTs, they did not find a difference in cognitive scores between depressed and non-depressed groups. And, importantly that there was no difference in the level of depression between passes and failures on the PVTs indicating that depression itself was not causing PVT failure. It is worth noting that the question of cognitive effort and depression has also been examined using a different method of comparing performance on: a) tests of cognition which are considered to rely more on automatic processes, with b) those requiring more conscious, deliberate input which might be considered more effortful (Den Hartog, Derix, Van Bemmel, Kremer, & Jolles, 2003; Hammar, Strand, Ardal, Schmid, Lund & Elliot, 2011). Neither of these studies found evidence to support this hypothesis. Furthermore, other studies looking at performance on PVTs in patients with depression have not found elevated failure rates (Lee, Boone, Lesser, Wohl, Wilkins & Parks, 2000; Rees, Tombaugh & Boulay, 2001).

Post-traumatic stress disorder

There is a similar literature relating to post-traumatic stress disorder (PTSD), which has also been associated with a reduction in cognitive function particularly in terms of attention (Qureshi, Long & Bradshaw et al., 2011). However, Gordon, Fitzpatrick and Hilsabeck (2011) compared cognitive test performance of veterans with mild traumatic brain injury (MTBI) and PTSD against veterans with MTBI alone, finding no difference between the groups. Demakis, Gervais and Rohling (2008) looked at the relationship between severity of PTSD symptoms and cognitive test performance in medico-legal claimants. When patients failing PVTs were excluded, no effect of symptoms severity on cognitive test performance was seen. Wisdom, Pastorek, Miller, Booth, Romesser, Linck & Sim (2014) looked at a sample of war veterans, and also found differences in cognitive performance between those with and without PTSD were no longer apparent after excluding those who scored below cut-off in a PVT. In sum therefore there appears to be an effect of PVT failure on cognitive performance that is likely independent of the presence of psychiatric disorder.

PVT failure without external incentive

There is now a considerable literature considering rates of PVT failure in clinical populations with no identified external incentive. McWirter, Ritchie,

Stone & Carson (2020) conducted a review of papers reporting PVT failure rates, acknowledging limitations in making comparisons due to factors such as different PVTs being used. A range of different populations were highlighted who often have high rates of scoring below cut-off on PVTs, but generally had no identified external incentives. These included mild cognitive impairment, functional disorders, epilepsy, intellectual disability, neurodegenerative disorders, and psychiatric conditions. Rates were considered to be highest for moderate to severe TBI, and for mild, moderate and severe dementia. However, it should be noted that the papers describing these high failure rates typically base this on a below cut-off score on a single PVT, which is not how a neuropsychologist would use PVTs clinically and there was no consideration of pattern of performance and whether this was consistent with severe impairment. It is often the case that, outside of a litigation context, there may be incentives that are not obvious or admitted, such as a benefit payment which affect the person's motivation. It is also important to bear in mind that poor effort may be due to a lack of incentive to perform well, as opposed to the presence of an incentive to perform badly. There are cases where an individual may feign dementia in pursuit of an external gain such as benefits payments (e.g. Crown Prosecution Service, 2019). However, the assumption that people failing PVTs is a 'false positive' because they are not felt to be malingering is a simplification and does not lead to the assumption that their results are valid.

McWirter et al. (2020) criticise the use of forced-choice tests which use a cut-off scores higher than chance; a practise adopted by most common PVTs. They argue that anybody with a functional attentional deficit would be vulnerable to failing such tests. Their stance is that failure on such tests only questions the validity of the results of the other neuropsychological tests, and will not always in itself allow us to fully understand the underlying reason. This aligns with our own view, although any suggestion that only below-chance scores should be considered is problematical and we would advocate this highlights the need to focus on context and consistency to interpret the test scores.

If these groups are known to experience significant cognitive impairment, how is it possible to tell if below cut-off scores on PVTs do indeed signify an invalid test profile? Green, Flaro, Brockhaus and Montijo (2012) recommended the use of comparisons to profiles for the specific diagnosis which the person has been given. For example, in the case of Alzheimer's disease the profile would include genuine tests of cognitive ability alongside PVTs, based on the finding that simulators tend to perform worse on the PVTs, but better on the genuine cognitive tests. This is thought to be because simulators tend to overestimate the effect of cognitive impairment on test performance. This is the same logic we advocate here, considering whether other test scores and the person's level of function is consistent with the severe level of cognitive impairment which would be necessary in order to fail the PVTs?

Some more controversial aspects of interpreting test performance

Implausible explanations

As discussed above, the effect of depression and PTSD on cognition is questionable once performance validity is controlled for and mood does not explain PVT failure. There are a number of explanations commonly given for PVT failure other than poor effort. Green and Merten (2013) outlined a number of these, along with arguments for why these explanations had questionable validity. The authors discuss specifically the case of a mild TBI (MTBI) patient who, as noted is demonstrated to have no long-term deficits post-injury. MTBI patients are nonetheless far more likely to score below cut-off on PVTs than those with severe TBI and those with developmental disabilities who have an incentive to perform well (e.g. in the context of childcare proceedings). Green and Merten (2013) also cited data showing the PVT failure rate was five time higher in cases of MTBI with no CT (computer assisted tomography) brain abnormality than in cases of severe TBI with confirmed abnormalities on CT brain scans. This is inconsistent with the notion that PVT failure is due to cognitive impairment. The key feature with these, and other clinical populations which demonstrate high levels of PVT failure, e.g. fibromyalgia (Gervais, Russell et al. 2001), chronic pain (Bianchini, Greve & Glyn, 2005), attention deficit/hyperactivity disorder (Harrison et al., 2007) is that the level of impairment required for the PVT failure to be due to cognitive problems is not consistent with other aspects of their presentation (e.g. other test results, level of everyday function). The explanations are implausible because of these inconsistencies.

Warning test takers

Warning test takers that an assessment might intuitively seem like a sensible strategy to ensure they produce full effort during an assessment. However, this strategy can be problematic if the patients are aware of which components of the assessment are in fact PVTs. Gervais, Green, Allen and Iverson (2001) looked at the PVT failure rates in a sample of chronic pain patients and reported an overall failure rate of 42%. They then compared this to another group for whom one of the tests in their assessment was identified as a PVT. The failure rate for that test dropped to 4%, whereas the failure rate on another PVT included within the same assessment battery was unaffected. A third group of patients were again given no warning that the assessment contained any PVTs, and the failure rate on both measures was comparable to that seen in the first condition. DenBoer and Hall (2007) demonstrated coaching enabled simulators to pass PVTs, whilst scoring poorly on the standard tests of neuropsychological function. Surveys of lawyers in America have indicated that nearly half consider it appropriate to provide their clients with information about psychological tests (Wetter & Corrigan, 1995), and this is done quite regularly in brain injury litigation (Essig, Mittenberg, Petersen, Strauman & Cooper, 2001). A survey conducted by the National Academy of Neuropsychology and Association of Trial Lawyers, suggested that 75% of attorneys provide clients with information about psychological tests and different ways to respond (Victor & Abeles, 2004). It is also possible for people to ascertain information regarding how to identify different PVT's via the internet (Bauer & McCaffrey, 2006). Whilst there is no way to prevent this from happening, it is possible for neuropsychologists to reduce the risk to some extent by not disclosing which PVTs they routinely use and ensuring that test data is only disclosed to those experts able to interpret the data.

Intermediate patients

Bigler (2014) has described a group he referred to as intermediate patients. These are patients whose test scores are *distinctly* above chance, but below the cut-off scores on PVTs. However, in this context the vast majority of known group studies (where people are classified on a range of criteria as having MND) and in simulator studies where people are asked to feign impairment, below-chance scores are relatively rare and failure below cut-offs on multiple PVTs is more common. As we have outlined it is important to consider the context and consistency of the findings and in such cases, one may rely more heavily on non-test related information to formulate the likely presence of cognitive impairment or the likely motivational or other factors at play.

Case studies

We will now consider a number of case studies in order to illustrate the process of interpretation of neuropsychological data and the integration of data from performance validity testing. We will also consider these cases in terms of the Frederick and Crosby (2000) illustrated in Figure 6.1 and the Sherman et al. (2020) criteria. As these are medico-legal cases, it could be considered they all have a potential external incentive to underperform.

Case study 1

In the first case study we illustrate of case of mild uncomplicated TBI with clear evidence of invalid responding. Mr Brown was a health care worker with a history of work-related stress who was involved in a low impact rear shunt collision 16 months prior to the assessment. He did not lose consciousness and following the accident proceeded to drive to work albeit having a stiff neck and headaches as well as some nausea. There was no post-traumatic amnesia (PTA) and no retrograde amnesia. On attendance at the ED two days later a CT brain scan was normal. Although there was no initial GCS score, from the description of his post-collision presentation it was likely 15/15. Dr Forbes (Neuropsychologist) concluded that this was a mild, uncomplicated TBI (Defined as a GCS 13–15 after 30 minutes, loss of consciousness of less than 30 minutes, Post Traumatic Amnesia < 24 hours and normal imaging). Numerous meta-analyses (e.g. Rohling, Binder, Demakis, Larrabee, Ploetz & Langhinrichsen-Rohling 2011; Larrabee et al., 2013) indicate that in the majority of cases no cognitive impairment would be expected beyond 3 months post-injury (*Injury Context*).

Despite this Mr Brown continued to complain of severely impaired memory, poor concentration and problem solving. On formal psychometric testing Mr Brown failed two well-validated stand-alone performance validity tests (PVTs) and two embedded validity measures. His performance on the 'easy' aspects of the stand-alone PVTs was well below people with dementia (*Internal Test Consistency*) and therefore inconsistent with the fact that he was still at work, independent in daily functioning, had driven alone to the appointments and was a good historian for recent and remote events (*Consistency of Tests with Functioning*). Furthermore, his performance on the harder aspects of the PVTs was disproportionately better than on the easier aspects. This pattern is inconsistent with severe cognitive impairment (*Internal Test Consistency*). On other measures, if taken at face value, Mr Brown obtained a Full Scale IQ of 70 (2nd percentile i.e. within the borderline learning disability range), memory index scores of 55 (<0.1st percentile) which were below that expected of many people with dementia and he had similarly poor executive functioning. Again, these were inconsistent with the known consequences of mild TBI (*Injury Context*) and also with the Claimant's reported day-to-day functioning and clinical presentation (*Consistency with Functioning*). Although Mr Brown reported some driving anxiety there was no evidence of PTSD and no evidence of significant depressive symptoms (*Comorbid context*). It was concluded that Mr Brown had not produced a valid set of results, and in the absence of valid results one would have to rely on the extant literature which would strongly indicate that there was no basis to conclude that there were organic impairments arising from the mild head injury sustained. Deliberate underperformance could not be concluded as the scores obtained were not below chance. Similarly, however, it was concluded that this could not be ruled out and failure on the validity tests was unlikely to be explained by Mr Brown's other reported symptoms of driving anxiety, tiredness and headaches. Dr Forbes noted that it was a matter for the Court to decide upon the Claimant's motivation for lack of engagement in the testing process, but possible reasons might include the potential for financial gain, the desire to escape a difficult work situation or the desire to 'prove' disability of which Mr Brown himself was convinced despite his objectively preserved functioning.

This case meets all four criteria for MND (Sherman et al., 2020). 1) presence of an external incentive, 2) evidence of an invalid presentation, 3) discrepancies between test data and other available forms of evidence, and 4) the invalid presentation cannot be accounted for by another developmental, medical or psychiatric condition. This case would also fall into the malingered quadrant of the Frederick and Crosby (2000) classification of invalid responses.

Case study 2

In our second case we illustrate the failure on PVTs but the likely presence of ongoing disability in the context of severe TBI. Mr West sustained a severe TBI in a road traffic accident (pedestrian versus truck) 2.5 years prior to his medico-legal assessment with Dr Hicks. He had an initial GCS of 5/15, a duration of PTA of over 3 months, and CT imaging showing bilateral frontal and temporal contusions. Such a severe TBI is associated with a high likelihood of significant cognitive impairment (e.g. Schretlen & Shapiro, 2003) and would be classed as 'extremely severe' by other classifications (Nakase-Richardson, Sepehri, Sherer, Yablon, Evans & Mani, 2009) with a high chance of reduced productivity (only 9% of this group returning to a normal level of productivity including employment) (*Injury Context*).

On formal testing Mr West was administered two stand-alone PVTs and five embedded validity measures. He failed 1 measure producing a pattern of performance inconsistent with severe impairment but scored only just below the established cut-off. He passed the other validity measures. On tests of cognitive ability, he showed no impairment of overall intellectual functioning, working memory or visual memory but showed impairment of verbal memory, processing speed and executive functioning. The pattern of performance and deficits would be consistent with the pattern seen in severe TBI but the results should be treated with some caution due to failure on a well-established PVT (*Injury Context; Internal Test Consistency*). Review of the contemporaneous records showed that Mr West was highly reliant on family for support post-accident and early acute and post-acute cognitive screening and functional assessments by OT showed early, severe cognitive deficits. An independent living trial with support workers and case management had shown repeated problems with memory and executive functioning with consequent effects on safety (e.g. when cooking complex meals), and he had failed a specialist driving assessment and been deemed unsafe to drive. His rehabilitation records were replete with examples of poor decision making, inability to stick to goals without support and the need for constant reminders and prompts to maintain a daily routine. Although Mr West could understand correspondence, he needed support to organise this, to diarise appointments and to manage his bills and weekly finances (*Consistency of Tests with Functioning*).

Dr Hicks was mindful that failure on any PVT can cause some suppression of the test data and can indicate variable engagement. However, whilst PVTs are designed to minimise false positives for poor effort a single failure still does lead to some false positive conclusions of invalid responding and the use of multiple PVTs and consideration of the rate of failure and passes on such measures has been recommended (e.g. Sherman et al., 2020). Failure on PVTs is not a dichotomous decision in that the suppression of performance on measures of cognitive ability is related to the number of fails and the extent of failure. In Mr West's case his single fail on 1/7 PVTs would not meet the recommended criteria for invalid responding overall and whilst some degree of suppression of the profile might be possible his pattern of performance on cognitive ability measures was consistent with both the severity of his TBI and the account given of his day-to-day cognitive functioning. Overall, Dr Hicks concluded that the results indicated severe cognitive impairment following TBI that would render Mr West unemployable and likely in need of ongoing care. There were no premorbid or comorbid conditions that would otherwise explain the Claimant's disability (*Premorbid and Comorbid Context*).

This case would not meet the criteria for MND (Sherman et al., 2000), because, as stated above, a borderline fail on 1/7 PVTs would not meet the criteria for invalid responding overall. All other data were consistent with a severe TBI. According to the Frederick and Crosby (2000) criteria, this might fall into the "careless" quadrant, if indeed the model were to apply at all.

Case study 3

In our third case study we illustrate the presentation of invalid responding with significant comorbidities.

Ms Lang sustained a mild complicated TBI in the index accident (car versus cyclist) 2 years prior to her medico-legal assessment with Dr Adams. Her initial GCS was 14/15 rising to 15/15 in the Emergency Department. Her PTA duration was likely invalidated by the prescription of significant opiate medication but even then was less than 24 hours. CT imaging revealed a 'tiny' subarachnoid haemorrhage. Ms Lang reported ongoing problems with symptoms of PTSD, depression balance problems and migraines and continued to take opiate medication which the Neurology experts felt was maintaining some of her symptoms. She described an inability to make even the most basic decisions such as what to have for breakfast or which news channel to watch. She stated she could not recall information which, for most brain-injured patients, would be very easy (such as what school her daughter had attended for 8 years pre-accident; the name of her mother-in-law and her own postcode for the home they had lived in for the last 15 years) (*Injury Context*). She was heavily reliant on her boyfriend to prepare meals and complete domestic chores and would not go out alone. The treating Neuropsychiatrist was of the view that she had likely developed a functional neurological disorder (FND) as well as a Major Depressive Disorder and PTSD (*Comorbid Context*).

Dr Adams opined that the neuropsychological literature (e.g. Dikmen, Machamer & Temkin, 2017) suggested that severe cognitive impairment after 12 months would be unlikely in someone with her injury characteristics (mild complicated TBI: *Injury Context*). Despite the a priori expectations of relatively good neuropsychological outcome Ms Lang scored within the grossly impaired range on some measures of memory (yet in the 'Average' range on other tests measuring similar abilities). Her pattern of performance was odd in that with repeated presentation of the stimuli she would initially improve and then worsen. She also showed markedly slowed processing on measures of mental speed, yet on other measures of executive functioning (that were also timed) she scored within largely normal limits (*Inconsistent test findings*). She scored particularly poorly on verbal fluency but examination of similar measures carried out in the acute hospital during her post-accident admission showed better and largely intact performance (*Inconsistent test findings over time*). There was therefore evidence of deteriorating scores over time which is not consistent with the trajectory of cognitive recovery from the organic effects of TBI (*Injury Context*).

Notably, across two assessments Ms Lang failed 4 stand-alone PVTs and also six embedded validity measures. Her scores on the individual measures were implausibly low for even severe TBI and closer to dementia (*Test inconsistency*), which were not consistent with her clinical presentation or her early cognitive screening scores. It was concluded that 10/10 PVT fails was clearly evidence of invalid responding. Given that this would lead to a very gross suppression of performance on other measures her results could not be relied upon. However, the severity of her initial injury, her best performances and the evidence of deterioration over time was not indicative of long-term organically mediated cognitive impairment arising from her TBI (*Injury context*). Dr Hicks raised the issue that the very extensive failure on multiple PVTs was highly unusual even for people with functional neurological disorders (Kemp, Coughlan, Rowbottom, Wilkinson, Teggert & Baker, 2008) and did indicate some awareness of her lack of valid responding. The Court was advised that any disability likely arose from her psychiatric difficulties rather than cognitive impairment post-TBI but that there was suspicion that Ms Lang had an awareness that she had not co-operated with the assessment process and a degree of litigation driven behaviour could not be ruled out.

Ms Lang would appear to fit the first three criteria for MND (Sherman et al., 2020), although possibly not the fourth, in that her difficulties might be best accounted for by a psychiatric condition (FND, major depressive disorder, PTSD). If considered there was sufficient evidence for deliberate underperformance, she would fit into the malingered quadrant of the Frederick and Crosby model (2000).

Case study 4

In our final case study we discuss the interpretation of extensive PVT failure in severe TBI and the need to rely on non-test data and 'best performance' data.

Mr Legget sustained an unequivocally severe TBI in the index accident. At the time of being seen by Dr Appleton he had already been seen twice by NHS neuropsychologists and, on each occasion had failed validity testing and produced quite differing results on other cognitive tests of ability (*Test inconsistency*). On the medico-legal assessment with Dr Appleton he failed all three of the stand-alone PVTs; on two of these there was a profile potentially consistent with severe impairment. On the other PVT, however, he produced a pattern of performance inconsistent with severe cognitive impairment, performing relatively better on more difficult tasks but below dementia patients on the validity measures (*Test inconsistency*). Furthermore, his performance across the PVTs was itself inconsistent in that when presented with twice as many items to remember he had performed better than on a test half the length (*Test inconsistency*).

Despite multiple tests being carried out over three separate assessments it was not possible to provide an accurate measure of his cognitive deficits and any low scores were uninterpretable on the basis of poor engagement in the testing process. However, more weight could be placed on areas of apparently intact cognitive functioning. With this in mind, across the three assessments, Mr Legget's best cognitive scores were indicative of intact cognitive function with the possible exception of verbal memory itself potentially only mildly reduced.

It was evident from Dr Appleton's review of the medical, case management and support worker records that, despite having support workers for his physical impairments arising from his orthopaedic injuries, he was able to access the community safely without supervision and was not under 24-hour care (*Consistency of tests with functioning*). He was driving, albeit the Case Manager had raised concerns over driving safety in terms of reckless manoeuvres and he had been found on occasion to not be wearing a seat belt. He did present as disinhibited in his comments being misogynistic, racist and generally lacking social graces. Of note he continued to be prescribed significant amounts of opiate medication for pain which would also be expected to affect his memory abilities (*Comorbid Context*). Indeed, it was notable that the treatment records from the very experienced treating neuropsychologist raised only issues relating to pain management and fatigue; although some degree of disinhibition was present it was commented that this appeared to be longstanding (*Premorbid Context*). There was little comment in the support records of poor day-to-day memory and in fact comments that at times he had reminded support staff of upcoming appointments that they had either not known about or forgotten, and he had been proven correct. It was concluded that Mr Legget had, despite his initially severe TBI, most likely made a largely full cognitive recovery and residual complaints of memory were either based on very subtle residual organic impairment that did not cause any significant disability or due to the ongoing effects of pain and opiate medication. There would be no cognitive barrier to independent living or employment. He concluded that Mr Legget's primary impairments post-accident were not neuropsychological in nature but rather related to pain and fatigue arising from his orthopaedic injuries.

In terms of MND criteria, there was evidence of an invalid presentation, discrepancies between test data and other forms of evidence, and no suggestion of any developmental, medical or psychiatric condition which could account for the invalid presentation. The Frederick and Crosby model (2000) might place Mr Legget in the malingered quadrant if it was felt his low scores were deliberate, or in the irrelevant quadrant if it was a case of variable effort determined by some other factor.

Conclusions

1. PVTs and SVTs are an essential component of neuropsychological evaluation to avoid misdiagnosis of cognitive impairment. PVT's have high specificity individually and few false positives in combination with regards to interpretive validity of performance on the cognitive test battery. However, validity and malingering and not synonymous. PVTs must be considered in the context of other patient information, and by paying attention to the degree of consistency across different sources of information.
2. Failure on PVTs will inform, with a high degree of certainty whether neuropsychological scores cannot be relied upon to be an accurate representation of a person's true cognitive ability. They may also act as one of many sources of information available to the Court to determine the Claimant's credibility. However, even in cases where deliberate underperformance is more probable than not, the motivation of the Claimant remains a matter for the Court.
3. When neuropsychological data is invalid, areas of apparently intact performance may give some indication of absence of impairment, but low scores will not be interpretable. The likelihood of neuropsychological difficulties will be determined by non-test data such as the mechanism of injury, nomothetic outcome data, medical records and treatment records and third-party information. It may be reasonable to re-assess after a period of rehabilitation if it is felt that engagement might improve.

References

American Psychiatric Association (APA) (2013). *Diagnostic and Statistical Manual of Mental Disorders*, 5th edn. DSM-5. Washington DC: APA.

Bass, C. & Halligan, P. (2014). Factitious disorder and malingering: Challenges for clinical assessment and management. *The Lancet, 383*:1422–1432.

Bass, C. & Wade, D. (2018). Malingering and factitious disorder. *Practical Neurology, 19(2)*, 95–105.

Bauer, L. & McCaffrey, R.L. (2006). Coverage of the test of memory malingering, Victoria Symptom Validity Test, and Word Memory Test on the internet: is test security threatened. *Archives of Clinical Neuropsychology, 21*, 121–126.

Ben-Porath, Y.S. & Tellegen, A. (2020). *Minnesota Multiphasic Personality Inventory-3 (MMPI-3): Manual for administration, scoring, and interpretation.* Minneapolis, MN: University of Minnesota Press.

Bianchini, K.J., Greve, K.W. & Glynn, G. (2005). On the diagnosis of malingered pain-related disability: Lessons from cognitive malingering research. *The Spine Journal, 5(4)*, 404–417.

Bigler, E.D. (2012). Symptom validity testing, effort and neuropsychological assessment. *Journal of the International Neuropsychological Society, 18*, 632–642.

Bigler, E.D. (2014). Effort, symptom validity testing, performance validity testing and traumatic brain injury. *Brain Injury, 28 (13–14)*, 1623–1638.

Boone, K.B. (2007). *Assessment of feigned cognitive impairment: A neuropsychological perspective.* New York: The Guilford Press.

Boone. K.B. (2009). The need for continuous and comprehensive sampling of effort/response bias during neuropsychological examinations. *The Clinical Neuropsychologist, 23(4),* 729–741.

Boone, K.B., Lu, P., Black, C., King, C., Lee, A., Philpott, L., Shamieh, E., Warner-Chacon, K. (2002). Sensitivity and specificity of the Rey Dot Counting Test in patients with suspect effort and various clinical samples. *Archives of Clinical Neuropsychology, 17(7),* 625–642.

Briere, J. (2001). *Detailed assessment of posttraumatic stress.* Odessa, FL: Psychological Assessment Resources.

Brooks, B.L., Ploetz, D.M & Kirkwood, M.W. (2015). A survey of neuropsychologists' use of validity tests with children and adolescents. *Child Neuropsychology, 22,* 1001–1020.

Burt, D.B., Zembar, M.J. & Niederehe, G. (1995). Depression and memory impairment: A meta-analysis of the association, its pattern, and specificity. *Psychological Bulletin,* 117, 285–305.

Carone, D.A. (2008). Children with moderate/severe brain damage/dysfunction outperform adults with mild-to-no brain damage on the medical symptom validity test. *Brain Injury, 22(12),* 960–971.

Christensen, H., Griffiths, K., MacKinnon, A. & Jacomb, P. (1997). A quantitative review of deficits in depression and Alzheimer-type dementia. *Journal of the International Neuropsychological Society, 3,* 631–651.

Crown Prosecution Service (2019). Available at https://www.cps.gov.uk/mersey-cheshire/news/update-dementia-faker-who-hid-her-fathers-death-faces-jail-ps750000.

Dandachi-FitzGerald, B., Ponds, R.W. & Merten, T. (2013). Symptom validity and neuropsychological assessment: a survey of practices and beliefs of neuropsychologists in six European countries. *Archives of Clinical Neuropsychology, 28(8),* 771–783.

Dean, A.C., Victor, T.L., Boone, K.B. & Arnold, G. (2008) The relationship of IQ to effort test performance. *The Clinical Neuropsychologist, 22(4),* 705–722.

Demakis, G.J., Gervais, R.O. & Rohling, M.L. (2008) The effect of failure on cognitive and psychological symptom validity tests in litigants with symptoms of post-traumatic stress disorder. *The Clinical Neuropsychologist, 22(5),* 879–895.

DenBoer, J.W. & Hall, S. (2007). Neuropsychological test performance of successful brain injury simulators. *The Clinical Neuropsychologist, 21,* 943–955.

Den Hartog, H., Derix, A., Van Bemmel, A., Kremer, B. & Jolles, J. (2003). Cognitive functioning in young and middle-aged unmedicated out-patients with major depression: testing the effort and cognitive speed hypotheses. *Psychological Medicine, 33,* 1443–1451.

Dikmen, S., Machamer, J. & Temkin, N. (2017). Mild traumatic brain injury: Longitudinal study of cognition, functional status, and post-traumatic symptoms. *Journal of Neurotrauma, 34,* 1524–1530.

Essig, S.M., Mittenberg, W., Peterson, R.S., Strauman, S., Cooper, J.T. (2001). Practices in forensic neuropsychology: Perspectives of neuropsychologists and trial attorneys. *Archives of Clinical Neuropsychology, 16,* 271–291.

Frederick, R.I. & Crosby, R.D. (2000). Development and validation of the Validity Indicator Profile. *Law and Human Behavior, 24(1),* 59–82.

Frencham, K.A., Fox, A.M. & Maybery, M.T. (2005). Neuropsychological studies of mild traumatic brain injury: A meta-analytic review of research since. *Journal of Clinical and Experimental Neuropsychology, 27*(3), 334–351.

Gervais, R.O., Green, P., Allen, L.M. & Iverson, G.L. (2001). Effects of coaching on symptom validity testing in chronic pain patients presenting for disability assessments. *Journal of Forensic Neuropsychology, 2*, 1–19.

Gervais, R.O., Russell, A.S., Green, P., Allen, M.L., Ferrari, R. & Pieschl, S.D. (2001). Effort testing in patients with fibromyalgia and disability incentives. *The Journal of Rheumatology, 28*(8), 1892–1899.

Goodrich-Hunsaker, N.J. & Hopkins, R.O. (2009). Word memory test performance in amnesic patients with hippocampal damage. *Neuropsychology, 23*(4), 529–534.

Gordon, S.N., Fitzpatrick, P.J. & Hilsabeck R.C. (2011) No effect of PTSD and other psychiatric disorders on cognitive functioning in veterans with mild TBI. *The Clinical Neuropsychologist, 25*(3), 337–347.

Gorissen, M., Sanz, J.C. & Schmand, B. (2005). Effort and cognition in schizophrenia patients. *Schizophrenia Research, 78*, 99–208.

Green, P. (2004). *Memory complaints inventory*. Edmonton, Canada: Green's Publishing.

Green, P. & Merten, T. (2013). Noncredible explanations of noncredible performance on symptom validity tests. In D.A. Carone & S.S. Bush (eds), *Symptom validity testing and Malingering*. pp.73–100. New York: Springer Publications.

Green, P., Montijo, J. & Brockhaus, R. (2011). High specificity of the word memory test and medical symptom validity test in groups with severe verbal memory impairment. *Applied Neuropsychology, 18*(2), 86–94.

Green, P., Flaro, L., Brockhaus, R. & Montijo, J. (2012). Performance on the WMT, MSVT, & NV-MSVT in children with developmental disabilities and in adults with mild traumatic brain injury. In C.R. Reynolds & A. Horton (Eds.) *Detection of Malingering During Head Injury Litigation* (2nd ed). New York, NY: Plenum Press.

Green, P., Rohling, M., Lees-Haley, P. & Allen, L. M. III (2001). Effort has a greater effect on test scores than severe brain injury in compensation claimants. *Brain Injury, 15*(12), 1045–1060.

Hammar, A., Strand, M., Årdal, G., Schmid, M, Lund, A. & Elliott, R. (2011). Testing the cognitive effort hypothesis of cognitive impairment in major depression. *Nordic Journal of Psychiatry, 65*(1), 74–80.

Harrison, A.G., Edwards, M.J. & Parker, K.C. (2007). Identifying students faking ADHD: Preliminary findings and strategies for detection. *Archives of Clinical Neuropsychology, 22*(5), 577–588.

Heilbronner, R.L., Sweet, J.J., Morgan, J.E., Larrabee, G.J., Millis, S.R. & Conference Participants (2009). American Academy of Clinical Neuropsychology Consensus Conference Statement on the Neuropsychological Assessment of Effort, Response Bias, and Malingering. *The Clinical Neuropsychologist, 23*, 1093–1129. https://doi.org/10.1080/13854046.2021.1896036

Holdnack, J., Drozdick, L., Weiss, L. & Iverson, G. (Eds), (2013). *WAIS-IV, WMS-IV, and ACS. Advanced Clinical Interpretations*. London: Elsevier.

Hunt, S., Root, J.C. & Bascetta, L. (2015). Effort testing in schizophrenia and schizoaffective disorder: validity indicator profile and test of memory malingering performance characteristics. *Archives of Clinical Neuropsychology, 29*(2), 164–172.

Kemp, S., Coughlan, A., Rowbottom, C., Wilkinson, K, Teggert, V. & Baker, G. (2008). The base rate of effort test failure in patients with medically unexplained symptoms. *Journal for Psychosomatic Research, 65*(4), 319–325.

Larrabee, G.J. (2007). *Assessment of malingered neuropsychological deficits.* New York: Oxford University Press.

Larrabee, G.J. (2012). Performance validity and symptom validity in neuropsychological assessment. *Journal of the International Neuropsychological Society, 18,* 625–630.

Larrabee, G.J., Binder, L.M., Rohling, M.L. & Ploetz, D.M. (2013). Meta-analytic methods and the importance of non-TBI factors related to outcome in Mild Traumatic Brain Injury: Response to Bigler et al (2013). *The Clinical Neuropsychologist, 27,* 215–237.

Lee, L.M., Boone, K.B., Lesser, I., Wohl, M., Wilkins, S. & Parks, C. (2000). Performance of older depressed patients on two cognitive malingering tests: false positive rates for the Rey 15-item memorization and dot counting tests. *The Clinical Neuropsychologist, 14,* 303–308.

Main, C., Wood, P., Hollis, S., Spanswick, C. & Weddell, G. (1992). The distress and risk assessment method. A simple patient classification to identify distress and evaluate the risk of poor outcome. *Spine, 17,* 42–52.

McDermott, L.M. & Ebmeier, K.P. (2009). A meta-analysis of depression severity and cognitive function. *Journal of Affective Disorders, 119(1–3),* 1–8.

McGuire, C., Crawford, S. & Evans, J.J. (2019). Effort testing in dementia assessment: A systematic review. *Archives of Clinical Neuropsychology, 34(1),* 114–131.

McMillan, T, Anderson, S., Baker, G., Berger, M., Powell, G. & Knight, R. (2009). Assessment of effort in clinical testing of cognitive functioning for adults. *British Psychological Society.* ISBN 978-1-85433-799-3

McWirter, L., Ritchie, C.W., Stone, S. & Carson, A. (2020). Performance validity test failure in clinical populations: A systematic review. *Journal of Neurology, Neurosurgery and Psychiatry, 91,* 945–952.

Millon, T., Grossman, S. & Millon, C. (2015). *MCMI-IV: Millon clinical multiaxial inventory manual* (1st ed.). Bloomington, MN: NCS Pearson, Inc.

Mittenberg, W., Patton, C., Canyock, E.M. & Condit, D.C. (2002). Base rates of malingering and symptom exaggeration. *Journal of Clinical and Experimental Neuropsychology, 24(8),* 1094–1102.

Morey, L.C. (2007). *The personality assessment inventory professional manual.* Lutz, FL: Psychological Assessment Resources.

Nakase-Richardson, R., Sepehri, A., Sherer, M., Yablon, S.A., Evans, C. & Mani, T. (2009). Classification schema of posttraumatic amnesia duration-based injury severity relative to 1-year outcome: Analysis of individuals with moderate and severe traumatic brain injury. *Archives of Physical Medicine and Rehabilitation, 90(1),* 17–19.

Quershi, S., Long, M., Bradshaw, M., et al. (2011). Does PTSD impair cognition beyond the effect of trauma? *The Journal of Neuropsychiatry and Clinical Neuroscience, 23,* 16–28.

Rees, L.M., Tombaugh, T.N. & Boulay, L. (2001). Depression and test of memory malingering. *Archives of Clinical Neuropsychology, 16,* 501–506.

Resnick, P.J. (1997). Malingering of posttraumatic disorders. In R. Rogers (Ed.), *Clinical assessment of malingering and deception* (2nd ed., pp. 130–152). New York: Guilford.

Rohling, M.L., Binder, L.M., Demakis, G.J., Larrabee, G.J., Ploetz, D.M. & Langhinrichsen-Rohling, J. (2011). A meta-analysis of neuropsychological outcome after mild traumatic brain injury. Re-analysis and re-considerations of Binder et al (1997), Frencham et al (2005) and Pertab et al (2009). *The Clinical Neuropsychologist, 25,* 608–623.

Rohling, M.L., Green, P., Allen, L.M. & Iverson, G. (2002). Depressive symptoms and neurocognitive test scores in patients passing symptom validity tests. *Archives of Clinical Neuropsychology, 17*, 205–222.

Rudman, N., Oyebode, J. R., Jones, C. A., & Bentham, P. (2011). An investigation into the validity of effort tests in a working age dementia population. *Aging & Mental Health, 15*, 47–57.

Schretlen, D.J. & Shapiro, A.M. (2003). A quantitative review of the effects of traumatic brain injury on cognitive functioning. *International Review of Psychiatry, 15*, 341–349.

Sherman, E., Slick, D. & Iverson, G.L. (2020). Multidimensional malingering criteria for neuropsychological assessment: A 20-year update of the malingered neuropsychological dysfunction criteria. *Archives of Clinical Neuropsychology, 35*(6), 735–764.

Sreenivasan, S., Eth, S., Kirkish, P. & Garrick, T. (2003). A practical method for the evaluation of symptom exaggeration in minor head trauma among civil litigants. *Journal of the American Academy of Psychiatry and Law, 31*, 220–231.

Tombaugh, T.N. (1997). The test of memory malingering (TOMM): Normative data from cognitively intact and cognitively impaired individuals. *Psychological Assessment, 9*, 260–268.

Van Dyke, S.A., Millis, S.R., Axelrod, B.N. & Hanks, R.A. (2013). Assessing effort: Differentiating performance and symptom validity. *The Clinical Neuropsychologist, 27*, 1234–1246.

Victor, T.L. & Abeles, N. (2004). Coaching clients to take psychological and neuropsychological tests: A clash of ethical obligations. *Professional Psychology: Research and Practice, 35*(4), 373–379.

Wetter, M.W. & Corrigan, S.K. (1995) Providing information to clients about psychological tests: a survey of attorneys' and law students' attitudes. *Professional Psychology: Research and Practice, 26*, 474–477.

Wisdom, N.M., Pastorek, N.J., Miller, B.I., Booth, J.E, Romesser, J.M., Linck, J.F. &. Sim, A.H. (2014). PTSD and cognitive functioning: Importance of including performance validity testing. *The Clinical Neuropsychologist, 28*(1), 128–145.

Zakzanis, K.K., Leach, L. & Kaplan, E. (1998). On the nature and pattern of neurocognitive function in major depressive disorder. *Neuropsychiatry, Neuropsychology & Behavioural Neurology, 11*, 111–119.

7 Mild traumatic brain injury and persistent neuropsychological symptoms

Andrew Worthington and Phil S. Moore

We have first raised a dust and then complain we cannot see[1]

Introduction

Mild traumatic brain injury (TBI) has long been a contentious area of clinical and medicolegal practice with increasing interest amongst some authorities in possible long-term effects matched by concern amongst others about the non-specificity of many symptoms and overlap with unrelated conditions. This chapter aims to provide a balanced appraisal of the evidence as it is relevant for medicolegal practice and specifically of the role of the neuropsychologist as expert. Our focus is on civil litigation and the use of science (neuropsychological constructs and methods) to assist the Courts in judgement by explaining the key issues or underlying principles in any given case. We discuss the importance of distinguishing between head injury and brain injury, highlight the relevance of extra-cerebral injuries for cognitive function and review psychological processes mediating symptom persistence. The difficulties of diagnosing mild TBI and potential implications of imaging technologies are considered and we conclude with a critical review of the notion of post-concussion syndrome and the current evidence base for treatment.

Mild traumatic brain injury as a population health problem

Historically the physiological basis for disturbances of cerebral function was not limited to injury to the head, some physicians arguing that damage to the spinal cord could elicit similar symptoms, whilst others were more sceptical about any putative organic basis to such complaints (Trimble, 1981). The

---

1 Berkeley G (1710/1996) *Principles of Human Knowledge and Three dialogues*. New York: Oxford University Press, p.8.

DOI: 10.4324/9781003105763-9

growth of rail travel gave impetus to the debate with references to an 'epidemic' of post-traumatic disability following commonly occurring shunts, sudden stops and derailments. Although symptom reports predated the availability of compensation, the notion of 'spinal concussion' as promoted by Queen Victoria's surgeon Sir John Erichsen, provided the basis for railway injury compensation in the 1870s. Approximately a third of his 42 cases reported cognitive symptoms without any loss of consciousness (Erichsen, 1875). Professional dispute about the nature of such injuries fed the appetite for expert medical opinion in compensation cases (Gasquoine, 2020). One British physician complained in 1881 that doctors rarely saw such patients clinically, only to assist with their claims for compensation (Evans, 2010) which is probably true of many neurologists today.

A century later and the 'silent epidemic' is now mild TBI (Goldstein, 1990) with a conservatively estimated incidence of 200–300/100,000 for hospitalised cases and population-based studies suggesting two to three times this rate (Lefevre-Dognin et al., 2020). Mild TBI represents approximately 70% to 90% of all-severity traumatic brain injuries (Cassidy et al., 2004), although this may be an underestimate as many people do not seek medical attention. Recognition of this 'silent epidemic' is changing, thanks in part to the increased recognition of mild TBI in sport (see McCrory et al., 2017) which has had significant legal implications in the US and is attracting similar interest in the UK. The question remains however, what relevance this relatively high incidence has for the Courts. Each case must be judged on its own merit but there can be little doubt that the higher profile of mild TBI encourages claimants and their lawyers to explore whether it should be included in a personal injury claim. The neuropsychologist is likely to play a key role in determining whether this is appropriate and, if so, how far it can be reasonably be said to have caused the losses claimed.

Cervical spine injury and whiplash

The term 'whiplash' originates from the idea of the spine moving like a whip following physical force. It is essentially a neck and upper back injury typically caused by a rear end vehicle shunt or sporting incident. Cognitive symptoms are often reported after such injuries (Takasaki et al., 2012) and may justifiably raise the question of an undiagnosed mild TBI. Ommaya et al. (1968) demonstrated in rhesus monkeys that a whiplash-type rotational force to the neck may lead to cerebral injury without direct head impact. Fisher (1982) described a 67-year-old woman who was wearing a seatbelt in a stationary car which was shunted from the rear. There was no direct impact to the head but she suffered transient memory loss lasting 72 hours which he termed 'whiplash amnesia'. A meta-analysis of 22 neuropsychological studies noted that abnormal results on measures of attention, working memory, immediate recall and visuomotor tracking were commonly observed after whiplash injury (Kessels et al., 2000). Whilst this is not evidence of Erichsen's 'spinal concussion' it suggests claimants' reports of cognitive disturbance should be taken seriously.

Yet evidence suggests such symptoms might well be caused by pain (Antepohl et al., 2003) and other somatic problems (Radanov et al., 1994). In a study of 98 whiplash patients, subjective cognitive complaints persisted after six months in 31 cases even though neuropsychological test results had returned to normal, with symptomatic patients reporting higher levels of neck pain (Radanov et al., 1993) but no evidence of cerebral dysfunction on SPECT/PET imaging (Radanov et al., 1999). Involvement in compensation was not recorded but Mayou and Bryant (1996) reported litigation status had no impact on cognitive complaints or outcome in their study of whiplash neck injury. Claimants using high levels of analgesia or self-medicating in other ways may also be exacerbating their cognitive symptoms. Therefore, for neuropsychologists the likelihood of an undiagnosed mild TBI has to be weighed against the possibility that cognitive complaints can more plausibly be attributed to other consequences of head injury or cervical spine damage, psychological trauma, litigation (and other stresses) and medication.

Head injury

Head injury refers to injury involving at the very least some tissue damage to a part of the head and usually involves some kind of trauma. Evidence for head injury is normally noted on hospital records during preliminary observations. Where hospitals use the Abbreviated Injury Scale (AIS) head and facial injury are distinguished with separate AIS codes but this may not occur in practice and head injury may simply describe a facial injury. The term head injury may be revised and used more specifically if a person reports an alteration of consciousness or memory around the time of the injury or if further evidence comes to light during investigation. Unfortunately, the terms brain injury and head injury are often used interchangeably by health professionals and may be synonymous in the public consciousness.

The neuropsychologist must take account of the potential for cranial nerve damage due to head or facial injury to affect performance on cognitive testing and contribute to neuropsychological symptoms in daily life. Head and facial injuries can damage cranial nerves, including cranial nerves I (olfactory), III (oculomotor), VI (abducens) and VIII (acoustic) which can affect hearing and balance. Damage to the bulbar cranial nerves (IX to XII) may cause dysarthria and dysphagia though these may be of less concern to the neuropsychologist than the pseudobulbar palsy associated with frontal lobe injury. Symptoms such as photosensitivity, diplopia and blurred vision can affect higher level visual information processing. Similarly, damage to the inner ear vestibular apparatus can occur in the absence of cerebral involvement. Cognitive complaints may reflect defects of hearing or interference from tinnitus. Labyrinthine disorders may also cause vertigo, disequilibrium and nausea, and in the absence of skull fracture may be considered a labyrinthine concussion (Bartholomew et al., 2020). Affective disturbance linked to vestibular symptoms may well mediate the relationship between symptoms and cognitive complaints (Gizzi et al., 2003). Not only are such conditions unpleasant and often distressing, evidence from dual-task experiments suggests cognitive processes may be recruited in efforts to compensate for imbalance (Andersson et al., 2003; Roberts et al., 2011).

Neuropsychological disturbances involving distortion of body schema, spatial orientation and dynamic sensory integration after mild TBI may be considered higher level vestibular disorders akin to the notion of higher visual disorders in perception (Brandt et al., 2014). Increasingly, evidence has implicated vestibular involvement in attention, memory, visuospatial ability and executive function (Bigelow & Agrawal, 2015). Consequently, in potential mild TBI cases it may be appropriate to consider an MRI scan of the internal auditory meatus alongside the more usual recommendation for a brain MR scan. In such matters the neuropsychologist will be considerably aided by the expert opinion of a consultant ENT surgeon, audiovestibular physician or neuro-otologist. Identification of audiovestibular pathology is of therapeutic as well as diagnostic relevance. Similar issues arise with disturbance of vision and ophthalmological examination is recommended to assess potentially confounding visual symptoms after mild TBI which may respond to intervention (Simpson-Jones & Hunt, 2019) particularly if there is a clinical history of trauma to the periorbital region.

Finally, if a concussed claimant has also suffered multiple serious injuries requiring a prolonged period in intensive care the neuropsychologist should also be alert to the possibility of critical illness-related cognitive impairment. Pandharipande et al. (2013) found one-third of patients with respiratory failure scored similarly to patients with moderate brain injury at 12 months, and sepsis may be a particular risk factor for lasting cognitive impairment amongst older adults (Iwashyna et al., 2010). If necessary neuropsychologists should seek guidance from their medical colleagues as to whether this is likely to be contributory factor rather than assume a hitherto unrecognised mild TBI as it may reflect a secondary mechanism of cognitive involvement.

Defining mild traumatic brain injury (mild TBI)

Just as head injury may not involve damage to the brain, a mild TBI can occur without any impact to the head and corresponding signs of external injury. A typical example is a seat-belted occupant in a car involved in a rear end or side-on shunt (Varney & Varney, 1995). Reference to mild TBI may be interpreted on the one hand to reflect a form of brain damage with connotations of permanent disability, and on the other as a synonym for concussion with implications of a brief disturbance of consciousness followed by a rapid return to normality. Language can be a powerful tool for determining beliefs and developing expectations under examination, in treatment and during litigation. The information people are given in hospital or access through the internet or other media often has a bearing on how they interpret their experiences. Noting what a person has been told previously, the neuropsychologist must appreciate how the diagnostic label has arisen and may need to correct any misunderstanding on the part of a claimant or their family. This can be very helpful for the Court and assists other experts in understanding the relevance of such matters for their own evidence. Other medical experts may revise their opinions on injury severity (upwards or downwards) on the basis of good neuropsychological evidence. In one study however neuropsychologists were more likely to anticipate post-concussive symptoms than A&E doctors and neurosurgeons, which may reflect the symptomatic bias in neuropsychologists' caseloads (Davies & McMillan, 2005). This suggests neuropsychologists relying only on their clinical experience rather than scientific literature may over-diagnose mild TBI. Equally, symptom base rate data need to be considered carefully in terms of their relevance for the individual under scrutiny.

Definitions of mild TBI vary (see review by Carroll et al., 2004). There have been proposals to grade severity in terms of clinical management or length of hospital stay but most criteria use three core clinical indices: (i) duration of loss of consciousness, (ii) disturbance of consciousness as measured by the Glasgow Coma Scale (GCS) score and (iii) post-traumatic amnesia (PTA). Not that this has produced a consensus. In the UK, Jennett and Teasdale (1981) proposed that mild TBI should be based on PTA less than one hour – most recently repeated by Agrawal (2020) – whilst the Medical Disability Society Working Party suggested that minor TBI (as distinct from moderate) should correspond to unconsciousness less than 15 minutes and PTA less than 6 hours (Medical Disability Society, 1988). In contrast, the American Congress of Rehabilitation Medicine (Kay et al., 1993), the World Health Organization (WHO) collaborating task force on mild TBI (Carroll et al., 2004), Lishman's Organic Psychiatry (Fleminger, 2009) and DSM 5 (American Psychiatric Association, 2013) all emphasise the following:

- Any loss of consciousness of 30 minutes or less
- GCS score of 13 to 15 after 30 minutes
- PTA less than 24 hours

These different indices do not always correspond; a person may recover consciousness before a GCS assessment is undertaken, or a GCS of 15 may be recorded though the person is still in PTA, orientation usually resolving before amnesia in mild injuries (Gronwall & Wrightson, 1980). This leaves open the question of how the neuropsychologist should use the information. Usually the more severe indicator is used but this can be misleading, for example, PTA may be artificially prolonged by use of strong analgesia especially if other serious injuries have been sustained which can cloud the assessment of mild TBI. The Mayo Clinic classification system (Malec et al., 2007) was developed to maximise use of positive evidence from reported symptoms, GCS, PTA and radiological evidence to classify TBI severity. Although it fails to differentiate between injuries at the moderate to severe end of the spectrum, this scheme distinguishes between a possible (mild) TBI where the only evidence is symptom report, classified as 'Symptomatic' (Possible) TBI; and a 'Probable' TBI based on the presence of loss of consciousness less than 30 minutes or PTA less than 24 hours or depressed, linear or basilar skull fracture. It should not be relied upon uncritically, however: of 1678 incidents, 906 were classified as Symptomatic (Possible) TBI and 633 as Mild (Probable) TBI but loss of consciousness was either absent or not recorded in 70% of cases, no GCS was recorded in 74% of cases, whilst 58% had no or unrecorded PTA. In addition, 49% had no CT scan which is an important omission as the WHO estimated the prevalence of intracranial abnormalities on CT scans in patients with a GCS of 13 as 30% or higher (Borg et al., 2004a) so some may have been misclassified. Furthermore, the presence of a depressed skull fracture or cerebral lesion elevates an otherwise mild TBI into the 'Moderate-Severe' category, whereas Williams et al., (1990) suggested a separate category of complicated mild TBI for those cases with depressed skull fracture or intracranial lesion otherwise meeting criteria for mild TBI. The authors justified this in terms of poorer cognitive function (verbal fluency, verbal recall, recognition memory and processing speed) for complicated versus uncomplicated mild TBI. Subsequent research on whether imaging abnormalities in mild TBI are associated with more symptoms or poorer outcomes has produced inconsistent results (Iverson, 2005, 2012).

Classification based on loss of consciousness, GCS and PTA may be misleading in cases of focal penetrating brain injury, where there may be significant localised damage without disturbance of consciousness. Radiological imaging in such cases is a more reliable guide to severity. Ultimately the neuropsychologist has to weigh the importance of severity indicators in the context of the broader clinical picture (for instance, intoxication at time of injury, serious extracranial injuries and communication difficulties) and the individual's prior status which may include pre-existing cognitive impairment. It is also important to bear in mind there is a range of outcomes for any given degree of severity and these two notions of severity of injury and of consequences need to be kept distinct. An unfortunate habit has crept into expert reports of referring to a 'significant' brain injury, a term which should be reserved for the injury sequelae. There are no objective scientific criteria for significant brain injury; if the term is used it should only be to clarify that the claimant X has suffered a brain injury of severity Y and this has led to significant (i.e. more than trivial) consequences Z.

A similar criticism may be levied at the increasing use of the notion of *subtle* brain injury. It may carry weight in hypoxic, metabolic or electrical injuries but in TBI cases where there are explicit criteria for establishing severity it has no diagnostic validity. It is used inconsistently to refer either to an injury too subtle to be identified objectively on scans or psychometric tests or to a subtle lasting effect from a more severe injury (Watt-Pringle & van den Broek, 2020). The potential for confusion inherent in arguing a 'severe subtle brain injury'[2] would be avoided if the term was restricted to the degree of measurable dysfunction on a defined outcome metric, avoiding any temptation to reason backwards from sequelae to initial severity. Thus mild TBI may cause subtle neuropsychological effects (which may have serious consequences), but subtle brain injury and mild TBI are not synonymous.

Mechanisms of mild TBI

Prins et al. (2019) stated, 'Perhaps the most challenging aspect of mild TBI is the limited ability to visualise the injury. The absence of bleeding, overt oedema and cell loss makes the brain appear deceptively normal' (p.608). This absence of structural pathology in many cases means that neuropsychological evidence may be critically important in assisting the Court. Although there is increasing understanding of the metabolic and ultrastructural pathologies associated with mild TBI which operate to affect blood flow, inflammation, cellular metabolism and degeneration, how far this explains failure to recover and whether brain lesions identified by imaging necessarily produce clinical symptoms are questions with no ready answer. In addition, given that certain psychological disorders have also been linked to abnormalities on brain imaging including Diffusion Tensor Imaging (DTI) (Lim & Helpern, 2002) any such anomalies may not be caused by the primary brain injury or even related to the index event. Neuropsychologists and others would do well to recognise these limits when translating the science into the legal arena.

Computed Tomography (CT) is still used for acute imaging of head trauma, the disadvantage of low resolution being offset by ready availability, cost and sensitivity to fluid and bone change. For mild injuries there is no link between findings on a CT scan and test results; de Guise et al. (2010) reported more post-concussion symptoms amongst 131 adults with a clear CT scan than in 45 patients with positive findings. In suspected mild TBI Magnetic Resonance Imaging (MRI) tends to be used at a later stage and more selectively in symptomatic cases. Different MR sequences are optimally sensitive to different trauma-related injuries (T2-weighted for blood and hemosiderin, FLAIR for gliosis and other white matter anomalies, SWI for microhemorrhages). As in the neuropsychological examination, there is rarely a pre-injury scan available for comparison but unlike neuropsychological investigations clinical CT and MRI is not used quantitatively to compare a patient study with a normative sample. Research studies may use different protocols than claimants utilise, but Wilde and Little (2019) warned,

> The issue of reliability (across sites and across time) is even more problematic in the promising quantitative MRI techniques that require significant post-processing, such as volumetric analysis, diffusion tensor imaging (DTI), magnetisation transfer imaging, magnetic resonance spectroscopy (MRS), arterial spin labelling (ASL) and functional (fMRI), as well as other techniques that further limit clinical application.
>
> (p.92)

2 *Siegel v Pummell* [2014] EWHC 4309 (QB)

Judges like what they can see and claimant lawyers may be seduced by brain imaging into believing it provides a definitive answer to persisting symptoms in a mild TBI case. An important question for the neuropsychologist is whether microscopic brain changes which require increasingly sophisticated technologies to identify are likely to have any behavioural concomitant. For example, in one MRI study at 12 months post-injury, whilst lesions were found in only 16% of patients with post-concussion symptoms, they were also noted in 11% of asymptomatic patients (Einarsen et al., 2019). In future more emphasis may be placed on functional and metabolic imaging (see Shin et al., 2017), but structural MRI remains the current standard. The most promising area of investigation in this respect is with relation to white matter (axonal) injury and diffusion tensor imaging (DTI) investigation, as confirmed in a recent meta-analysis by Wallace et al. (2018). It is not enough to show mild TBI can produce brain changes on DTI however, they have to be causally related to neuropsychological sequelae and several studies have shown that DTI changes at different times post mild TBI are unrelated to symptoms and neuropsychological test performance (Miles et al., 2008; Lange et al., 2012; Panenka et al., 2015). In a study of 75 cases and 40 matched orthopaedic controls no abnormalities were evident in simple or complicated mild TBI, but age-related axonal changes were found (Ilvesmaki et al., 2014). DTI protocols are not standardised for use in the Courts, and few neuroradiologists (yet alone neurologists) have expertise in their interpretation. Incidental (asymptomatic) findings on brain MRI were noted in 34% of patient participants and 27% of normal controls in a review of 641 research cases (Royal & Peterson, 2008) whilst Illes et al. (2004) reviewed 151 MR scans and found 45% of healthy volunteers showed incidental anomalies. There have been calls for the development of a population imaging database, as with neuropsychological investigations, to provide an understanding of normal variation (Wintermark et al., 2015). Without this the situation was succinctly summarised by Asken et al. (2018, p.603) in a systematic review: 'DTI can sensitively detect difference in mTBI patients but evidence for the specificity of these findings is currently low'. The neuropsychologist should therefore adopt a cautious approach to imaging, remembering that the presence or absence of lesions on a scan does not make or break the neuropsychological evidence. Expert neuropsychological opinion has contributed to favourable judgments for claimants in mild TBI cases who experience persistent disabling and distressing symptoms where there is no radiological indication of brain injury.[3][4][5]

Concussion and the post-concussion syndrome

There is no universal consensus on the definition of concussion which has been considered alternatively to be an entity separate from mild TBI and as a

---

3 *Siegel v Pummell* [2014] EWHC 4309 (QB).
4 *Williams v Jervis* [2008] EWHC 2346 (QB).
5 *Gale v Esure Services Ltd* [2019].

consequence of mild TBI. Anderson et al. (2006) for example distinguished the adverse pathophysiological impact of biomechanical trauma to the brain which underpins mild TBI from the transiently impaired functional status characteristic of concussion. Conversely Smith and Stewart (2020) argued concussion is not a diagnostic label and should be replaced with terms that reflect the underlying pathophysiology, notably diffuse axonal injury.

A subset of mild TBI patients develop persistent and distressing sensory, somatic psychological, cognitive and behavioural symptoms which have assumed an increasingly questionable syndromal status as Post-concussion syndrome (PCS). Estimates vary with the oft-repeated 15% symptom rate at 12 months which derives from the neurosurgeon Rutherford's work in the 1970s (Rutherford, 1989; Alexander, 1995) reflecting a common myth that this reflects brain damage (Greiffenstein, 2009) and which has been criticised methodologically in favour of a much lower 3–5% estimate (Iverson, 2005; McCrea, 2008). The actual prevalence is unknown, rates being influenced by the population studied, failure to control for factors such as age or depression (Garden & Sullivan, 2010) and methods of measuring symptoms, checklists being particularly likely to result in higher base rates (Edmed & Sullivan, 2012, 2014)

Estimates of higher symptom rates in mild TBI are beset by methodological problems with McCullagh and Feinstein (2003) suggesting that patients who engage with outcome studies may well be unrepresentative of the wider mild TBI population. Certainly, base rates are often ignored. In a questionnaire follow-up study of 110 non-litigating adults diagnosed with concussion Hiployee et al. (2017) reported remarkable figures of just 30 recovered and 80 not recovered cases, many still 'symptomatic' after 10 years. Critically however, the categorisation was based on self-reported symptoms with a high base rate (69% of the 'not recovered' group reported headaches, 67.5% reported concentration difficulties and 52.5% fatigue). The TRACK-TBI study reported 53% of mild TBI describing functional limitations at 12 months compared to 38% of orthopaedic trauma cases (Nelson et al., 2019). This also reflects the overinclusive nature of such complaints. For example, similar results could be demonstrated in a Lithuanian study based on presence of 3 symptoms at 12 months (78% of mild TBI vs 47% of orthopaedic controls) whereas there was no difference based on six core symptoms (only one patient from each group), raising doubt as to the validity of a 'syndrome' status (Mickeviciene et al., 2004). Significantly the authors noted,

> more subjective cognitive dysfunction in patients with concussion compared with controls 1 year after concussion seems to be related to sociodemographic factors and awareness of persisting symptoms caused by repeated questionnaires rather than to persisting effects of a mild traumatic brain injury.
>
> (p.418)

The fact that 'post-concussion' symptoms are regularly elicited in the absence of concussion also militates against a neurological basis for persistent symptoms (Meares et al., 2008; Iverson & Lange, 2010; Dean et al., 2012). For reference McCaffrey et al. (2006) produced an excellent review of almost 200 studies of symptom base rates in the general population. More recently population base rates in a large pan-European study of over 11,750 ranged from 49.9% for fatigue to 10.7% for double vision (Voormolen et al., 2019). Furthermore, in healthy individuals post-concussion-like symptoms are not associated with poorer cognitive performance on testing (Chan, 2001; Yang et al., 2006).

Beyond post-concussion syndrome

In relation to the diagnosis of PCS ICD-10 acknowledges, 'the etiology of these symptoms is not always clear ... The nosological status of this condition is thus somewhat uncertain. There is little doubt, however, that this syndrome is common and distressing to the patient' (World Health Organization, 1992, p.67). Whilst recognising a phenomenon in need of an explanation, we believe the days of PCS are numbered, noting that the DSM IV diagnosis of post-concussional disorder has not survived DSM 5 and its equivalent will disappear in ICD 11. In potential mild TBI cases evaluated by neuropsychologists the notion of Mild Neurocognitive Disorder will increasingly take centre stage.

The distinction between Major and Mild Neurocognitive Disorder is acknowledged in DSM 5 as being inherently arbitrary, but psychometric criterion for the latter is typically between one and two standard deviations (3rd to 16th percentile). This focus on the neuropsychological data is consistent with a move away from a post-concussion 'syndrome' towards defining the severity of the injury and seeking to establish the precise mechanisms underlying the cause of persisting symptoms, much as Sharp and Jenkins (2015) argued in relation to the concept of concussion. Neuropsychologists and others have long struggled with the cause of post-concussion symptoms but Iverson (2019) has recently proposed a network model which eliminates the need for a cause independent of the symptoms and instead recognises the interaction between symptoms as constituting the syndrome. This fits well with the shift we have described towards a three-step medicolegal process of (i) first identifying the likelihood of mild TBI, then (ii) determining the presence or absence of cognitive disorder on testing and, finally, (iii) establishing the likely cause of persisting neuropsychological complaints (Figure 7.1). This also allows for a truly neuropsychological formulation in understanding the uniqueness of mild TBI in each the individual case.

Diagnostic labels help to put people into categories which are more readily understood by doctors and lawyers but for post-concussion symptoms this approach is problematic as there is no specific marker for the condition and

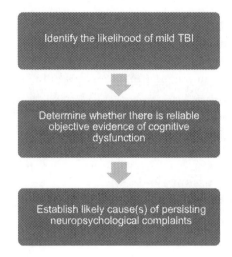

Figure 7.1 Stages in medicolegal neuropsychological evaluation of mild TBI

it does not represent a single entity. Following the steps set out in Figure 7.1 the neuropsychologist's skills in formulation are likely to be more important in identifying predisposing factors, triggers and maintaining influences that go beyond the injury itself. In a similar vein Rickards et al. (2020) refer to predisposing, precipitating and perpetuating factors. Psychology has always favoured a dimensional approach to understanding mental disorder and this is gaining traction even with the gold standard of psychiatric taxonomy DSM 5 which states, 'dimensional approaches to diagnosis … will likely supplement or supercede current categorical approaches in coming years' (American Psychiatric Association, 2013, p.13).

From diagnosis to formulation: Biopsychosocial factors

The notion that PCS evolves from a neurological condition to an increasingly psychological disorder (Lishman, 1988) has given way to multifactorial models. These recognise psychological and physical aspects may play a role from the outset in combination with individual predispositions and vulnerabilities and post-injury beliefs and experiences (Jacobson, 1995; Wood, 2004). Thus Iverson (2012) stated, 'The only reasonable approach to understanding poor outcome from mTBI is a biopsychosocial perspective' (p.53). In advising the Court on why a particular claimant presents in the way they do neuropsychologists should be aware of the potential contributions of sensory and motor pathologies to neuropsychological complaints and recognise known psychosocial predictive factors for persistent symptoms. Unfortunately, most mild TBI follow-up studies do not extend later than 12 months post-injury whereas many claimants are examined beyond this time. Established premorbid factors for symptoms at one year include prior psychiatric history (Booker et al., 2019), concurrent physical health status (McLean et al., 2009), female gender and being somewhat older (King, 2014). Of mild TBI patients who reported no cognitive complaints after two weeks De Koning et al. (2018) found 57% later reported symptoms at one year, a group which was predicted on the basis of higher initial hospital anxiety and depression scale (HADS) scores of anxiety and depression. In one 4-year study persistence of cognitive symptoms was more likely in those with a prior TBI, who sought acute medical attention initially, experienced poor sleep quality and had high levels of anxiety or depression (Theadom et al., 2018).

Psychological symptoms may have their origin in experiences in intensive care and this should be considered as a possible cause of both cognitive and psychological symptoms, but patchy recollection of this period should not be confused with brain injury. Post-traumatic stress disorder (PTSD) may include memory gaps for the trauma and can contribute to persisting cognitive symptoms thereby clouding the clinical picture. Bryant and Harvey (1998) reported a 14% rate of acute stress disorder in mild TBI of whom 82% met diagnostic criteria for PTSD at 6 months. Rates vary widely however with research involving military veterans likely to skew the association of PTSD and mild TBI (Carlson et al., 2011).

A range of mechanisms have been posited as explaining the onset or persistence of symptoms after mild TBI in the absence of major psychological disorder. For example, Hou et al. (2012) reported an initial all-or-nothing response was the key predictor of post-concussion symptoms at 3 months. Whilst these have varying degrees of face validity, theoretical plausibility and empirical support, the neuropsychologist should consider the most likely reasons in each case which involves an evidence-based formulation rather than simply rehearsing a list of possible causes. Anything is possible, but what are the most likely causes in the individual's case? Amongst the most commonly cited explanations are that people tend to report fewer premorbid difficulties after mild TBI (the 'good old days' hypothesis). Thus claimants rated their pre-injury function as superior to non-claimants (Lees-Haley & Brown, 1993). This bias is not specific to all litigants (Lange et al., 2010) but is more common amongst those showing poor effort on testing (Iverson et al., 2010). Alternatively, people may deliberately or unwittingly draw attention to their symptoms, catastrophising their circumstances, often referred to as a 'cry for help' (Young, 2019).

Misattribution of symptoms to brain damage by various means is a common theme, attributed to a nocebo effect. Symptom profile may reflect implicit notions of brain injury (illness representations), Whittaker et al. (2007) reporting that people who initially (at 1 to 3 weeks) believe a mild TBI will have serious repercussions were more likely to report persistent symptoms at 3 months. Similarly Snell et al. (2011) modified the revised Illness Perceptions Questionnaire for use with mild TBI and reported poor outcomes at 3 months were associated with a stronger injury-identity and greater emotional impact. Another potential factor is anxiety sensitivity, which is the fear of arousal-related sensations due to a belief such sensations have adverse consequences. Higher levels of anxiety sensitivity correlate with increased symptom reporting (Wood et al., 2011) and may mediate the gender difference in persisting symptoms after mild TBI (Albanese et al., 2017).

The power of a label to affect behaviour is well recognised in psychology. Suhr and Gunstad (2005) suggested that 'diagnosis threat' explained why people whose attention was drawn to their history of mild head injury obtained poorer cognitive test scores than others who were not subject to this manipulation. Ozen and Fernandes (2011) suggested the effect is greater on reported complaints than on objective testing. This may be an extension of the expectation-as-aetiology (Mittenberg et al., 1992) or self-fulling prophecy notion whereby people are over-sensitised to normal cognitive lapses (or lapses due to non-cognitive factors) and act accordingly, Mulhern and McMillan (2006) observing that advice given in hospital may itself influence the outcome. Belanger et al. (2013) reported that knowledge, self-efficacy and attributions each contributed independently to symptom report with greater complaints overall being found in people who attributed their symptoms to brain injury. Cultural factors are poorly researched but may also mediate symptom presentation (Zakanis & Yeung, 2011).

Research has also demonstrated that people involved in litigation tend to report more symptoms than closely matched non-litigants (Feinstein et al., 2001; Hanks et al., 2019). In their meta-analysis Binder and Rohling (1996) noted, 'financial incentives assume importance in inverse relation to the severity of the brain injury' (p.9) but the nature of the association between litigation and symptoms is difficult to determine. Patients who failed performance validity testing reported a greater sense of injustice after mild TBI and perceived injustice correlated with greater symptoms and negative expectations of recovery but also with traumatic stress and depression (Iverson et al., 2018). Persistent symptomatic cases may be more likely seek redress, litigation may encourage a focus on symptoms or litigation stresses may prolong and exacerbate symptoms. In an interesting early study Fee and Rutherford (1988) followed up 44 mild TBI claimants (PTA 60 minutes or less) after 3 to 4 years, noting that 57% were symptomatic at the time of the medicolegal report (13 months post-accident on average), 39% had symptoms on settlement of their claim and 34% remained symptomatic 1 year later. Notably the post settlement litigation group had more symptoms than a general minor TBI group, leading the authors to speculate that litigation stresses may persist beyond settlement.

Loss of future earnings can be a key aspect of claim and an evidence-based neuropsychological opinion is especially important for assessing this aspect of damages. Outcomes are generally but not universally favourable. Englander et al. (1992) reported a return to work or school rate of 88% in an insured US sample and a Canadian study described a median time to return to work of 7 months in patients litigating at 12 months compared to just 4 days for those not in litigation (Reynolds et al., 2003). Hurt (2000) described a return to work rate of 90% with the aid of a vocational counsellor. An international systematic review concluded that overall mild TBI per se is not a significant risk factor for long-term work disability though 5% to 20% experience problems in the longer term (Cancelliere et al., 2014). A meta-analysis and systematic review by Bloom et al., (2018) reported more than half return to work within 1 month and 80% were back at work by 6 months. In one long-term mild TBI study after an average of 8 years, return to full time work was twice as likely in males of average premorbid cognitive ability than lower ability, and four times as likely for men of above average ability (Vanderploeg et al., 2003) though overall contribution to the variance was small indicating many factors influence outcomes.

Implications for assessment

Neuropsychological assessment of mild TBI is as much an evaluation of psychological factors as of neuropsychological deficits and calls for a different approach than examination of people with unequivocal severe brain injury. Lawyers should understand such cases are not in principle any easier to examine and the scope for a diverse range of opinion means the expert's involvement can be complex and time-consuming. Both pre- and post-injury medical records may shed light on factors which help to explain how symptoms have arisen and persisted, as may school or employment records. Cognitive tests should focus on aspects most commonly disrupted by brain trauma and on the claimant's cognitive complaints, supplemented by measures of performance validity (see chapter by Gerhand and colleagues within this volume). Self-report inventories should be treated cautiously and should either include validity measures or be interpreted alongside other evidence of reliability of self-report. These may include measures of pain, fatigue, personality, coping styles and self-efficacy in addition to the evaluation of mood and post-traumatic symptoms. We echo the advice of Ettenhofer and Abeles (2008) that neuropsychologists and others 'are urged to exercise great caution in ascribing cognitive, postconcussive or emotional symptoms to neurological injury without fully evaluating the possible relevance of nonneurological factors' (p.370). The many injury-related and psychosocial aspects outlined in this chapter should help the neuropsychologist ensure all relevant factors are considered in reaching an expert opinion and assisting the Court to understand the claimant's condition and prognosis.

Neuropsychological intervention

Interventions to address neuropsychological sequelae of mild TBI need to be based on an individualised formulation. Some people focus only on their label of *brain injury* and fail to appreciate the *mild* whilst others are frustrated that a mild injury can have far from mild consequences and by an uncertain prognosis (Buck et al., 2012). Many treatment studies conflate mild and moderate brain injury. Of those focussed only on mild TBI one systematic review (Al Sayegh et al., 2010) suggested education and reassurance alone may be of less benefit than originally considered, with limited evidence for more comprehensive treatment. There is modest evidence for psycho-education using cognitive behavioural therapy (CBT) concepts applied as soon as possible following a mild TBI (Nygren-de Boussard et al., 2014) and some evidence this may prevent onset of a PCS in people at risk (Silverberg et al., 2013; Caplain et al., 2019). Vanderploeg et al. (2019) found CBT to be five to six times more effective than cognitive rehabilitation in reducing chronic symptoms. A recent systematic review and meta-analysis found that CBT for PCS showed small effects for anxiety, depression and social integration (Chen et al., 2020). Economic costs of mild TBI are poorly researched but likely to be high (Borg et al., 2004b) suggesting intervention may well be cost-effective although routine intervention may not be productive (Snell et al., 2009). Getting people mobilising again may improve function and probably has psychological as well as physical benefits (Baker et al., 2012). Other approaches such as Acceptance and Commitment Therapy (ACT) may help people adjust to chronic symptoms such as pain and vestibular disorder (*cf.* Whiting et al., 2012) but evidence in mild TBI is lacking. Eye Movement Desensitisation Re-Processing (EMDR) to alleviate psychological trauma associated with either the injury or its aftermath, also shows promise although it is very early days (Moore, 2021). Ultimately if disability is underpinned by a complex pattern of symptoms a more comprehensive programme may be required addressing pain, sleep, audiovestibular and visual disorders for which Marshall et al. (2012) provide helpful clinical practice guidelines.

Conclusion

This chapter has described how a silent epidemic of mild TBI presents a challenge for the Courts and to the expert neuropsychologist. For a significant minority the consequences of mild TBI can be anything but mild and views amongst neuropsychologists remain polarised, exemplified on the one hand by Bigler et al. (2013) '… there is incontrovertible evidence that some patients with mTBI will have permanent structural brain damage to the brain and experience neurobehavioral sequelae…' (p.204) and by the response of Larrabee et al. (2013) that

> the evidence is weak for biomarkers of mTBI such as diffusion tensor imaging and for demonstrable neuropathology in uncomplicated mTBI. Postconcussive symptoms and reduced neuropsychological test scores are not specific to mTBI but can result from pre-existing psychosocial and psychiatric problems, expectancy effects and diagnosis threat.
>
> (p.215)

Our review of the evidence leads us to the latter conclusion but each expert needs to reach an opinion based not on dogma but a systematic analysis of the merits of a range of potential causative factors. Promising though newer imaging technologies may be in research settings, it remains to be seen how far the latest methods will really alter the medicolegal landscape, evidence to date being stronger in showing that mild TBI may cause brain anomalies than in demonstrating they have any role in persisting chronic symptoms. Base rate data can be compelling in neuropsychology but have had less impact so far in brain imaging research. That a wide range of neuropsychological complaints may follow mild TBI is not in doubt but the complexity of mild TBI symptoms cannot be predicted by a scan. Once satisfied that a claimant has sustained a mild TBI, the neuropsychologist must then establish whether the relationship with the reported symptoms is causal and determine the mostly likely means by which the symptoms have arisen. In this way expert neuropsychological opinion will frequently be important in providing the Courts with a comprehensive scientific analysis of the most likely symptom etiologies in the individual case.

References

Agrawal, N. (2020) Brain injury. In Agrawal, N., Faruqui, R., & Bodani, M. (Eds) *Oxford textbook of neuropsychiatry*. Oxford: Oxford University Press, 171–180.

Albanese, B., Boffa, J., Macatee, R., & Schmidt, N. (2017) Anxiety sensitivity mediates gender differences in post-concussive symptoms in a clinical sample. *Psychiatry Research 252*: 242–246.

Alexander, M. P. (1995) Mild traumatic brain injury: Pathophysiology, natural history, and clinical management. *Neurology* 45: 1253–1260.

Al Sayegh, A., Sandford, D., & Carson, A. (2010) Psychological approaches to treatment of post-concussion syndrome: A systematic review. *Journal of Neurology, Neurosurgery and Neuropsychiatry 81* (10): 1128–1134.

American Psychiatric Association (2013) *Diagnostic and statistical manual of mental disorders fifth edition: DSM-5*. Washington: American Psychiatric Association.

Anderson, T., Heitger, M., & Macleaod, A. (2006) Concussion and mild head injury. *Journal of Neurology, Neurosurgery and Psychiatry* 6: 342–357.

Andersson, G., Hagman, J., Taliamzadeh, T., Svedberg, A., & Larsen, H. C. (2003) Dual-task study of cognitive and postural interference in patients with vestibular disorders. *Otology and Neurotology* 24: 289–293.

Antepohl, A., Kiviloog, L., Andersson, J., & Gerdle, B. (2003) Cognitive impairment in patients with chronic whiplash-associated disorder – A matched study. *NeuroRehabilitation, 18* (4): 307–315.

Asken, B., DeKosky, S., Clugston, J., Jaffee, M., & Bauer, R. (2018) Diffusion tensor imaging (DTI) findings in adult civilian, military and sport-reported mild traumatic brain injury (mTBI): A systematic critical review. *Brain Imaging and Behavior 12*: 585–612.

Baker, J., Freitas, M., Leddy, J., Kozlowski, K., & Willer, B. (2012) Return to full functioning after graded exercise assessment and progressive exercise treatment of postconcussion syndrome. *Rehabilitation Research and Practice* 1–7 doi:10.1155/2012/705309.

Bartholomew, R., Lunber, R., Knoll, R., Gghanad, I., Jung, D., Nadl, J., Alvarez, V., Remenschneider, A. & Kozin, E. (2020) Labyrinthine concussion: Historic otopathological antecedents of a challenging diagnosis. *Laryngoscope Investigative Otolaryngoloist 5*: 267–277.

Belanger, H., Barwick, F., Kip, K., Kretzmer, T., & Vanderploeg, R. (2013) Post-concussive symptom complaints and potentially malleable positive predictors. *The Clinical Neuropsychologist 27 (3)*: 343–355.

Berkeley, G. (1710/1996) *Principles of Human Knowledge and Three dialogues.* New York: Oxford University Press.

Bigelow, R.T., & Agrawal, Y (2015) Vestibular involvement in cognition: Visuospatial ability, attention, executive function and memory. *Journal of Vestibular Research 25*: 73–89.

Bigler, E., Farrer, T., Pertab, J., James, K., Petrie, J., & Hedges, D. (2013) Reaffirmed limitations of meta-analytic methods in the study of mild traumatic brain injury: A response to Rohling et al. *The Clinical Neuropsychologist 27 (2)*: 176–214.

Binder, L. M., & Rohling, M.L. (1996). Money matters: A meta-analytic review of the effects of financial incentives on recovery after closed-head injury. *American Journal of Psychiatry 153*: 7–10.

Bloom, B., Thomas, S., Ahrensberg, J., Weaver, R., Fowler, A., Bestwick, J., Harris, T., & Pearse, R. (2018) A systematic review and meta-analysis of return to work after mild traumatic brain injury. *Brain Injury 32 (13–14)*: 1623–1636.

Booker, J., Sinha, S., Choudhari, K., Dawson, J., & Singh, R. (2019) Description of the predictors of persistent post-concussion symptoms and disability after mild traumatic brain injury: The SHEFBIT cohort. *British Journal of Neurosurgery 33*: 367–375.

Borg, J., Holm, L., Cassidy, D., Peloso, P., Carroll, L., von Holst, H., & Ericson, K. (2004a) Diagnostic procedures in mild traumatic brain injury: Results of the WHO collaborating centre task force on mild traumatic brain injury. *Journal of Rehabilitation Medicine Supp 43*: 61–75.

Borg, J., Holm, L., Pelso, P., Cassidy, D., Carroll, L., von Holst, H., Paniak C, & Yates D (2004b) Non-surgical intervention and cost for mild traumatic brain injury: Results of the WHO collaborating centre task force on mild traumatic brain injury. *Journal of Rehabilitation Medicine Suppl 43*: 76–83.

Brandt, T., Strupp, N., & Dieterich, M. (2014) Towards a concept of disorders of higher vestibular function. *Frontiers in Integrative Neuroscience 8*: 47.

Bryant. R., & Harvey, A. (1998) Relationship between acute stress disorder and posttraumatic stress disorder following mild traumatic brain injury. *American Journal of Psychiatry 155*: 625–629.

Buck. P., Laster, R., Sagrati, J., & Kirzner, R. (2012) Working with mild traumatic brain injury: Voices from the field. *Rehabilitation Research and Practice 7*: 1–6.

Cancelliere, C., Kristman, V., Cassidy, D., Hincapie, C. A., Cote, P., Boyle, E., Carroll, L. J., Stalnacke, B., Nygren-de Boussard, C., & Borg, J. (2014) Systematic review of return to work after mild traumatic brain injury: Results of the international collaboration on mild traumatic brain injury prognosis. *Archives of Physical Medicine and Rehabilitation 95 (3 Supp 2)*: S201–209.

Caplain, S., Chenuc, G., Blancho, S., Marque, S., & Aghakhani, N. (2019) Efficacy of psychoeducation and cognitive rehabilitation after mild traumatic brain injury for preventing post-concussional syndrome in individuals with high risk of poor prognosis: A randomized clinical trial. *Frontiers in Neurology 10*: 929.

Carroll, L., Cassidy, J. D., Holm, L., Kraus, J., & Coronado, V. (2004) Methodological issues and research recommendations for mild traumatic brain injury: The WHO collaborating centre task force on mild traumatic brain injury. *Journal of Rehabilitation Medicine Supp: 43*: 113–125.

Carlson, K., Kehle, S., Meis, L. A., Greer, N., MacDonald, R., Rutks, I., Sayer, N. A., Dobscha, S. K., Wilt, T. J. (2011) Prevalence, assessment and treatment of mild traumatic brain injury and posttraumatic stress disorder: A systematic review of the evidence. *Journal of Head Trauma Rehabilitation 26 (2)*: 103–115.

Cassidy, J. D., Carroll, L. J., Peloso, P. M., Borg, J., von Holst, H., Holm, L., Kraus, J., & Coronado, V. G. (2004) Incidence, risk factors and prevention of mild traumatic brain injury: Results of the WHO Collaborating Centre Task Force on Mild Traumatic Brain Injury. *Journal of Rehabilitation Medicine (43* Suppl): 28–60.

Chan, R. K. (2001) Base rate of post-concussion symptoms among normal people and its neuropsychological correlates. *Clinical Rehabilitation 15*: 266–273.

Chen, C., Lin, M., Huda, M., & Tsai, P. (2020) Effects of cognitive behavioural therapy for adults with post-concussion syndrome: A systematic review and meta-analysis of randomized controlled trials. *Journal of Psychosomatic Research 136*: 110190.

Davies, R., & McMillan, T. (2005) Opinion about post-concussion syndrome in health professionals. *Brain Injury 19 (11)*: 941–947.

Dean, P. J., A., O'Neill, D., & Sterr, A. (2012). Post-concussion syndrome: Prevalence after mild traumatic brain injury in comparison with a sample without head injury. *Brain Injury 26 (1)*: 14–26.

De Koning, M. E., Scheenen, M., E., Van Der Horn, H., Spikman, J., & Van Der Naalt, J. (2018) From 'miserable minority' to fortunate few': The other end of the mild traumatic brain injury spectrum. *Brain Injury 32 (5)*: 540–543.

Edmed, S., & Sullivan, K. (2012) Base rates of post concussion syndrome by method of symptom report. *Applied Neuropsychology 19 (3)*: 164–170.

Edmed, S., & Sullivan, K. (2014) Method of symptom assessment influences cognitive, affective and somatic post-concussion-like symptom base rates. *Brain Injury 28 (10)*: 1277–1282.

Einarsen, C., Moen, K., Haberg, A., Eikenes, L., Kvisrad, K., Xu, J., Moe, H., Tollfsen, M., Vik, A., & Skandsen, T. (2019) Patients with mild traumatic brain injury recruited from both hospital and primary are settings: A controlled longitudinal magnetic resonance imaging study. *Journal of Neurotrauma 36*: 3172–3182.

Englander, J., Hall, K., Stimpson, T., & Chaffin, S. (1992) Mild traumatic brain injury in an insured population: Subjective complaints and return to employment. *Brain Injury 6 (2)*: 161–166.

Erichsen, J. (1875) *On concussion of the spine nervous shock and other obscure injuries of the nervous system in their clinical and medico-legal aspects*. London: Longmans, Green & Co.

Ettenhofer, M., & Abeles, N. (2008) The significance of mild traumatic brain injury to cognition and self-reported symptoms in long-term recovery from injury. *Journal of Clinical and Experimental Neuropsychology 31 (3)*: 363–372.

Evans, R.W. (2010) Persistent post-traumatic headache, Postconcussion syndrome and whiplash injuries: The evidence for a non-traumatic basis with an historical review. *Headache: The Journal of Head and Face Pain 50(4)*: 716–724.

Fee, C., & Rutherford, W. (1988) A study on the effect of legal settlement on post-concussion symptoms. *Archives of Emergency Medicine* 5: 12–17.

Feinstein, A., Ouchterlony, D., Someville, J., & Jardine, A. (2001) The effects of litigation on symptom expression: A prospective study following mild traumatic brain injury. *Medicine, Science and Law* 41 (2): 116–121.

Fisher, C. M. (1982) Whiplash amnesia. *Neurology* 32 (6): 667–668.

Fleminger, S. (2009) Head Injury. In: David, A.S., Fleminger, S., Kopelman, M., Lovestone, S., & Mellers, J. (Eds) *Lishman's organic psychiatry.* Chichester: Wiley-Blackwell, 167–279.

Garden, N., & Sullivan, K. (2010) An examination of the base rates of post-concussion symptoms: the influence of demographics and depression. *Applied Neuropsychology* 17 (1): 1–7.

Gasquoine, P.G. (2020) Railway spine: The advent of compensation for concussive symptoms. *Journal of the History of the Neurosciences* 29 (2): 234–245.

Goldstein, M. (1990). Traumatic brain injury: A silent epidemic. *Annals of Neurology* 27(3): 327–327.

Gronwall. D., & Wrightson, P. (1980) Duration of post-traumatic amnesia after mild head injury. *Journal of Clinical Neuropsychology* 2 (1): 51–60.

De Guise, E., Lepage, J-L., Tinawai, S., LeBlanc, J., Dagher, J., Lamoureux, J., & Feyz, M. (2010) Comprehensive clinical picture of patients with complicated vs uncomplicated mild traumatic brain injury. *The Clinical Neuropsychologist* 24 (7): 1113–1130.

Greiffenstein, M. F. (2009) Clinical Myths of Forensic Neuropsychology. *The Clinical Neuropsychologist* 23 (2): 286–296.

Gizzi, M., Zlotnik, M., Cicerone, K., & Riley, E. (2003) Vestibular disease and cognitive dysfunction. No evidence for a causal connection. *Journal of Head Trauma Rehabilitation* 18 (5): 398–407.

Hanks, R., Rappaport, L., Seagly, K., Millis, S., Scott, C., & Pearson, C. (2019) Outcomes after concussion recovery education: Effects of litigation and disability status on maintenance of symptoms. *Journal of Neurotrauma* 36 (4): 554–558.

Hiployee, C., Dufot, P., Davis, H., Wennberg, R., Tartaglia, M., Mikulis, D., Hazrati, L, & Tator, C. (2017) Longitudinal study of post-concussion syndrome: Not everyone recovers. *Journal of Neurotrauma* 34: 1511–1523.

Hou, R., Moss-Morris, R., Pebveler, R., Mogg, K., Bradley, B., & Belli, A. (2012) When a minor head injury results in enduring symptoms: A prospective investigation of risk factors for postconcussional syndrome after mild traumatic brain injury. *Journal of Neurology, Neurosurgery and Psychiatry* 83 (2): 217–223.

Hurt, G. (2000) Vocational Rehabilitation. In: Raskin, S. A. and Mateer, C. A. (Eds) *Neuropsychological management of mild traumatic brain injury.* New York: Oxford University Press, 215–230.

Illes, J., Rosen, A., Huang, L. et al. (2004) Ethical consideration of incidental findings on adult brain MRI in research. *Neurology* 62 (6): 888–890.

Ilvesmaki, T., Luoto, T. M., Hakulinen, U., Brander, A., Ryymin, P., Eskola, H., Iverson, G. L., & Ohman, J. (2014) Acute mild traumatic brain injury is not associated with white matter change on diffusion tenor imaging. *Brain* 137 (7): 1876–1882.

Iverson, G. L. (2005) Outcome from mild traumatic brain injury. *Current Opinion in Psychiatry* 18: 301–317.

Iverson, G. L. (2012) A biopsychosocial conceptualisation of poor outcome from mild traumatic brain injury. In: Vasterling, J., Bryant, R., & Keane, T. (Eds) *PTSD and mild traumatic brain injury*. New York: The Guilford Press.

Iverson, G. L. (2019) Network analysis and precision rehabilitation for the postconcussion syndrome. *Frontiers in Neurology 10*: 489.

Iverson, G. L., & Lange, R. T. (2010) Examination of 'Postconcussion-like' symptoms in a healthy sample. *Applied Neuropsychology 10 (3)*: 137–144.

Iverson, G. L., Lange, R., Brooks, B., & Ashton Rennison, V. L. (2010) 'Good old days' bias following mild traumatic brain injury. *The Clinical Neuropsychologist 24 (1)*: 17–37.

Iverson, G. L, Terry, D., Karr, J., Panenka, W., & Silverberg, N. (2018) Perceived injustice and its correlates after mild traumatic brain injury. *Journal of Neurotrauma 35 (10)*: 1156–1166.

Iwashyna, T., Ely, E., Smith, D., & Langa, K. (2010) Long-term cognitive impairment and functional disability among survivors of severe sepsis. *Journal of the American Medical Association 304 (16)*: 1787–1794.

Jacobson, R. (1995) The post concussional syndrome: Physiogenesis, psychogenesis and malingering. An integrated model. *Journal of Psychosomatic Research 39*: 675–693.

Jennett, B., & Teasdale, G. (1981) *Management of head injuries*. Philadelphia: Davis.

Kay, T., Harrington, D., Adams, R. et al., (1993) Definition of mild traumatic brain injury. *Journal of Head Trauma Rehabilitation 8 (3)*: 86–87.

Kessels, R., Aleman, A., Verhagen, W., & Van Luijtelaar, E. (2000) Cognitive functioning after whiplash injury: A meta-analysis. *Journal of the International Neuropsychological Society 6*: 271–278.

King, N. (2014) A systematic review of age and gender factors in prolonged postconcussion symptom after mild head injury. *Brain Injury 28*: 1639–1645.

Lange, R., Iverson, G. L., & Rose, A. (2010) Post-concussion symptom reporting and the 'Good-Old-Days' bias following mild traumatic brain injury. *Archives of Clinical Neuropsychology 25*: 442–450.

Lange, R., Iverson, G. L., Brubacher, J., Madler, B., & Heran, M. (2012) Diffusion tensor imaging findings are not strongly associated with post concussional disorder 2 months following mild traumatic brain injury. *Journal of Head Trauma Rehabilitation 27 (3)*: 188–198.

Larrabee, G., Binder, L., Rohling, M., & Ploetz, D. (2013) Meta-analytic method and the importance of non-TBI factors related to outcome in mild traumatic brain injury: Response to Bigler et al., (2013). *The Clinical Neuropsychologist 27 (2)*: 215–237.

Lees-Haley, P., & Brown, R. (1993) Neuropsychological complaint base rates of 170 personal injury claimants. *Archives of Clinical Neuropsychology 8 (3)*: 203–209.

Lefevre-Dognin, C, Cogne, M., Perdrieau, V., Granger, A., Helsot, C., & Azouvi, P. (2020) Definition and epidemiology of mild traumatic brain injury. *Neurochirurgie 6*: S0028–3770, doi.org/10.1016/j.neuchi.2020.02.002

Lim, K., & Helpern, J. (2002) Neuropsychiatric applications of DTI – a review. *NMR in Biomedicine 15*: 587–593.

Lishman, W. A. (1988) Physiogenesis and psychogenesis in the 'post-concussional syndrome'. *British Journal of Psychiatry 153*: 460–469.

Malec, J., Brown, A., Leibson, C., Flaada, J., Mandrekar, J., Diehl, N., & Perkins, P. (2007) The Mayo classification system for traumatic brain injury severity. *Journal of Neurotrauma 24*: 1417–1424.

Marshall, S., Bayley, M., McCullagh, S., Velikonja, D., & Berrigan, L. (2012) Clinical practice guidelines for mild traumatic brain injury and persistent symptoms. *Canadian Family Physician 58*: 257–267.

Mayou, R., & Bryant, B. (1996) Outcome of 'whiplash' neck injury. *Injury 29 (9)*: 617–623.

McCaffrey, R., Bauer, L., O'Bryant, S., & Palav, A. (2006) *Practitioner's guide to symptom base rates in the general population.* New York: Springer, pp.236.

McCrea, M. (2008) *Mild traumatic brain injury and postconcussion syndrome.* New York: Oxford University Press.

McCrory, P., Feddermann-Demont, N., Dvořák, J., Cassidy, J. D., McIntosh, A., Vos, P. E., Echemendia, R. J., Meeuwisse, W. & Tarnutzer, A. A. (2017). What is the definition of sports-related concussion: A systematic review. *British Journal of Sports Medicine 51 (11)*, 877–887.

McCullagh, S., & Feinstein, A. (2003) Outcome after mild traumatic brain injury: An examination of recruitment bias. *Journal of Neurology, Neurosurgery and Psychiatry 74*: 39–43.

McLean, S., Kirsch, N., Tan-Schriner, C. et al. (2009) Health status, not head injury, predicts concussion symptoms after minor injury. *American Journal of Emergency Medicine 27*: 182–190.

Meares, S., Shores, E., Taylor, A., Batchelor, J., Bryant, R. A., Baguley, J., Chapman, J., Gurka, J., Dawson, K., Capon, L., & Marosszeky, J. E. (2008) Mild traumatic brain injury does not predict acute postconcusison syndrome. *Journal of Neurology, Neurosurgery and Psychiatry 79*: 300–306.

Medical Disability Society (1988) *Report of the Working Party on the Management of Traumatic Brain Injury.* London: Development Trust for the Young Disabled on behalf of the Medical Disability Society.

Mickeviciene, D., Shrader, H., Obelieniene, D., Surkiene, D., Kunickas, R., Stovner, L. J., & Sand, T. (2004) A controlled prospective inception cohort on the post-concussion syndrome outside the medico-legal context. *European Journal of Neurology 11*: 411–419.

Miles, L., Grossman, R., Johnson, G., Babb, J., Diller, L., & Inglese, M. (2008) Short-term DTI predictors of cognitive dysfunction in mild traumatic brain injury. *Brain Injury 22 (2)*: 115–122.

Mittenberg, W., DiGiulio, D., Perrin, S., & Bass, A. (1992) Symptoms following mild head injury: Expectation as aetiology. *Journal of Neurology, Neurosurgery and Psychiatry 55*: 200–204.

Moore, P. S. (2021) EMDR treatment for persistent post concussion symptoms following mild traumatic brain injury. *Journal of EMDR Practice and Research, 15 (3)*.

Mulhern, S., & McMillan, T. (2006) Knowledge and expectation of postconcussion symptoms in the general population. *Journal of Psychosomatic Research 61*: 439–445.

Nelson, L., Temkin, N., Dikmen, S., Barber, J., Giancino, J. T., Yuh, E., Levin, H. S., McCrea, M. A., Stein, M. B., Mukherjee, P., Okonkwo, D. O., Robertson, C. S., Diaz-Arrastia, R., Manley, G. T., and the TRACK-TBI Investigators. (2019) Recovery after mild traumatic brain injury in patients presenting to US level I trauma Centers. *JAMA Neurology 76 (9)*: 1049–1059.

Nygren-de Boussard, C., Holm, L. W., Cancelliere, C., Godbolt, A. K., Boyle. E., Stålnacke. B. M., Hincapie, C., Cassidy, J. D., & Borg, J. (2014) Nonsurgical interventions after mild traumatic brain injury: A systematic review. Results of the international collaboration on mild traumatic brain injury prognosis. *Archives of Physical Medicine and Rehabilitation* 95 (*3*): S257–S264.

Ommaya, A, Faas, F., & Yarnell, P. (1968) Whiplash injury and brain damage: An experimental study. *Journal of the American Medical Association* 204 (*4*): 285–289.

Ozen, L., & Fernandes, M. (2011) Effects of 'diagnosis threat' on cognitive and affective functioning long after mild head injury. *Journal of the International Neuropsychological Society* 17: 219–229.

Pandharipande, P., Girard, T., Jackson, J, Moprandi, A., Thompson, J. L., Pun, B. T., Brummel, N. E., Hughes, E. E., Vasilevskis, A. K., Shintani, A. K., Moons, K. G., Geeverghese, S. K. et al. for the BRIAN-ICU Study Investigators (2013) Long-term cognitive impairment after critical illness. *New England Journal of Medicine* 369: 1306–1316.

Panenka, W., Lange, R., Bouix, S., Shewchuck, J., Manraj, K., Heran, S., Brubacher, J., Eckbo, R., Shenton, M., & Iverson, G. L. (2015) Neuropsychological outcome and diffusion tensor imaging in complicated versus uncomplicated mild traumatic brain injury. *PLoS ONE* 19 (*4*): e0122746.

Prins, M., Giza, C., & Mannix, R. (2019) Pathophysiology of mild traumatic brain injury. In: Silver, J., McAllister, T., & Arciniegas, D. (Eds) *Textbook of Traumatic Brain Injury* (3rd edition). Washington: American Psychiatric Association, 607–621.

Radanov, B., Di Stefano, G., & Schnidrig, A. (1993) Cognitive functioning after common whiplash. A controlled follow-up study. *Archives of Neurology* 50 (*1*): 87–91.

Radanov, B., Di Stefano, G., Schnidrig, A., & Sturzenegger, M. (1994) Common whiplash: Psychosomatic or somatopsychic. *Journal of Neurology, Neurosurgery and Psychiatry* 57: 486–490.

Radanov, B., Bicik, I., Dvorak, J., Antinnes, J., von Schulthess, G., & Buck, A. (1999) Relation between neuropsychological and neuroimaging findings in patients with late whiplash syndrome. *Journal of Neurology, Neurosurgery and Psychiatry* 66: 485–489.

Reynolds, S., Paniak, C., Toller-Lobe, G., & Nagy, J. (2003) A longitudinal study of compensation-seeking and return to work in a treated mild traumatic brain injury sample. *Journal of Head Trauma Rehabilitation* 18 (*2*): 139–147.

Rickards, T., Cranston, C., & McWhorter, J. (2020) Persistent post-concussive symptoms: A model of predisposing, precipitating and perpetuating factors. *Applied Neuropsychology* 1–11.

Roberts, J., Cohen, H., & Sangi-Haghpeykar, H. (2011) Vestibular disorders and dual task performance: Impairment when walking a straight path. *Journal of Vestibular Research* 21 (*3*): 167–174.

Royal, J., & Peterson, B. (2008) The risks and benefits of searching for incidental findings in MRI research scans. *Journal of Law, Medicine and Ethics* 36: 356–360.

Rutherford, W. H. (1989) Postconcussion symptoms: relationship to acute neurological indices, individual differences, and circumstances of injury. In: Leving, H. S., Eisenberg, H. M., Benton, A. L. (Eds) *Mild Head Injury*. New York: Oxford University Press, 217–228.

Sharp, D. J., & Jenkins, P. O. (2015) Concussion is confusing us all. *Practical Neurology* 15: 172–186.

Shin, S., Bales, J., Dixon, C., & Hwang, M. (2017) Structural imaging of mild traumatic brain injury may not be enough: Overview of functional and metabolic imaging of mild traumatic brain injury. *Brain Imaging and Behavior* 11: 591–610.

Silverberg, N., Hallam, B., Rose, A., Underwood, H., Whitfield, K., Thornton, A., & Whittal, M. (2013) Cognitive-behavioural prevention of postconcussion syndrome in at-risk patients. A pilot randomized controlled rial. *Journal of Head Trauma Rehabilitation 28* (4): 313–322.

Simpson-Jones, M. & Hunt, A. (2019) Vision rehabilitation interventions following mild traumatic brain injury: a scoping review. *Disability and Rehabilitation 41* (18): 2206–2222.

Smith, D. H., & Stewart, W. (2020) 'Concussion' is not a true diagnosis. *Nature Reviews Neurology 16*: 457–458.

Snell, D., Surgenor, L., Hay-Smith, E., & Sigert, R. (2009) A systematic review of psychological treatments for mild brain injury: An update on the evidence. *Journal of Clinical and Experimental Neuropsychology 31* (1): 20–38.

Snell, D., Siegert, R., Hay-Smith, J., & Surgenor, L. (2011) Associations between illness perceptions, coping styles and outcomes after mil traumatic brain injury: Preliminary results from a cohort study. *Brain Injury 25* (11): 1126–1138.

Suhr, J., & Gunstad, J. (2005) Further exploration of the effect of 'diagnosis threat' on cognitive performance in individuals with mild head injury. *Journal of the International Neuropsychological Society 11*: 23–29.

Takasaki, H., Chien, C., Johnstone, V., Treleaven, J., & Jull, G. (2012) Validity and reliability of the Perceived Deficit Questionnaire to assess cognitive symptoms in people with chronic whiplash-associated disorders. *Archives of Physical Medicine and Rehabilitation 93*: 1774–1781.

Theadom, A., Starkey, N., Barker-Collo, S., Jones, K., Ameratunga, S., & Feigin, V. (2018) Population-based cohort study of the impacts of mild traumatic brain injury in adults four years post-injury. *PLoS ONE 13* (1): e0191655.

Trimble, M. R. (1981) *Post traumatic Neurosis: from railway spine to the whiplash*. New York: John Wiley.

Vanderploeg, R., Curtiss, G., Duchnick, J., & Luis, C. (2003) Demographic, medical and psychiatric factors in work and marital status after mild head injury. *The Journal of Head Trauma Rehabilitation 18* (2): 148–163.

Vanderploeg, R., Belanger, H., Curtiss, G., Bowles, A., & Cooper, D. (2019) Reconceptualising rehabilitation of individuals with chronic symptoms following mild traumatic brain injury. *Rehabilitation Psychology 64* (1): 1–12.

Varney, N., & Varney, R. (1995) Brain injury without head injury: Some physics of automobile accidents with particular reference to brain injuries occurring without physical head trauma. *Applied Neuropsychology 2*: 47–62.

Voormolen, D., Cnossen, M., Polinder, S., Gravesteijn, B., von Steinbuchel, N., Real, R., & Haagsma, J. (2019) Prevalence of post-concussion-like symptoms in the general population in Italy, The Netherlands and the United Kingdom. *Brain Injury 33* (8): 1078–1086.

Wallace, E., Mathias, J., & Ward, L. (2018) Diffusion tenor imaging changes following mild, moderate and severe adult traumatic brain injury: A meta analysis. *Brain Imaging and Behavior 11* (2): 591–610.

Watt-Pringle, J. & van den Broek, M. (2020) Subtle brain injury claims. In: van den Broek, D., & Sembi, S. (Eds) *Brain Injury Claims* (2nd edition). London: Sweet & Maxwell, 353–397.

Whiting, D., Simpson, G., Mcleod, H., Deane, F., & Ciarrochi, J. (2012). Acceptance and Commitment Therapy (ACT) for psychological adjustment after traumatic brain injury: reporting the protocol for a randomised controlled trial. *Brain Impairment 13*: 360–376.

Whittaker, R., Kemp, S., & House, A. (2007) Illness perceptions and outcome in mild head injury: A longitudinal study. *Journal of Neurology, Neurosurgery and Psychiatry 78*: 644–646.

Wilde, E., & Little, D. (2019) Clinical Imaging. In: Silver, J., McAllister, T., & Arciniegas, D. (Eds) *Textbook of Traumatic Brain Injury* (3rd edition). Washington: American Psychiatric Association, 89–126.

Williams, D., Levin, H., & Eisenberg, H. (1990) Mild head injury classification. *Neurosurgery 27*: 422–428.

Wintermark, M., Coombs, L., & Druzgall, T. (2015) Traumatic brain injury imaging research roadmap. *American Journal of Neuroradiology 36*: E12–E23.

Wood, R. L. (2004) Understanding the "miserable minority": A diathesis-stress paradigm for post-concussional syndrome. *Brain Injury 18 (11)*: 1135–1153.

Wood. R. L., McCabe, M., & Dawkins, J. (2011) The role of anxiety sensitivity in symptom perception after minor head injury: An exploratory study. *Brain Injury 25 (13–14)*: 1296–1299.

World Health Organization (1992) *The ICD-10 classification of mental and behavioural disorders*. Geneva: World Health Organization.

Yang, Y., Chan, R., & Deng, Y. (2006) Examination of postconcussion-like symptoms in healthy university students: relationships to subjective and objective neuropsychological function performance. *Archives of Clinical Neuropsychology 21*: 339–347.

Young, G. (2019) The Cry for Help in psychological injury and law: Concepts and review. *Psychological Injury and Law 12*: 225–237.

Zakanis, K., & Yeing, E. (2011) Base rates of Post-concussive symptoms in a non-concussed multicultural sample. *Archives of Clinical Neuropsychology 26*: 461–465.

8 The frontal lobe paradox

Samantha Fisher-Hicks, Rodger Ll. Wood and Bill Braithwaite QC

A primary function of neuropsychological assessment in a medico-legal context is not simply to inform the Court about the impact of a brain injury on person's cognitive abilities, or the nature and degree of impairment, as measured by cognitive tests, but also how performance on clinical tests translates into everyday functions or abilities that underpin community independence. However, as Ponsford et al. (1995) noted, 'it is frequently difficult to predict how results on psychometric tests reflect an individual's daily life and roles in society' (p 134). Manchester, Priestley and Jackson (2004) expressed a similar view with regard to executive test results. They suggest that, taken in isolation, such test results can be poor predictors of a person's ability to function in everyday life.

It is not unusual to find an apparent dislocation between *good* performance on clinical tests and (reported or observed) *poor* performance in everyday social or functional activities, especially those that involve social judgement, anticipation of consequences, or emotive reasoning. This apparent dislocation has been labelled *The Frontal Paradox* or the *Frontal Lobe Paradox*. The term was first coined by Walsh (1985) in his book *Understanding Brain Damage*. It has important implications for the value of a neuropsychological assessment in any context. However, in a medico-legal context, the implications of not understanding the frontal paradox are probably more significant. This is because if test results do not have good ecological value, then there will inevitably be questions about whether a court report that relies too heavily (or entirely) on the results of neuropsychological tests, as a basis for explaining or predicting psychosocial outcome, could be considered 'fit for purpose'. In this chapter we will therefore endeavour to explain the nature of the frontal paradox and the implications for presenting neuropsychological information in court.

Role of the prefrontal cortex

Changes in cognition and behaviour are frequent legacies following injury to the prefrontal cortex (Stuss et al., 1983). Such changes are particularly evident when injury involves the ventromedial prefrontal cortex (Bechara et al., 1994). This is an area of the brain that is particularly vulnerable to traumatic brain injury (TBI) and therefore, the type of injury frequently encountered in medico-legal assessments. However, it has been recognised for some time that patients with prefrontal injury can perform equally as well on neuropsychological tests when compared with healthy controls, even when there is very extensive frontal pathology (Newcombe & Fortuny, 1979; Diller & Gordon, 1981; Lezak, 1983; Eslinger & Damasio, 1985; Bigler, 1988; Shallice & Burgess, 1991). Mesulam (1986) commented on the 'surprising paucity of [measured] cognitive deficits in patients with substantial frontal lobe damage' (p.320). Lezak (1995) also noted that many patients with prefrontal pathology, when placed in situations in which they should be able to function (based on their measured cognitive ability) fail to, a) adapt skills to the task at hand; b) make errors they do not detect; c) fail to adjust behaviour as the situation changes; d) lack the ability to anticipate or plan ahead; e) respond badly to negative feedback; and f) fail to execute tasks properly for procedural, not task-content reasons.

Lezak's comments mainly refer to executive failures in real-life settings. She, like Damasio et al. (1991), emphasised that impairment of executive functioning can exist even when other cognitive domains are normal, or relatively unaffected. Similar arguments have been made by Burgess and Alderman (2003), who noted that 'People with executive impairment can exhibit serious difficulties performing everyday tasks when neuropsychological test performance suggests only minor cognitive changes have occurred' (p. 388). Wood and Liossi (2006, 2007) have also questioned the ecological validity of many neuropsychological tests, especially when estimating or predicting a person's potential for informed decisions on employment, mental capacity, and future quality of life.

Efforts have been made to develop more specialised tests of executive ability, with a greater emphasis on ecological validity (Burgess & Shallice, 1997; Shallice & Burgess, 1991). For example, the Behavioural Assessment of the Dysexecutive Syndrome [BADS] (Wilson et al,. 1996) was considered to be more sensitive to executive impairment compared with other traditional executive measures (Wilson, 1993). However, it has not proved as sensitive as originally hoped (Bennett et al., 2005). An evaluation by Norris and Tate (2000) found that only one of the BADS subtests (Zoo Map) correlated with independent ratings on the DEX, but this was not in the expected direction. Another study found the BADS to be insensitive to executive function impairments in relatively high functioning individuals (Sohlberg & Mateer, 2001) and in a group of patients who were reported to have planning deficits by care staff (McGeorge et al., 2001).

The identification of executive impairments in daily life may best be achieved through more naturalistic assessment measures, utilising information provided by significant others. One example of a naturalistic approach is the Multiple Errands Test (MET; Shallice & Burgess, 1991). The MET utilises a complex, real-life setting (e.g. an unfamiliar shopping precinct) and requires participants to complete a series of tasks (e.g. purchasing items, writing down specific information, travelling to a specific location at a set time) whilst following a set of predetermined rules (e.g. spend as little money as possible). The examiner observes the patient's performance. Several studies have established that control participants perform significantly better than individuals with executive dysfunction arising from a variety of aetiologies, including acquired brain injury (Knight et al., 2002; Dawson et al., 2009; Morrison et al., 2013). Although, the MET is not without its drawbacks (Rand et al., 2009; Logie et al., 2011) and is not suitable for all patients (Knight et al., 2002), it has potential to capture executive difficulties which may elude traditional neuropsychological testing. In the context of medico-legal assessment, Priestley and Manchester (2014) conclude:

> Use of a test of this type may prove cost effective in reducing the need for lengthy argument between various experts concerning the existence of executive functions, deficits, and the likely effect of any impairment on independent living, employment and social functioning.

Case examples

The following clinical case studies offer examples of how clinical neuropsychological tests administered to patients who have suffered prefrontal injury can lack the ability to fully reflect the psychosocial impact of prefrontal dysfunction.

Case study 1

The disparity between *normal* performance on clinical tests and *poor* performance in everyday activities was illustrated in a classical case study by Eslinger and Damasio (1985), who reported the case of a patient, EVR. He was a 35-year-old man who underwent surgery to remove a cerebral tumour, resulting in a bilateral lesion involving the ventromedial prefrontal cortex. He subsequently developed a profound change in his ability to fulfil his personal and professional responsibilities, in contrast to his premorbid functioning. He lost his job, due to his unreliability and disorganisation; he became bankrupt after an ill-fated business venture (reflecting a lack of judgement); his marriage failed, and he was forced to move in with his parents. The constellation of personality and behavioural changes he exhibited were described as 'acquired sociopathy' by Eslinger and Damasio (1985). However, despite his impaired function in everyday life, he demonstrated intact or superior performance on virtually all conventional neuropsychological measures of language, attention, intellectual abilities, and executive functioning.

Case study 2

Wood and Rutterford (2004b) outlined a similar case, that of MN, whose progress was monitored for 18 years. MN suffered a serious prefrontal injury as the result of a road traffic accident in 1982. He subsequently appeared to make an excellent recovery, mainly because he presented as bright and articulate during clinical interview. Prior to discharge he completed a neuropsychological assessment without exhibiting any abnormality. However, within a year of the injury it became evident that his behaviour in the community was erratic, impulsive, and characterised by executive dysfunction. His articulate and plausible manner meant that he had no difficulty getting employment, but he lost one job after another because of his inability to plan, organise, and initiate actions. He could not recognise errors in his performance (so could not make adjustments in his behaviour) and could not maintain goal-directed activities. He failed to manage his finances, spent money irresponsibly, and had to be bailed out by his parents. When these aspects of his behaviour were pointed out to him, he appeared indifferent. He was always able to provide very plausible reasons for his failures, giving the impression that he was going to deal with these issues in the future.

However, although MN's cognitive (executive) failures in a community setting became increasingly obvious over time, there was no corresponding neuropsychological abnormality on formal assessment. When a full neuropsychological assessment was carried out 12 months post-injury, it recorded intellectual abilities in the superior range, commensurate with his estimated premorbid abilities. There were a few observational signs of attention weaknesses, but not to the extent that they translated into memory, or executive deficits on standardised tests. He was reassessed several times over 16 years, using more specialised tests as they became available, but his scores were always in the normal range. When the case went to court four years post-injury (~1986), the senior barrister, a Queens Counsel, who was very experienced in personal injury work, recommended that the claimant accept a modest settlement because of fears that a High Court Judge would (1) be influenced by the claimant's very articulate and plausible manner when he gave evidence in the witness box; (2) be influenced by his normal neuropsychological test results, and (3) fail to realise that in the real world, MN was unable to function at a level commensurate with his appearance and measured cognitive abilities.

> **Case study 3**
>
> Stuss and Knight (2002) provide a similar case example of JL who suffered bilateral orbital damage as the result of a fall, 13 years previously. He had initially completed an extensive neuropsychological examination without exhibiting any impairment. However, with the passage of time he began to exhibit a range of psychosocial problems, including aggression, sexual disinhibition, and financial mismanagement. When reassessed again after 13 years, both neurological and neuropsychological examinations were normal, with the exception of poor performance on theory of mind tests.

The role of language

It has been postulated that the frontal lobe paradox might arise from the failure of language to mediate actions, leading to a dissociation between measured cognitive ability and the means of translating that ability into action. The potential role of language in the dissociation between *knowing and doing* has been recognised since Luria (1973) proposed that human activity is evoked by intentions formulated by speech to define a certain goal. He proposed that intentions are initially mediated by external speech, and later by internal speech. This has important implications for attention control because, in Luria's view, 'inner-speech' directs attention to salient features of an activity, then mediates the monitoring of performance by comparing the outcome with the original intention (reflecting an important component of executive function).

Analogies have been made with learning in childhood. When learning a task, children (and many adults) often use language overtly to focus attention and regulate their actions. As complex actions sequences become more familiar (through practice and repetition), the control over the sequence of discrete units of action changes from overt speech to covert (or inner) speech. Luria therefore argued that inner speech is responsible for mediating complex forms of behaviour by creating an internal plan to achieve a goal. However, after frontal injury, Luria noted that many patients failed to act upon their stated intentions, 'the verbal command remained in their memory, but it no longer controlled the initiated action and lost its regulating influence' (p. 200).

Stuss and Benson (1986) also commented on speech having an important programming and regulating role in behaviour. They noted that frontal damage can disturb this regulatory role, pointing out that patients may verbalise correctly but fail to use the information to direct behaviour. The dislocation between an ability to verbalise an intention and a failure or inability to act on that intention, suggests that the term *Strategy Application Disorder* offered by Burgess (2000) might have been a better way of describing some features of neurobehavioural disability, than incorporating them under the general rubric of *executive dysfunction*.

Case study 4: An example of 'knowing versus doing'.

Teuber (1964, p. 333) referred to what we now call the frontal paradox as 'the curious dissociation between knowing and doing'. An example of this dissociation between knowing how to do something yet failing to implement that knowledge, is provided by one of the authors (RLW). The case of SS involved a highly intelligent man, employed as a computer programmer. He suffered a blast injury in 1989, at the age of 28 years, that resulted in bilateral prefrontal contusions, evident on an MRI scan. He was neurologically intact and verbally fluent but exhibited an impulsive and disinhibited pattern of behaviour, with impulsive aggression. A comprehensive neuropsychological assessment was conducted whilst the man was an in-patient at an acute rehabilitation unit. He recorded a superior level of intellectual ability in both the verbal and visual domains. Memory functions, as measured by the Wechsler Memory Scale, 3rd Edition (WMS III) ranged from average to high average with some features suggesting that delayed recall was poorly organised, even though it was accurate. Tests of speed of information processing and flexibility of attention were broadly in the normal range, with some minor weaknesses on a task involving the need to switch attention between two stimulus categories. All executive tests from the BADS were performed normally.

SS was about to be discharged as 'neuropsychologically intact' when his Occupational Therapist (OT) pointed out that irrespective of his measured cognitive abilities, he still had difficulty carrying out activities of daily living, even though he understood, and could explain procedurally, what he needed to do. An assessment was therefore organised in the OT kitchen to see how well SS could make a cheese and tomato sandwich. Initially, he was asked to state what steps he would take to make the sandwich. This led to some irritability and accusations of being patronised. However, with some persuasion, SS set out each step in the procedure:

- I get two pieces of bread.
- I spread Mayonnaise on each piece.
- I take two slices of cheese from the packet and lay them on the bread.
- I cut up the tomato and lay it on the cheese.
- Then I eat the sandwich.

Once procedural knowledge was established, SS was asked to carry out the task. He began by opening cupboards and draws, taking out a knife from a draw but then leaving it on the counter. He continued pacing up and down the kitchen. He finally opened the door of the refrigerator and took out the cheese, but not the tomato or the mayonnaise.

After further pacing, during which he was becoming extremely agitated, he again opened the door of the refrigerator and removed the mayonnaise, but not the tomatoes. He then started to pick up and put down items or move them around on the counter-top without executing any action that would lead to the preparation of a sandwich, except that he pulled off the plastic tie that held together the cellophane wrapper that covered the bread. He then stared at the rounds of bread but did not attempt to start making the sandwich. His increasing level of agitation made it necessary to verbally guide him each step of the way (using the steps previously stated by him) in order to complete the task. Thereafter, a programme of verbal mediation training commenced to help him complete several basic routines linked to life in sheltered accommodation. However, it was some months before he learned to use check lists in order to verbally mediate actions that allowed him to perform simple activities of daily living tasks. He never recovered community independence.

Case study 5: How 'knowing verses doing' can influence mental capacity

JT was assessed by one of the authors (SFH) in relation to her ability to manage her financial affairs. She was born prematurely and displayed mild cognitive developmental difficulties which had an impact on her educational achievements. Later, during adolescence, she started to exhibit behavioural and social problems. JT's financial affairs were managed by a court appointed deputy. However, JT disputed the need for a deputy and requested a mental capacity assessment to determine if she could take control of her financial affairs.

During clinical interview, JT presented as a bright and articulate lady, who gave a very plausible and considered account of her life. She stated that she was able to shop independently and had no difficulty with financial transactions. On neuropsychological assessment, there was little evidence of abnormality. When presented with various financial scenarios, she was able to work out approximate totals when asked to consider hypothetical purchases and could calculate what change she would expect to have. She showed an adequate understanding of the value of money, understood her bank statements, had knowledge of the value of her settlement, and her monthly incomings and outgoings. She described how she used internet banking to check her balance and work out a monthly budget. She reported that she regularly transferred money to her savings account for various social events. When presented with a series of hypothetical scenarios aimed at assessing her ability to weigh up and identify potential financial risk, she performed relatively well, although one of her answers was superficial and poorly reasoned.

However, when her activities were subsequently discussed at a meeting attended by a family member, her Case Manager and her legal team, information emerged to reveal a much more chaotic picture. In everyday life, JT was disorganised, impulsive and demonstrated difficulties with planning, initiation and judgment. In contrast to JT's plausible account of her financial management, her deputy revealed that she typically spent her generous monthly budget within the first week or so, resulting in several requests for more money to buy food or other necessary items. As such, payments into her account had to be made on a weekly basis. On a number of occasions, significant sums of money were noted to be missing from her account, for which she could give no explanation. Concerns were expressed by her care team about the volume of clothes she ordered online. Many of these were never opened, or were the wrong size, but were never returned. Concerns were also raised because there were several examples of situations where she had been taken advantage of financially. JT had failed to engage with her care and legal team's attempts to improve her financial management skills (e.g. by completing budgeting forms and having regular review meetings), even though she plausibly expressed a desire and intent to become independent in respect of her financial management.

These two case studies show that it is imperative that experts are mindful of the perils of sole reliance on a person's verbal explanation of their real-life behaviour or *intended* actions without investigating the extent to which such stated intentions actually translate into purposeful behaviour.

Problems with office-based assessments

Test structure and environment

The highly structured nature of a typical neuropsychological assessment, combined with the conditions of the testing environment, may be counter-productive when trying to identify salient but subtle features of executive dysfunction that can have an impact on psychosocial functioning. Shallice and Burgess (1991) addressed the problems with office-based assessments in the following way: a) the examiner prompts test behaviour, preventing an assessment of the patients ability to self-initiate an action; b) tests are of short duration, whereas in real-life people have to maintain goal-directed behaviour over long time spans; c) only one problem is addressed at any time, compared to real life when people have to balance several ideas or activities simultaneously; d) the person being assessed is not required to set priorities or to deal with competing task demands, which is usually a requirement of community living; e) there is no requirement to activate an intention after a delay therefore, there is no need to use prospective memory.

Shallice and Burgess added that the examiner decides the order in which tests are administered and gives instruction when to start each test undermines the assessment's ability to identify problems of initiative, or a lack of drive and motivation. Another basic assumption that underpins most clinical assessments is that tests need to be administered in a quiet environment, free of distraction, at a pace, or over time, that does not cause excessive fatigue, and delivered in such a way that minimises the stressful nature of the assessment experience. This may have ethical value, but it also ignores the fact that many people who suffer TBI describe distractibility and fatigue as frequent and intrusive problems affecting prospective memory, the continuity of thinking, and the ability to follow-through on a task and achieve an intended goal.

All, or any of these factors may impose limitations on a neuropsychologist's opinion about a person's psychosocial potential, emphasising the need to consider neuropsychological test results in the broader context of observations obtained collateral sources, for example, family and friends of the claimant, employers and treating clinicians.

The role of attention

The context in which assessments are carried out, and the procedural weaknesses referred to above, emphasise a problem intrinsic to many existing tests – their failure to assess attention control. Stuss and Alexander (2007) argue that many features of what we refer to as executive dysfunction, can be explained as impairments in attentional control. In real life a person continually has to direct and re-direct attention, based on changing environmental circumstances and intentions. It is usually necessary to monitor several ideas or actions simultaneously and then select and react to relevant stimuli. By contrast, in a clinical assessment a person is only asked to focus upon one thing at a time and the demands are for serial processing, whereas real life requires parallel processing (Schneider & Shiffrin, 1977; Wood & Grafman, 2003). When one examines the role of attention in everyday life we can see that the attentional loading required for many routine everyday activities is far greater than can usually be captured on clinical tests, which is a reason why many people with frontal brain injury can succeed on tests yet fail to cope in the community. The conditions under which a neuropsychological assessment is administered can therefore minimise attentional loading, allowing patients to focus all their available attention on a single task, rather than divide and switch attention across and between several simultaneous activities, such as they need to do in real life, to keep track of changing situations.

Impact of intelligence

Wood and Rutterford (2004a) suggested that highly intelligent patients seem to employ powers of reasoning more effectively when completing consulting room executive tests, even though they exhibit a lack of reasoning ability to cope with comparable cognitive demands in real life. Shuren and Grafman (2002) addressed this by exploring the contrasting nature of deductive and inductive reasoning, to distinguish how these different reasoning processes are employed during a clinical assessment, as opposed to everyday life.

Deductive reasoning, they argue, is largely the responsibility of the left hemisphere, which mediates abstract and logical thinking. They propose that such abilities are amenable to assessment using standardised tests. Inductive reasoning on the other hand is more difficult to assess using standardised tests because it takes the form of hypothesis testing, which often relies on a person's past (usually emotional) experience to make decisions. However, when an event is entirely novel, deductive reasoning may be unreliable and decisions need to be made on the basis of inductive reasoning, a process predominantly involving the right hemisphere and medial frontal cortex, areas that only play a minor role in many of the cognitive abilities routinely assessed by standardised clinical tests (Goel et al., 1998; Osherson et al., 1998). These differences in reasoning ability, therefore suggest that a variety of tests are needed to assess the range of reasoning processes that people rely on for day-to-day decision making (Shuren & Grafman, 2002; Burgess, 2003).

Impulsive decision making

An approach to measuring the impact of impulsivity on reasoning and decision making has involved reward-choice paradigms, where impulsivity is defined as a preference for a smaller-sooner rewards (SSR) versus a larger-later reward (LLR), a process described as *temporal discounting*. An exploratory study (McHugh & Wood, 2008) employed a temporal discounting paradigm to examine decision making for hypothetical monetary reward in a group of brain injured patients and age-matched controls. Participants were asked to choose between a larger reward available at a specified time in the future and smaller reward available immediately. Each of the two groups demonstrated temporal discounting; that is, the subjective value of the reward decreased with increasing delay before gratification. However, the TBI group discounted more than the controls, suggesting that their decision making was more impulsive, possibly reflecting a need for immediate gratification.

Wood and McHugh (2013) proceeded to examine whether *temporal discounting* was related to impulsivity, intellectual factors, poor memory, or executive dysfunction, either measured by clinical tests, or on the basis of ratings made by relatives. As in the original pilot study, they found that the rate of temporal discounting was higher for TBI participants than healthy controls matched for age, gender and estimated pre-accident IQ, even though both groups discounted the LLR more as temporal factors increased. When the influence of cognitive factors was examined, there was no relationship between WAIS III subtest scores and discounting performance. Memory functions, as measured by the WMS III did not make any contribution to the scores and there was no relationship with executive ability, even though they employed a selection of executive tests that were currently used as ecological measures of executive function. Possibly more surprising was the absence of any relationship between discounting performance and relative's ratings of executive dysfunction on the DEX-O (Dysexecutive Questionnaire (proxy version) Burgess et al. 1996). They considered that was probably explained by the generalised nature of ratings on the DEX-O, whilst temporal discounting measures a specific aspect of judgement and decision making. The temporal discounting procedure therefore seemed to offer something new in the assessment of decision making after TBI, particularly the ability to calculate relative monetary values when temporal factors are involved. As such, the paradigm could be a useful addition to existing neuropsychological test batteries, especially in the context of assessing mental capacity to manage a financial award.

The role of emotion

Damasio (1996), and Bechara et al. (2000), explained failures in different types of reasoning by using the concept of somatic markers, or *'gut feelings'*, that emotionally evaluate potential outcomes, and act as a guide to adaptive decision making (Damasio, 1996). As an alternative to cognitive tests that rely on deductive reasoning they developed the Iowa Gambling Task (IGT) as a method of measuring inductive (emotional) reasoning (Bechara et al., 1994). The IGT is believed to mimic real-life decision making in that it incorporates the experience of rewards and losses, as well as factoring uncertainty of outcomes and risk (Bechara et al., 1997; Bechara et al., 1994).

Evidence has suggested that individuals with damage to the ventromedial prefrontal cortex (VMPFC) exhibit relatively poor performance on the IGT, despite retaining intellectual capabilities that allow them to perform well on more traditional cognitive tests (Bechara et al., 1994). They found that individuals with VMPFC damage tend to make more disadvantageous and fewer advantageous choices than both healthy controls and patients with lesions to other brain areas. The IGT has also been considered sensitive to some aspects of executive dysfunction after TBI (e.g. Bonatti et al., 2008; Cotrena et al., 2014; MacPherson et al., 2009; Sigurdardottir et al., 2010). However, it should be noted that this paradigm is not without criticism (Alvarez & Emory, 2006), even the extent to which it relies more heavily on cognitive than emotional abilities (Torralva et al. 2007; Demaree et al., 2010; Gansler et al., 2011).

The use of rating scales

Behavioural rating scales have been developed to elicit information about cognitive-behaviour deficiencies that have an impact on community independence. However, many of these have poor psychometrics, which render them unreliable when trying to establish a profile of neurobehavioural disability (see the reviews by Wood et al., 2008; Tate, 2010). To correct this, Alderman et al developed the St Andrew's Swansea Neurobehavioural Outcome Scale [SASNOS] (Alderman et al., 2011). This was designed specifically for individuals with acquired brain injury, to address some of the shortcomings of earlier measures. When considering the frontal lobe paradox, a major strength of the SASNOS is the inclusion of a patient and a proxy version (the latter can be completed by significant others and/or by clinicians who know the patient well). To counter the potential lack of awareness exhibited by many individuals, leading to a tendency to underreport the frequency and severity of neurobehavioural problems (Prigatano & Schacter, 1991; Bivona et al., 2014). Evidence has suggested that concordance between patient and proxy ratings differs across functional domains. For example, a higher level of concordance is reached on items related to physical functioning and self-care, whereas ratings on emotional and behavioural items reach lower levels of agreement and appear to be perceived differently by patients and proxies (Seel et al., 1997; Weddell & Wood, 2018). Therefore, the importance of including the perspective of an informant when assessing neurobehavioural disability cannot be overemphasised, although it should also be borne in mind that proxy ratings can also be biased.

The legal perspective by Bill Braithwaite QC of Exchange Chambers

The disconnect emphasised in this chapter is one of the most important and most overlooked problems in compensation claims following significant brain injury. The case of MN demonstrates this point – although he tested well, the claimant's behaviour in the community was described as erratic, impulsive, and characterised by executive dysfunction. His articulate and plausible manner meant that he had no difficulty getting employment, but he lost one job after another. That account emphasises the problem for lawyers of relying on test results, to the exclusion of evidence of functionality.

It is the lawyers' duty to recognise this issue, and to ensure that experts have all information necessary to enable them to form an informed opinion. That means lawyers should anticipate this issue, and explore it with family, and with all others who see the claimant in daily life – e.g. friends, therapists, financial deputy, work colleagues, employers.

All relevant evidence should be recorded, and made available as appropriate to the experts. Whether it can and should be done before the first neuropsychological examination will depend on the timescale of the rehabilitation and the litigation process.

Experts should be instructed to consider as part of the interview and examination process whether they can uncover relevant evidence of the claimant's ability to function in the real world – their enquiry might be more focussed than the lawyers.

Because mental capacity has to be considered in all cases of severe or moderate/severe brain injury, the process of gathering evidence of function can go hand in hand with exploration of mental capacity i.e. the thought processes involved in decision making. Of course, here again there is a functionality issue; very often, people who have suffered severe brain injury are protected by their family from the process of making decisions, so that evidence may be hard to find.

Experts should be litigation literate, i.e. they should understand the litigation process, and they should know that it is their duty to make sure that they have all available information to enable them to form a sound opinion. If they feel that evidence is lacking, they should ask for it to be obtained.

And that leads me on to the last area of comment, but one which is particularly important; the duties of experts. I have been lecturing and writing on this topic for almost 30 years, and the basic principles have remained the same throughout that time.

The expert, whether reporting for claimant or defendant, is required to give an independent opinion. Of course the expert must see and consider the issues from the view of who is instructing him or her, so that all relevant arguments can be canvassed and discussed, but that does not detract from the basic principle of independence. Reinforcing that point, the expert's report is addressed to the Court, and the Court has expectations of so called 'experts', some of whom have relatively little experience of the issues at stake in the compensation claim.

An expert's report should provide a comprehensive review of all factors that contribute to a claimant's condition and psychosocial potential, and the expert should include and evaluate information from all who are able to give an informed view of the claimant's functionality.

Instructing solicitors should take a dim view of experts who provide reports that offer a narrow perspective on the claimant's condition, and do not reflect a range of opinion, especially if the solicitors and barristers find, at settlement meetings or mediations, or, far worse, at trial, that they have to back down in an argument because factors, other than purely tests scores, have not been considered, when explaining how impairment and disability following brain injury have an impact on social handicap. If a case goes badly because the expert has not comprehensively addressed all the relevant issues, the expert may be open to serious criticism from a judge, with inevitable knock-on effects for his or her medico-legal practice.

Of course, the other side of that coin is that good lawyers should protect experts from making significant mistakes. As lawyers, we should have good questioning and analytical skills, which ought to enable us to detect problems before they become embarrassing, correct them, and ensure that the expert performs to the best of his or her ability. Good, sensible, appropriate teamwork between lawyers and experts usually or always produces good results!

Conclusions

This chapter has highlighted some of the limitations of neuropsychological testing and specifically the perils of relying solely on neuropsychological test data to inform opinion. These issues have been comprehensively discussed by George and Gilbert (2018). The case examples we have provided will be familiar to many clinical neuropsychologists and other disciplines who act as 'Experts' in the medico-legal arena. They illustrate how some individuals can perform well on clinical tests in a quiet, highly structured environment, and can also be very plausible when they express their intentions. Yet, they lack the ability to utilise their measured cognitive abilities in real-life settings and fail to implement their intentions in a meaningful and sustained way (see Priestley & Manchester, 2014). Wood and Bigler (2017) proposed that it would be unwise to form opinions about a person's level of everyday functioning solely on test performance or a person's verbal explanation of their *intended* actions, without knowing if stated intentions will actually translate into purposeful behaviour: 'it would be unwise, even negligent, to form opinions on how test performance is likely to influence everyday behaviour, without carefully interviewing those with direct experience of the person's real-world behaviour over a period of time' (p. 93).

Such experiences emphasise that a neuropsychologist's opinion should be based on a convergence of evidence derived from a variety of sources, including careful, semi-structured interviews with relatives and/or friends who observe such individuals in everyday activities, in order that performance on neuropsychological tests can be compared and contrasted with real-life behaviours. We recommend that performance on standardised cognitive tests should be balanced by self and proxy ratings on psychometrically robust and specialised rating scales that can potentially capture the real-life impact of executive dysfunction (see Draper & Ponsford, 2009).

References

Alderman, N., Wood, R. L., & Williams, C. (2011). The development of the St Andrew's-Swansea Neurobehavioural Outcome Scale: Validity and reliability of a new measure of neurobehavioural disability and social handicap. *Brain Injury, 25(1)*, 83–100. doi:10.3109/02699052.2010.532849.

Alvarez, J., & Emory, E. (2006). Executive function and the frontal lobes: A meta-analytic review. *Neuropsychology Review, 16*, 17–42.

Bechara, A., Damasio, H., & Damasio, A. R. (2000). Emotion, decision making and the orbitofrontal cortex. *Cerebral cortex (New York, N.Y.: 1991), 10(3)*, 295–307. https://doi.org/10.1093/cercor/10.3.295.

Bechara, A., Damasio, A. R., Damasio, H., & Anderson, S. W. (1994). Insensitivity to future consequences following damage to human prefrontal cortex. *Cognition, 50*, 7–15. doi:10.1016/0010–0277(94)90018-3.

Bechara, A., Damasio, H., Tranel, D., & Damasio, A. R. (1997). Deciding advantageously before knowing the advantageous strategy. *Science (New York, N.Y.), 275(5304)*, 1293–1295. https://doi.org/10.1126/science.275.5304.1293.

Bennett, P. C., Ong, B., & Ponsford, J. (2005). Measuring executive dysfunction in an acute rehabilitation setting: Using the dysexecutive questionnaire (DEX). *Journal of the International Neuropsychological Society, 11*(4), 376–385. https://doi.org/10.1017/S1355617705050423.

Bigler, E. D. (1988). Frontal lobe damage and neuropsychological assessment. *Archives of Clinical Neuropsychology, 3*(3), 279–297. https://doi.org/10.1016/0887-6177(88)90020-0.

Bivona, U., Riccio, A., Ciurli, P., Carlesimo, G., Donne, V., Pizzonia, E., et al. (2014). Low self-awareness of individuals with severe traumatic brain injury can lead to reduced ability to take another person's perspective. *Journal of Head Trauma and Rehabilitation, 29*, 157–171. doi:10.1097/HTR.0b013e3182864f0b.

Bonatti, E., Zamarian, L., Wagner, M., Benke, T., Hollosi, P., Strubreither, W., & Delazer, M. (2008). Making decisions and advising decisions in traumatic brain injury. *Cognitive and Behavioural Neurology, 21*(3), 164–175. doi:10.1097/WNN.0b013e318184e688.

Burgess P. W. (2000). Strategy application disorder: The role of the frontal lobes in human multitasking. *Psychological Research, 63*(3–4), 279–288. doi:10.1007/s004269900006.

Burgess, P. W. (2003). Assessment of executive function. In P. W. Halligan, U. Kischka, & J. C. Marshall (Eds.), *Handbook of clinical neuropsychology* (pp. 322–340). Oxford: Oxford University Press.

Burgess, P. W., & Shallice, T. (1997). The relationship between prospective and retrospective memory: Neuropsychological evidence. In M. A. Conway (Ed.), *Studies in cognition. Cognitive models of memory* (pp. 247–272). The MIT Press.

Burgess, P. W., & Alderman, N. (2003). Executive dysfunction. In L. H. Goldstein and J. E. McNeil (eds) *Clinical Neuropsychology.* https://doi.org/10.1002/0470013338.ch9.

Burgess, P. W., Alderman, N., Evans, J., Emslie, H., & Wilson, B. A. (1998). The ecological validity of tests of executive function. *Journal of the International Neuropsychological Society: JINS, 4*(6), 547–558. https://doi.org/10.1017/s1355617798466037

Cotrena, C., Branco, L. D., Zimmermann, N., Cardoso, C. O., Grassi-Oliveira, R., & Fonseca, R. P. (2014). Impaired decision-making after traumatic brain injury: the Iowa Gambling Task. *Brain Injury, 28*, 1070–1075. doi:10.3109/02699052.2014.896943.

Damasio, A. R. (1996). The somatic marker hypothesis and the possible functions of the prefrontal cortex. *Philosophical Transactions of the Royal Society of London (series B) 351*(1346), 1413–1420.

Damasio A. R., Tranel D., & Damasio H. C. (1991) Somatic markers and the guidance of behaviour: therapy and preliminary testing (pp. 217–229). In H. S. Levin, H. M. Eisenberg, & A. L. Benton (Eds) *Frontal lobe function and dysfunction.* New York: Oxford University Press.

Dawson, D. R., Anderson, N. D., Burgess, P., Cooper, E., Krpan, K. M., & Stuss, D. T. (2009). Further development of the Multiple Errands Test: Standardized scoring, reliability, and ecological validity for the Baycrest version. *Archives of Physical Medicine and Rehabilitation, 90*(11 Suppl), S41–S51. https://doi.org/10.1016/j.apmr.2009.07.012.

Demaree, H. A., Burns, K. J., & DeDonno, M. A. (2010). Intelligence, but not emotional intelligence, predicts Iowa gambling task performance. *Intelligence, 38*(2), 249–254. https://doi.org/10.1016/j.intell.2009.12.004.

Diller, L., & Gordon, W. A. (1981). Interventions for cognitive deficits in brain-injured adults. *Journal of consulting and clinical psychology, 49*(6), 822–834. https://doi.org/10.1037//0022-006x.49.6.822.

Draper, K., & Ponsford, J. (2009). Long-term outcome following traumatic brain injury: A comparison of subjective reports by those injured and their relatives. *Neuropsychological Rehabilitation*, *19*(5), 645–661. https://doi.org/10.1080/17405620802613935

Eslinger, P. J., & Damasio, A. R. (1985). Severe disturbance of higher cognition after bilateral frontal lobe ablation: Patient EVR. *Neurology*, *35*(12), 1731–1741. https://doi.org/10.1212/WNL.35.12.1731.

Gansler, D. A., Jerram, M. W., Vannorsdall, T. D., & Schretlen, D. J. (2011). Comparing alternative metrics to assess performance on the Iowa Gambling Task. *Journal of Clinical and Experimental Neuropsychology*, *33*(9), 1040–1048. https://doi.org/10.1080/13803395.2011.596820.

George, M. S., & Gilbert, S. (2018). Mental Capacity Act (2005) assessments: Why everyone needs to know about the frontal lobe paradox. *The Neuropsychologist*, *5*, 59–66.

Goel, V., Gold, B., Kapur, S., & Houle, S. (1998). Neuroanatomical correlates of human reasoning. *Journal of Cognitive Neuroscience*, *10*(3), 293–302. https://doi.org/10.1162/089892998562744.

Knight, R. T., Alderman, N., & Burgess, P. W. (2002). Development of a simplified version of the Multiple Errands Test for use in hospital settings. *Neuropsychological Rehabilitation*, *12*, 231–255.

Lezak, M. D. (1983). *Neuropsychological Assessment* (2nd ed). New York: Oxford University Press.

Lezak, M. D. (1995). *Neuropsychological Assessment* (3rd ed.). New York: Oxford University Press.

Logie, R. H., Trawley, S., & Law, A. (2011). Multitasking: multiple, domain-specific cognitive functions in a virtual environment. *Memory & Cognition*, *39*(8), 1561–1574. https://doi.org/10.3758/s13421-011-0120-1.

Luria, A. R. (1973). The frontal lobes and the regulation of behaviour. In K. H. Pribram & A. R. Luria, *Psychophysiology of the frontal lobes*. Academic Press.

MacPherson, S. E., Phillips, H. L., Della Sala, S., & Cantagallo, A. (2009). Iowa gambling task impairment is not specific to ventromedial prefrontal lesions. *The Clinical Neuropsychologist*; *23*: 510–522.

Manchester, D., Priestley, N., & Jackson, H. (2004). The assessment of executive functions: Coming out of the office. *Brain injury*, *18*(11), 1067–1081. https://doi.org/10.1080/02699050410001672387.

McGeorge, P., Phillips, L. H., Crawford, J. R., Garden, S. E., Della Sala, S., Milne, A. B., Hamilton, S. W., & Callender, J. S. (2001). Using virtual environments in the assessment of executive dysfunction. *Presence: Teleoperators and Virtual Environments*, *10*(4), 375–383. https://doi.org/10.1162/1054746011470235.

McHugh, L., & Wood, R. L. (2008). Using a temporal discounting paradigm to measure decision-making and impulsivity following traumatic brain injury: A pilot study. *Brain Injury*, *22*, 715–721.

Mesulam, M. M. (1986). Frontal cortex and behaviour. *Annals of neurology*, *19*(4), 320–325. https://doi.org/10.1002/ana.410190403.

Morrison, M. T., Giles, G. M., Ryan, J. D., Baum, C. M., Dromerick, A. W., Polatajko, H. J., & Edwards, D. F. (2013). Multiple Errands Test-Revised (MET-R): A performance-based measure of executive function in people with mild cerebrovascular accident. *The American journal of occupational therapy: official publication of the American Occupational Therapy Association*, *67*(4), 460–468. https://doi.org/10.5014/ajot.2013.007880.

Newcombe, F., & Fortuny, L.A. (1979). Problems and perspectives in the evaluation of psychological deficits after cerebral lesions. *International Rehabilitation Medicine*, *1(4)*, 182–192. doi:10.3109/03790797909164041.

Norris, G., & Tate, R. L. (2000). The Behavioural Assessment of the Dysexecutive Syndrome (BADS): Ecological, concurrent and construct validity. *Neuropsychological Rehabilitation*, *10(1)*, 33–45. https://doi.org/10.1080/096020100389282.

Osherson, D., Perani, D., Cappa, S., Schnur, T., Grassi, F., & Fazio, F. (1998). Distinct brain loci in deductive versus probabilistic reasoning. *Neuropsychologia*, *36(4)*, 369–376. https://doi.org/10.1016/s0028-3932(97)00099-00097.

Ponsford, J., Sloan, S., & Snow P. (1995). *Traumatic brain injury: Rehabilitation for everyday adaptive living*. London: Erlbaum.

Priestley, N., & Manchester, D. (2014). Presenting evidence of executive functions deficit in court. Why is behaviour so important? *Personal Injury Brief Update Law Journal*, 1 March.

Prigatano, G. P., & Schacter, D. L. (Eds.). (1991). *Awareness of deficit after brain injury: Clinical and theoretical issues*. Oxford: Oxford University Press.

Rand, D., Weiss, P. L., & Katz, N. (2009). Training multitasking in a virtual supermarket: A novel intervention after stroke. *The American Journal of Occupational Therapy: Official Publication of the American Occupational Therapy Association*, *63(5)*, 535–542. https://doi.org/10.5014/ajot.63.5.535.

Schneider, W., & Shiffrin, R. M. (1977). Controlled and automatic human information processing: I. Detection, search, and attention. *Psychological Review*, *84(1)*, 1–66. https://doi.org/10.1037/0033-295X.84.1.1.

Seel, R. T., Kreutzer, J. S., & Sander, A. M. (1997). Concordance of patients' and family members' ratings of neurobehavioral functioning after traumatic brain injury. *Archives of physical medicine and rehabilitation*, *78(11)*, 1254–1259. https://doi.org/10.1016/s0003-9993(97)90340-90343.

Shallice, T., & Burgess, P. W. (1991). Deficits in strategy application following frontal lobe damage in man. *Brain: A Journal of Neurology*, *114 (Pt 2)*, 727–741. https://doi.org/10.1093/brain/114.2.727.

Shuren, J. E., & Grafman, J. (2002). The neurology of reasoning. *Archives of Neurology*, *59(6)*, 916–919. https://doi.org/10.1001/archneur.59.6.916.

Sigurdardottir, S., Jerstad, T., Andelic, N., Roe, C., & Schanke, A. K. (2010). Olfactory dysfunction, gambling task performance and intracranial lesions after traumatic brain injury. *Neuropsychology*, *24(4)*, 504–513. https://doi.org/10.1037/a0018934.

Sohlberg, M. M., & Mateer, C. A. (2001). *Cognitive rehabilitation: An integrative neuropsychological approach*. Guilford Press.

Stuss, D. T., & Alexander, M. P. (2007). Is there a dysexecutive syndrome? *Philosophical Transactions of the Royal Society of London. Series B, Biological Sciences*, *362(1481)*, 901–915. https://doi.org/10.1098/rstb.2007.2096.

Stuss, D. T., & Knight, R. T. (Eds.). (2002). *Principles of frontal lobe function*. Oxford: Oxford University Press. https://doi.org/10.1093/acprof:oso/9780195134971.001.0001.

Stuss, D. T., Benson, D. F., Kaplan, E. F., Weir, W. S., Naeser, M. A., Lieberman, I., & Ferrill, D. (1983). The involvement of orbitofrontal cerebrum in cognitive tasks. *Neuropsychologia*, *21*: 235–248.

Stuss, D. T., & Benson, D. F. (1986). *The frontal lobes*. New York: Raven Press.

Tate, R. L. (2010). *A compendium of tests, scales and questionnaires: The practitioner's guide to measuring outcomes after acquired brain impairment* (1st ed.). Psychology Press. https://doi.org/10.4324/9781003076391.

Teuber, H. L. (1964). The riddle of frontal lobe function in man. In J. M. Warren, & K. Akert (Eds) *The frontal granular cortex and behaviour* (pp.410–444). New York: McGraw-Hill.

Torralva, T., Kipps, C. M., Hodges, J. R., Clark, L., Bekinschtein, T., Roca, M., Calcagno, M. L., & Manes, F. (2007). The relationship between affective decision-making and theory of mind in the frontal variant of fronto-temporal dementia. *Neuropsychologia, 45*(2), 342–349. https://doi.org/10.1016/j.neuropsychologia.2006.05.031.

Walsh, K. W. (1985). *Understanding brain damage: A primer of neuropsychological evaluation*. London: Churchill Livingstone.

Weddell, R. A., & Wood, R. L. (2018). Perceived personality change after traumatic brain injury II: comparing participant and informant perspectives. *Brain Injury, 32*(4), 442–452. https://doi.org/10.1080/02699052.2018.1429657.

Wilson, B. A. (1993). Ecological validity of neuropsychological assessment: Do neuropsychological indexes predict performance in everyday activities? *Applied & Preventive Psychology, 2*(4), 209–215. https://doi.org/10.1016/S0962-1849(05)80091-80095.

Wilson, B. A., Alderman, N., Burgess, P. W. Emslie, H., & Evans, J. J. (1996). *Behavioural assessment of the dysexecutive syn-drome (BADS)*. Bury St. Edmunds: Thames Valley Test Company.

Wood, R. L., & Bigler, E. (2017). Problems assessing executive dysfunction in neurobehavioural disability. In T. M. McMillan & R. L. Wood (Eds.), *Brain, behaviour and cognition. Neurobehavioural disability and social handicap following traumatic brain injury* (pp. 87–100). London: Routledge/Taylor & Francis Group. https://doi.org/10.4324/9781315684710-7.

Wood, J. N., & Grafman, J. (2003). Human prefrontal cortex: Processing and representational perspectives. *Nature Reviews Neuroscience, 4*(2), 139–147. https://doi.org/10.1038/nrn1033.

Wood, R. L., & Liossi, C. (2006). The ecological validity of executive tests in a severely brain injured sample. *Archives of Clinical Neuropsychology, 21* (5), 429–437.

Wood, R. L., & Liossi, C. (2007). The relationship between general intellectual ability and performance on ecologically valid executive tests in a severe brain injury sample. *Journal of the International Neuropsychological Society: JINS, 13*(1), 90–98. https://doi.org/10.1017/S1355617707070129.

Wood, R. L., & McHugh, L. (2013). Decision making after traumatic brain injury: A temporal discounting paradigm. *J Int Neuropsychol Soc.* February; *19*(2):181–188. doi:0.1017/S135561771200118X.

Wood, R. L., & Rutterford, N. (2004a). 20-Year Follow-Up of Serious Head Trauma. *Journal of the International Neuropsychological Society, 10*(4), 12.

Wood, R. L., & Rutterford, N. (2004b). Relationships between measured cognitive ability and reported psychosocial activity after bilateral frontal lobe injury: An 18-year follow-up. *Neuropsychological Rehabilitation, 14*(3), 329–350.

Wood, R. L., & Rutterford, N. A. (2006). Long-term effect of head trauma on intellectual abilities: a 16-year outcome study. *Journal of neurology, neurosurgery, and psychiatry, 77*(10), 1180–1184. https://doi.org/10.1136/jnnp.2006.091553.

Wood, R. L., Alderman, N., & Williams, C. (2008). Assessment of neurobehavioural disability: A review of existing measures and recommendations for a comprehensive assessment tool. *Brain Injury, 22*(12), 905–918. doi:10.1080/02699 05080249127.

9 Assessing mental capacity in brain injury litigation

Ian P. Brownhill

Introduction

The Mental Capacity Act 2005 (herein: 'the Act') came into force in England and Wales in 2007. A core aim of the Act is to empower and protect people who may not be able to make some decisions for themselves. Some of those decisions are every day and mundane for example what to wear or eat, others are more major and include life sustaining treatment. Since the Act came into force the court has been asked on more than one occasion to consider and adjudicate upon how a person who lacks capacity is to participate in a judicial process. The starting point, quite properly, in the majority of the jurisprudence is how the Act applies to the relevant decision: does P[1] have the mental capacity to conduct the proceedings in which they are involved?

The presumption of capacity

The simple fact that a person has sustained a brain injury ought not lead automatically to an assessment of their mental capacity. To do otherwise would be to act contrary to the principles of the Act. In particular, section 1(2) a person (P) must be assumed to have capacity unless it is established that he/she lacks capacity.

It follows that there must be a reason to assess P's capacity beyond the fact that he or she has sustained a brain injury. It was put this way by Swift J in *Royal Bank of Scotland Plc v AB*:[2]

> 26.This leaves the Tribunal's reliance on the section 1(2) presumption of capacity. The presumption of capacity is important; it ensures proper respect for personal autonomy by requiring any decision as to a lack of capacity to be based on evidence. Yet the section 1(2) presumption like any other, has logical limits. When there is good reason for cause for concern, where there is legitimate doubt as to capacity to litigate, the presumption cannot be used to avoid taking responsibility for assessing

1 The letter 'P' is used as shorthand to describe a protected party in litigation.
2 [2020] UKEAT 0266_18_2702.

DOI: 10.4324/9781003105763-11

and determining capacity. To do that would be to fail to respect personal autonomy in a different way.

Personal autonomy is not only protected by the presumption of capacity but by the requirement that P is not to be treated as unable to make a decision unless all practicable steps to help him to do so have been taken without success: section 1(3) of the Act.

Some common practicable steps are set out in detail in chapter 3 of the Mental Capacity Act Code of Practice. These include: providing the relevant information to the decision being made,[3] adapting methods of communication,[4] assessing capacity at a time and in place where a person is most likely to be able to make the decision.[5]

The obligation to take practicable steps applies as much to expert assessors as it does any other. Poole J recently reminded experts of their responsibilities in *AMDC, AG, CI*,[6] he stated:

> 28(h). If on assessment P does not engage with the expert, then the expert is not required mechanically to ask P about each and every piece of relevant information if to do so would be obviously futile or even aggravating. However, the report should record what attempts were made to assist P to engage and what alternative strategies were used. If an expert hits a "brick wall" with P then they might want to liaise with others to formulate alternative strategies to engage P. The expert might consider what further bespoke education or support can be given to P to promote P's capacity or P's engagement in the decisions which may have to be taken on their behalf. Failure to take steps to assist P to engage and to support her in her decision-making would be contrary to the fundamental principles of the Mental Capacity Act 2005 ss 1(3) and 3(2).

Who should assess P's capacity?

The Act imposes no qualification requirement as to who is qualified to assess P's capacity. This is as much the case in everyday decisions as it is in serious medical treatment cases or in litigation at any level.

The Code of Practice provides[7] that:

> The person who assesses an individual's capacity to make a decision will usually be the person who is directly concerned with the individual at the time the decision needs to be made. This means that different people

---

3 Paragraphs 3.7 to 3.9 of the Code.
4 Paragraph 3.10 to 3.11 of the Code.
5 Paragraph 3.13 to 3.14 of the Code.
6 [2020] EWCOP 58.
7 4.38.

will be involved in assessing someone's capacity to make different decisions at different times.

In respect of litigation, the Code of Practice specifies[8] that a formal assessment of capacity should be conducted:

> to establish whether a person who might be involved in a legal case needs the assistance of the Official Solicitor or other litigation friend (somebody to represent their views to a court and give instructions to their legal representative) and there is doubt about the person's capacity to instruct a solicitor or take part in the case
>
> if there may be legal consequences of a finding of capacity (for example, deciding on financial compensation following a claim for personal injury).

In brain injury litigation, that formal assessment of capacity will tend to be conducted by a professional. That assessment of capacity is not a clinical assessment[9]. Rather, it is an assessment to assist the court as to particular specific issues. In the context of brain injury litigation, that will often be whether:

- P is able to conduct the proceedings;
- P is able to make decisions as to their property and affairs.

Important too is the assessment as to whether steps could be taken so as to enable P to make capacious decisions in these regards. Likewise, assessors will often be asked to provide evidence as to how to enable P to participate in proceedings.

Who does the capacity assessment will depend on the particular case. The assumption held by some that all capacity assessments must be conducted by psychiatrists is incorrect. Likewise, the working assumption that medical evidence is required in all civil cases where issues of capacity are raised is also incorrect. In *Hinduja v Hinduja & Ors*,[10] Falk J stated:

> 37. There is no requirement in the [Civil Procedure Rules] to provide medical evidence. The absence of any such requirement was commented on by Chadwick LJ in Masterman-Lister at [66]. There is no reference to medical evidence in CPR 21.6. The only reference to medical evidence is in paragraph 2.2 of PD 21, which applies where CPR 21.5(3) is being relied on. That requires the grounds of belief of lack of capacity to be stated and, "if" that belief is based on medical opinion, for "any relevant document" to be attached. So the Practice Direction provides that

---

8 4.54.
9 See 28(a) of *AMDC, AG, CI*.
10 [2020] EWHC 1533 (Ch).

medical evidence of lack of capacity must be attached only if (a) it is the basis of the belief, and (b) exists in documentary form. It does not require a document to be created for the purpose.

Falk J considered that the comments in the judgments in *Masterman-Lister*[11] and the *Folks v Faizey*[12] in respect of medical evidence being necessary were not:

> 39. [....] intending to lay down any rigid principle under which medical evidence is required unless the circumstances are exceptional. The question will always depend on what the circumstances are. For example, Folks v Faizey was a personal injury claim where the claimant had suffered a severe head injury in a road traffic accident. The issue of capacity arose during the proceedings, the Court of Protection was involved (which would have required at least some medical evidence in any event), and there was a real dispute between medical experts about whether the claimant had capacity. The need for medical evidence was obvious. Similarly in Masterman-Lister, which like Folks v Faizey related to serious injuries following a road traffic accident, there was a real issue about capacity.

Advantages of neuropsychological assessment

In brain injury litigation, where it is considered necessary for a formal assessment of capacity to be completed, it will be necessary for P's lawyers to identify the appropriate expert, or experts to perform that assessment. For lawyers conducting brain injury litigation, it can be difficult to identify the correct assessor to complete the assessment. Whomever is appointed, they need to have a good command of the statutory framework around capacity and be able to evidence how they have come to a particular conclusion.[13]

Inevitably, there is some overlap between professional disciplines and expertise. However, when deciding on an appropriate assessor it is helpful to consider the emphasis and experience of the different professions, such as whether to instruct a neuropsychologist, neurologist or psychiatrist/neuropsychiatrist. The medical professions of neurology and psychiatry have their strengths and share some overlap in expertise. However, an important attribute of the neuropsychologist is that they are uniquely trained in the administration and interpretation of objective cognitive and psychological measures. Neuropsychologists are also traditionally trained in working with a range of psychological matters that may pre-date or follow P's brain injury. Neuropsychological opinion is formulation driven (see conclusion chapter), meaning that the cognitive, emotional and behavioural components are framed according to

---

11 [2002] EWCA Civ 1889.
12 [2006] EWCA Civ 1381.
13 For more details see paragraph 28 of Poole J's judgment in *AMDC v AG & Anor* [2020] EWCOP 58.

162 *Current condition*

predisposing, precipitating, perpetuating and protective factors. Neuropsychologists synthesise their findings with their knowledge of brain injury and psychosocial scientific evidence. Neuropsychologists undertake regular training in mental capacity and are guided by key documents, such as the British Psychological Society's 'What makes a good assessment of capacity?', [14] key texts such as Ryan-Morgan's (2019) Mental Capacity Casebook, [15] and have access to legal updates – such as the 39 Essex Chambers briefing updates.[16] Neuropsychologists are often good at triangulating additional sources of information, as we see in Worthington and Moore's chapter on testing, and in recognising hidden cognitive disability in the form of 'frontal paradox' phenomena, as we appreciate in Fisher-Hicks and Wood's chapter.

Neuropsychologists are also skilled in assisting P's decision making, and are well versed in consultation with others, including liaising with other experts on matters such as speech or language problems, neurological illness or psychiatric illness. In circumstances where this happens, there is a requirement to record in their report the nature and provenance of such advice they have obtained.[17]

Where an expert produces an assessment for the court, their overriding duty is to the court, not the party who has instructed them.[18] In circumstances where an expert does not act with the necessary independence, they may be held personally liable for wasted costs, [19] referred to their professional regulator[20] or even subject of a referral to the Director of Public Prosecutions.[21]

How to assess capacity

Ahead of any capacity assessment, the assessor is best advised to remind themselves of sections, 1, 2, 3 of the Act. For each assessment, the assessor is required to answer three questions, in this order:[22]

1. Is P unable to make a decision? If so:
2. Is there an impairment or disturbance in the functioning of P's mind or brain? If so:
3. Is P's inability to make the decision because of the identified impairment or disturbance?

---

14 Retrieved on 19/06/2021: https://www.bps.org.uk/sites/www.bps.org.uk/files/Policy/Policy%20-%20Files/What%20makes%20a%20good%20assessment%20of%20capacity.pdf.
15 Ryan-Morgan, T. (2019). *Mental capacity casebook: Clinical assessment and legal commentary.* Routledge.
16 Retrieved on 19/06/2021: https://www.39essex.com/resources-and-training/mental-capacity-law/.
17 *R. v Pabon* [2018] EWCA Crim 420; [2018] Lloyd's Rep. F.C. 258 (CACD) at para.52.
18 Rule 35.3 of the Civil Procedure Rules.
19 *Phillips v Symes (A Bankrupt) (Expert Witnesses: Costs)* [2004] EWHC 2330 (Ch).
20 *Meadow v General Medical Council* [2007] Q.B. 462.
21 *Hussein v William Hill Group* [2004] EWHC 208 (QB).
22 This order does not accord with the Code of Practice. However, it does accord with the caselaw, for example see *Kings College NHS Foundation Trust v C and V* [2015] EWCOP 80 at paragraph 35.

In answering the first question, it is necessary to identify the relevant information for the purposes of the decision before determining whether P is able to understand, retain, use or weigh that information.

Two common decisions which are assessed during the course of brain injury litigation are whether P has:

1. The mental capacity to conduct the proceedings;
2. The mental capacity to make decisions as to their property and financial affairs.

In respect of the relevant information relating to those decisions, the court has given indications as to what they consider to be relevant information for purposes of the decisions. It must be remembered that each decision is specific, so that the information outlined here must be tailored to the particular assessment.[23]

Conduct of proceedings

To have capacity to conduct proceedings, P must have capacity to understand, retain information (including advice by lawyers) relevant to the issues on which their instructions or decision is likely to be necessary in the course of the proceedings, sufficient to enable them to make decisions based upon this information. This includes the ability to use or weigh information (and advice) in the balance as part of the process of making decisions within the proceedings and the ability to communicate those decisions (whether by talking, using sign language or any other means).

Paragraph 4.33 of the Mental Capacity Act Code of Practice states that the Act's definition of capacity accords with the existing common law tests. The common law authorities on capacity to litigate continue to provide a helpful guide when applying the test in sections 2 and 3 in the context of litigation capacity.

The common law approach to litigation capacity has been considered and developed in a number of cases. The leading case is *Masterman-Lister v Brutton & Co*[24] in this case, Chadwick LJ stated:

> ...the test to be applied....is whether the party to legal proceedings is capable of understanding, with the assistance of such proper explanation from legal advisors and experts in other disciplines as the case may require, the issues on which his consent or decision is likely to be necessary in the course of those proceedings. If he has capacity to understand that which he needs to understand in order to pursue or defend a claim, I can see no reason why the law whether substantive or procedure should require the

---

23 *B v A Local Authority* [2019] EWCA Civ 913.
24 [2003] 3 All ER 162.

imposition of a next friend or guardian ad litem (or, as such person is now described in the Civil Procedure Rules, a litigation friend...)

(para. 75)

...a person should not be held unable to understand the information relevant to a decision if he can understand an explanation of that information in broad terms and simple language; and that he should not be regarded as unable to make a rational decision merely because the decision which he does in fact make is a decision which would not be made by a person of ordinary prudence.

(para. 79)

Kennedy LJ stated at paragraph 26:

...the mental abilities required include the ability to recognise a problem, obtain and receive, understand and retain relevant information, including advice; the ability to weigh the information (including that derived from advice) in the balance in reaching a decision, and the ability to communicate that decision...

He further observed at paragraph 27:

...What, however does seem to me to be of some importance is the issue-specific nature of the test; that is to say the requirement to consider the question of capacity in relation to the particular transaction (its nature and complexity) in respect of which the decisions as to capacity fall to be made... Of course as Boreham J said in White's case, capacity must be approached in a common sense way, not by reference to each step in the process of litigation, but bearing in mind the basic right of any person to manage his property and affairs for himself, a right with which no lawyer and no court should rush to interfere.

The Court of Appeal had cause to revisit the *Masterman-Lister* test in *Bailey v Warren*.[25] At paragraph 126 of the judgment Arden LJ set out the matters to be considered when assessing P's capacity to conduct proceedings:

...The assessment of capacity to conduct proceedings depends to some extent on the nature of the proceedings in contemplation. I can only indicate some of the matters to be considered in assessing a client's capacity. The client would need to understand how the proceedings were to be funded. He would need to know about the chances of not succeeding and about the risk of an adverse order as to costs. He would need to have

25 [2006] EWCA Civ 51.

capacity to make the sort of decisions that arise in litigation. Capacity to conduct such proceedings would include the capacity to give proper instructions for and to approve the particulars of claim, and to approve a compromise. For a client to have capacity to approve a compromise, he would need insight into the compromise, an ability to instruct his solicitors to advise him on it, and an understanding of their advice and an ability to weigh their advice....

In *The NHS Trust v Ms T*[26] Bracewell J stated the following when addressing the issue of litigation capacity:

> ...There is no problem in this case in respect of Miss T's intellectual capacity. She is able to instruct solicitors, articulating well and with an approach which demonstrates that she knows there is a problem. But her difficulties arise in relation to processing information in order to give meaningful instructions to legal advisers. ...her wishes as expressed to her legal advisers are solely driven by a desire to kill herself which arises from mental disorder, that disorder involving a delusional belief that the blood within her body is evil.... Intellectually, she is able to acknowledge that that is a delusional belief, but she is driven by that belief by reason of her mental illness, which prevents her from processing information and giving reasoned instructions on the basis of that which she intellectually knows, but cannot understand by reason of her disability....
>
> (at para. 4)

It follows that whether or not the person has capacity to conduct the proceedings it is necessary to focus on the particular proceedings in relation to which the issues arise, the complexity of that litigation and the issues to be determined. In *Sheffield City Council v (1) E (2) S.*[27] Munby J went on to observe:

> There is no principle either of law or of medical science, which necessarily makes it impossible for someone who has litigation capacity at the same time to lack subject-matter capacity. That said, however, it is much more difficult to imagine a case where someone has litigation capacity whilst lacking subject-matter capacity than it is to imagine a case where someone has subject-matter capacity whilst lacking litigation capacity.... I suspect that cases where someone has litigation capacity whilst lacking subject-matter capacity are likely to be very much more infrequent, indeed pretty rare. Indeed, I would go so far as to say that only in unusual circumstances will it be possible to conclude that someone who lacks subject-matter capacity can nonetheless have litigation capacity....

26 [2004] EWHC 2195 (Fam).
27 [2004] EWHC 2808 (Fam).

166 Current condition

Capacity to conduct proceedings is not always straight forward. The phraseology used[28] in assessments had led to the issue being hard fought in court. As too must it be remembered that simply identifying a legal issue and seeking out lawyers is not proof of capacity to conduct proceedings.[29]

Property and affairs

Decisions in respect of P's property and affairs are rarely one-off decisions. On occasion they are, for example whether P has the capacity to make a gift, or to sell a property. However, instead it has been described as:[30]

> The management of affairs relates to a continuous state of affairs whose demands may be unpredictable and may occasionally be urgent.

In respect of the relevant information, the oft quoted passage[31] predates the Act. However, it continues to be applied[32] and remains helpful:

> The expression 'incapable of managing her own affairs and property' must be construed in a common sense way as a whole. It does not call for proof of complete incapacity. On the other hand, it is not enough to prove that the plaintiff is now substantially less capable of managing her own affairs and property than she would have been had the accident not occurred. I have no doubt that the plaintiff is quite incapable of managing unaided a large sum of money such as the sort of sum that would be appropriate compensation for her injuries. That, however, is not conclusive. Few people have the capacity to manage all their affairs unaided.... It may be that she would have chosen, and would choose now, not to take advice, but that is not the question. The question is: is she capable of doing so? To have that capacity she requires first the insight and understanding of the fact that she has a problem in respect of which she needs advice ... Secondly, having identified the problem, it will be necessary for her to seek an appropriate adviser and to instruct him with sufficient clarity to enable him to understand the problem and to advise her appropriately.... Finally, she needs sufficient mental capacity to understand and to make decisions based upon, or otherwise give effect to, such advice as she may receive.

The issue has been considered specifically in the context of brain injury litigation. A distinction is often drawn between the overall management of a

---

28 See for example paragraph 142 of *King v The Wright Roofing Company Ltd* [2020] EWHC 2129 (QB).
29 See for example paragraph 18 of *Dunhill v Burgin (Nos 1 and 2)* [2014] UKSC 18.
30 Paragraph 41 of *A,B,C,X,Z* 2012 EWHC 2400 (COP).
31 *White v Fell*, 12th November 1987 unreported.
32 See for example paragraph 18 of *Masterman-Lister v Brutton & Co* [2002] EWCA Civ 1889.

person's estate compared to making day to day financial decisions.[33] Whilst P may not have capacity to manage a large award that follows brain injury litigation, they may still have capacity to make everyday financial spending decisions.

The concept of whether P has capacity to be told the extent of their estate does not sit comfortably with the Act. The Act is not focused on whether P has capacity to have knowledge about a particular issue, but rather instead whether they can make a particular decision. To frame that decision as "being informed of one's assets" is not a decision that a person would normally make. However, the court has made determinations as to whether P has capacity to know about their estate.[34]

Fluctuating capacity

Fluctuating capacity is not an unusual feature when P has a brain injury.[35] Those fluctuations can vary depending on the nature of the brain injury. Whilst fluctuating capacity is a well-known phenomenon with which lawyers are familiar, it does not appear on the face of the Act. The approach in the Code of Practice is simply to wait until such a time as the person may be able to make the particular decision. However, that approach does not work in all cases. Instead, it is necessary to focus on the nature of the relevant decisions and the nature (and potentially cause) of the fluctuations in capacity. Neuropsychologists assess how fluctuations in arousal levels, fatigue, mood, alcohol/substance use, pain and changing social circumstances are likely to affect capacity at a specific point in time. The courts have showed a willingness to zoom out and to consider closely linked decisions as to forming a macro-question.[36]

The restoration of capacity

Whilst in some cases a person will never be restored to capacity, in other cases they do so. That restoration of capacity may come through education, training, or neuropsychological treatment. The neuropsychologist is again well placed to consider if and how P can be supported to restore capacity. Neuropsychological treatment work sometimes includes psychological approaches to reduce pain or alcohol use, or using P's requisite cognitive strengths to enable P to understand information relevant to a decision. The restoration of capacity is another area that a neuropsychologist may be asked to re-assess.

---

33 See paragraphs 284 to 298 of *Ali v Caton & Anor* [2013] EWHC 1730 (QB).
34 *PBM v TGT & Anor* [2019] EWCOP 6.
35 See *Fluctuating capacity and impulsiveness in acquired brain injury: the dilemma of "unwise" decisions under the Mental Capacity Act*, Chris Lennard, The Journal of Adult Protection 8 August 2016.
36 *Royal Borough of Greenwich v CDM (Rev 1)* [2019] EWCOP 32.

That assessment may be as simple as a new interview with P and reporting afresh, or it may require a full neuropsychological assessment review.

Conclusion

The Mental Capacity Act (2005) came into force in England and Wales two years later and the law has developed from that point onwards. It is important that mental capacity continues to be explored in textbooks, particularly case law and our understanding of brain injury and its consequences. The presumption of capacity is fundamental, but where reasonable doubt is raised as to mental capacity for a specific decision, an assessment is warranted. There has been a tradition to instruct medically trained professionals to assess capacity, but this chapter has argued that neuropsychologists have the benefit of objective cognitive assessments to assist opinion. As we see in other chapters, even objective tests can sometimes miss hidden cognitive disability, but expert interpretation is key to accurate opinion. This chapter has provided a concise guide to the legal aspects of mental capacity to conduct proceedings and to make decisions as to property and financial affairs. The issues raised in the present chapter on the Mental Capacity Act reflect many of the complexities that are illustrated throughout the book and which commonly arise in neuropsychological assessment in brain injury claims.

Part 3
Loss, disability and impact

10 Legal principles of quantum

William Latimer-Sayer QC

Introduction

Compensation claims have a single aim: to recover damages for the claimant. In this chapter I discuss the legal principles which apply to the assessment of such claims. In order to value the appropriate level of award, there is a complex interplay between legal rules, practice and procedure; the available factual evidence; and the parties' respective expert medical and quantum evidence. Neuropsychologists often play a key role in determining the current and long-term needs of those who have suffered from brain injury and provide helpful guidance regarding additional costs and expenses which may arise. This chapter summarises the main guiding principles and heads of loss that commonly apply and considers several case examples by way of illustration.

The fundamental aim

The vast majority of claims for personal injury are brought in tort.[1] The overarching principle is known as 'restitutio in integrum'. In other words, so far as possible from a financial perspective, the claimant should be put back into the position he or she would have been in had the tort not occurred.[2]

Relevant legal principles

When assessing damages, the court will have regard to a number of important rules and concepts. Naturally, many of these rules are complicated by exceptions or caveats, which may be relevant in certain cases. Whilst a detailed understanding of all the applicable principles and their nuances is not necessary for the preponderance of medico-legal work, knowledge of the

---

1 Slight differences may apply to claims brought for trespass to the person or in contract where the object of compensation is to put the claimant into the position as if the contract had been properly performed.
2 *Livingstone v Rawyards Coal Co* (1880) 5 App Cas 25.

DOI: 10.4324/9781003105763-13

following essential elements may assist in understanding the approach that will be taken by the court.

Distinction between past and future expenses and losses

Past expenses and losses are those incurred up to the date of assessment or trial. Future expenses and losses are those expected to be incurred after the date of settlement or trial. Although similar general principles apply to the assessment of both past and future losses, there are additional factors which influence the calculation of future losses. In particular since future losses have not yet been incurred and are therefore more inherently uncertain than past losses, additional considerations will apply. Often discounts will need to be applied to take account of contingencies and the chance of the anticipated expenditure not being incurred. However, such discounts are unusual in respect of neuropsychological costings and are more common to reflect say the 50% chance of needing a hip replacement in 20 years' time. The salient point for practitioners to note is that it is not necessary to establish a definite or certain need for an item of future expenditure for it to be recoverable. The claimant can recover damages in relation to a real or significant chance of anticipated expenditure. For example, in a brain injury case, the claimant may be at risk of suffering a psychiatric disorder requiring in-patient treatment in the future or his or her marriage might be at increased risk of breakdown resulting in the need for paid care.

Distinction between losses and expenses

As regards pecuniary losses, the claimant is entitled to recover 100% of his or her net loss. This is known as the 100% principle.[3] Therefore, a claimant previously employed as a banker or professional footballer who suffers from a traumatic brain injury is entitled to recover their full loss of earnings (net of tax and National Insurance) even though the level of their lost earnings may be considered to be obscene by others. Such losses are not constrained by principles such as reasonableness and proportionality. However, the assessment of expenses (both past and future) is different. Here the touchstone is reasonableness and to be recoverable, claimed expenses must objectively be reasonable, both in type and amount.

Reasonableness

Reasonableness is a pervasive concept in the assessment of damages for personal injury. Before an item of loss or damage can be recoverable, the type of

---

3 *Wells v Wells* [1999] AC 345.

loss must be reasonably foreseeable.[4] Crucially, in respect of past and future expenses, to be recoverable in full, the court must be persuaded that not only the nature of the expense incurred is reasonable, but also the amount of claimed expenditure is reasonable. As regards past expenditure, if the claimant has acted unreasonably and has either purchased items which were not required or were unreasonably expensive or has undergone unnecessary treatment, such items will be disallowed and a more appropriate level of expenditure will be allowed instead.

As regards future expenses, the claimant is entitled to claim the reasonable costs or additional costs or meeting his or her reasonable needs.[5] The claimant is not necessarily restricted to claiming the 'cheapest' option out of a range of reasonable options.[6] But what should the court do when faced with a number of reasonable options for proposed future expenditure? Arguably the court has a wide discretion, particularly where the costs of the various options differ. Albeit technically obiter, it is submitted that Foskett J accurately summarised the law regarding the approach to assessing damages and reasonableness in *Robshaw v United Lincolnshire Hospitals NHS Trust*[7] where he said at para [166]:

> To my mind, in assessing how to provide full compensation for a claimant's reasonable needs, the guiding principle is to consider how the identified needs can reasonably be met by damages – that flows from giving true meaning and effect to the expression "reasonable needs". That process involves, in some instances, the need to look at the overall proportionality of the cost involved, particularly where the evidence indicates a range of potential costs. But it all comes down eventually to the court's evaluation of what is reasonable in all the circumstances: it is usually possible to resolve most issues in this context by concluding that solution A is reasonable and, in the particular circumstances, solution B is not. Where this is not possible, an evaluative judgment is called for based upon an overall appreciation of all the issues in the case including (but only as one factor) the extent to which the court is of the view that the compensation sought at the top end of any bracket of reasonable cost will, in the event, be spent fully on the relevant head of claim. If, for example, the claimant seeks £5,000 for a particular head of claim, which is accepted to be a reasonable level of compensation, but it is established that £3,000 could achieve the same beneficial result, I do not see that the court is bound to choose one end of the range or the other: neither is wrong, but neither is forced upon the court as the "right" answer unless there is some binding principle that dictates the choice. It would be open to the court to choose

---

4 *Page v Smith* [1996] AC 155; *Simmons v British Steel plc* [2004] ICR 585.
5 *Sowden v Lodge* [2004] EWCA Civ 1370.
6 *Rialis v Mitchell* (1984) Times, 17 July approved in *Sowden v Lodge* [2004] EWCA Civ 1370.
7 [2015] EWHC 923 (QB).

one or other (for good reason) or to choose some intermediate point on the basis that the claimant would be unlikely to spend the whole of the £5,000 for the purpose for which it would be awarded and would adopt a cheaper option or for some other reason.

In practice this means that a judge is not bound to accept one expert's view regarding a recommended care package or predicted level of treatment costs. The court may prefer one expert over another and accept his or her views in their entirety. However, when assessing quantum, the court may well find that the most appropriate level of award is somewhere between the parties' respective positions.

Proportionality

In relation to past and future losses, the principle of proportionality has no application. It is no defence to argue that a reasonably foreseeable loss occasioned by the defendant's negligence is excessive: the claimant is entitled to be put back into the position as if the loss had not occurred. However, as regards past and future expenses, the position is more nuanced.

In *Whiten v St George's Healthcare NHS Trust*[8] Mrs Justice Swift stated at para [27]:

> In considering what is "reasonable", I have had regard to all the relevant circumstances, including the requirement for proportionality as between the cost to the defendant of any individual item and the extent of the benefit which would be derived by the claimant from that item.

Subsequently, in the case of *Ellison v University Hospitals of Morecambe Bay NHS Foundation Trust*[9] Mr Justice Warby accepted that proportionality was a relevant factor to this extent: in determining whether a claimant's reasonable needs require that a given item of expenditure should be incurred, the court must consider whether the same or a substantially similar result could be achieved by other, less expensive, means. However, he rejected the more general proposition that a claimant should not recover compensation for the cost of a particular item which would achieve a result that other methods could not, if the cost of that item was disproportionately large by comparison with the benefit achieved. He held that such a general proposition regarding proportionality would be at odds with the basic rules as to compensation for tort ie the claimant is entitled to full compensation as if the tort had not occurred. On the facts of the case, he allowed a home hydrotherapy pool, since despite its expense, hydrotherapy was the only way of ameliorating the claimant's

---

8 [2011] EWHC 2066 (QB).
9 [2015] EWHC 366 (QB).

agonising pain due to frequent spasms and there were no other viable options providing a similar level of symptomatic relief.

The claimant's loss

Only the claimant may claim for his or her losses and expenses. Apart from some recognised exceptions, for example in respect of gratuitous care and travel expenses incurred to provide such care, third parties may not recover for losses or expenses they may have suffered. Therefore, the claimant's husband, wife, mother, father or other close family or friend cannot claim for their own personal losses such as the mental suffering they endue as a consequence of the claimant's injuries or for any loss of earnings they may have suffered. Generally speaking, this means that the claimant will be unable to claim for psychological treatment for family members affected by his or her injuries. For this reason, instead of seeking compensation directly for the claimant's family members, claimant lawyers might encourage describing the treatment as 'family treatment' if the treating might be for the family as a whole or to help improve family dynamics. Arguably, if the treatment involves the claimant or indirectly benefits him or her, it may be recoverable.

Foreseeability and remoteness

As described above, technically only reasonably foreseeable losses can be recovered. Losses or expenses that are too 'remote' will be disallowed. However, fortunately this restriction on the recoverability of damages rarely arises in the context of neuropsychology evidence to be recoverable. All that needs to be foreseen is a slight risk of the broad nature or type of injury or loss in question, not the exact type of injury or loss, nor the extent or severity of the same.[10] For instance, where it is reasonably foreseeable that a defendant's conduct would expose the claimant to risk of personal injury, the claimant will be able to recover for any personal injury, whether physical or psychiatric, resulting from the defendant's wrongdoing, even if psychiatric injury was not foreseeable.[11] Likewise, all that needs to be anticipated is that in light of his or her injuries, the claimant might require some assistance, medical treatment or property adaptations. It does not need to be foreseen specifically that the claimant requires 24-hour care from qualified psychiatric nurses, EMDR (eye movement desensitisation and reprocessing) therapy or the installation of a lift and carers' accommodation before damages can be claimed for these items.

---

10 *Smith v Leech Brain & Co Ltd* [1962] 2 QB 405; *Hughes v Lord Advocate* [1963] AC 837; *Overseas Tankship (UK) Ltd v Miller Steamship Co Pty (The Wagon Mound (No 2)* [1967] 1 AC 617; *Ogwo v Taylor* [1988] 1 AC 431; *Corr v IBC Vehicles Ltd* [2008] UKHL 13.
11 *Page v Smith* [1996] AC 155; *Simmons v British Steel plc* [2004] ICR 585.

Causation and pre-existing illness or ill-health

To be recoverable, all expenses and losses must be directly or indirectly attributable to the injuries which the claimant has suffered. In most cases, causation will not be controversial and the standard 'but for' test will be satisfied. In other words, already incurred and expected future losses and expenses will usually be recoverable because in the absence of the injuries, such losses and expenditure would not have been necessary.

The position is more difficult where the claimant has a relevant past medical history which may have resulted in some needs in any event. Whilst the law relating to causation is complicated, where the claimant was already suffering from a pre-existing illness/condition at the time of the accident, a number of interrelated principles come into play. These may be summarised as follows:

- The eggshell skull principle – it is no defence to say that the injuries sustained by the proposed claimant are out of proportion to the defendant's wrongdoing. The defendant must take his or her victim as he or she finds them.[12] Therefore, where personal injury was a foreseeable outcome of the defendant's conduct, he or she will be responsible for the entirety of the damage caused notwithstanding the unusually severe reaction suffered by the claimant who was particularly vulnerable to suffering injury by reason of his or her pre-existing condition. For example, in *Smith v Leech Brain*[13] the claimant's husband was struck by a piece of molten metal and suffered a small burn on his lip. Thereafter, because of a predisposition to cancerous cells, he developed cancer and died. The defendant was held liable for his death: some injury was to be foreseen, even if the extent of it was not.
- The eggshell personality principle – there is no difference in principle between pre-existing psychiatric vulnerability factors and pre-existing physical vulnerability factors. Therefore, where a claimant suffers from pre-existing psychological problems, the defendant will be responsible for the entirety of the damage caused notwithstanding that the extent of the same could not have been foreseen. This principle is known as the eggshell personality principle.[14]
- Supervening illnesses principle – the defendant will not be liable for the consequences of any supervening illnesses which would have occurred in the absence of the defendant's wrongdoing in any event.[15] This is an extension of the principle that the defendant is not responsible for damage which would have occurred irrespective of his or her wrongdoing.[16]

---

12 *Bourhill v Young* [1943] AC 92, per Lord Wright at 109–110: 'If the wrong is established the wrongdoer must take the victim as he finds him'. See also *Smith v Leech Brain* [1962] 2 QB 405.
13 [1962] 2 QB 405.
14 *Malcolm v Broadhurst* [1970] 3 All ER 508. See also *Mullins v Gray* [2004] EWCA Civ 1483.
15 *Jobling v Associated Dairies Ltd* [1982] AC 794; *Kenth v Heimdale Hotel Investments Ltd* [2001] EWCA Civ 1283; *Morgan v Millett* [2001] EWCA Civ 1641; and *Gray v Thames Trains Ltd v anor* [2009] 3 WLR 167.
16 See further *Barnett v Chelsea and Kensington Hospital Management Committee* [1969] 1 QB 428; and *Hotson v East Berkshire Health Authority* [1987] AC 750.

Therefore, the defendant is not responsible for any symptoms or deterioration in the claimant's health that would have been expected to occur in the absence of the material injury.
- The aggravation/exacerbation principle – where a claimant already suffered some symptoms arising from a pre-existing illness or condition prior to the accident, the defendant is only liable for the additional injury he or she has caused.[17]
- The acceleration principle – where a claimant suffered from a pre-existing condition the symptoms of which have been brought forward or accelerated by reason of the defendant's negligence, the claimant is restricted to claiming damages for injuries, expenses and losses for the duration of the 'acceleration period'.[18] Of course, the expenses and losses arising after the relevant acceleration period would have occurred in any event and will therefore not be recoverable. This principle is often applied when quantifying neck and back injuries, but also equally applies to psychological disorders e.g. a claimant suffers an accelerated breakdown which would have occurred in any event or early onset dementia due to a neurological injury.
- Discount for pre-existing risk of injury principle – where a claimant had a pre-existing condition at the time of the accident which made it possible that he or she would suffer from similar injuries to those complained of in any event, it is possible that the claim for future loss will be discounted to reflect the chance that the injuries, expenses and losses complained of may have occurred notwithstanding the defendant's negligence.[19]
- The 'more of the same' principle. Where a claimant is already injured or disabled, he or she is only entitled to be compensated for the extent that his or her condition has been worsened by the defendant's negligence. Where the defendant causes additional care needs which are qualitatively different from the claimant's pre-existing needs, these can be compensated in their entirety. However, where the care needs are quantitatively, but not qualitatively, different from what would have been required but for the negligence (i.e. more of the same), then the claimant may only recover for the additional care required.[20]

Quality of life

The claimant's 'quality of life' is another somewhat controversial factor in the assessment of damages. Many judges will refer to the potential for a particular

---

17 *Page v Smith (No 2)* [1996] 1 WLR 855; *Vernon v Bosley* [1997] PIQR P255.
18 *Kenth v Heimdale Hotel Investments Ltd* [2001] EWCA Civ 1283; *Smithurst v Sealant Construction Services Ltd* [2011] EWCA Civ 1277; *Hayden v Maidstone & Tunbridge Wells NHS Trust* [2016] EWHC 3276 (QB).
19 *Page v Smith* [1996] AC 155; *Heil v Rankin* [2001] PIQR Q3.
20 *Reaney v University Hospital of North Staffordshire NHS Trust & anor* [2015] EWCA Civ 1119.

loss or expense to improve or restore the claimant's 'quality of life', [21] 'enjoyment of life'[22] or 'level of independence'[23] as a way of justifying the recovery of that particular head of loss. This may just be seen as shorthand for the exercise which the court is performing, i.e. attempting so far as money can to put the claimant back in the position he or she would have been but for the injury, when the claimant had a much greater ability to enjoy life. However, not all judges have accepted this approach and a few have adopted a more technical and less sympathetic view regarding the relevance of this concept. For example, in *Thrul v Ray*,[24] Burton J (as he then was) stated at [Q47]:

> It is therefore important in assessing the [claimant's] claim for compensation to bear in mind that it is not the purpose of this court to make allowance for anything which would, as it was put on various occasions by, I think, all the witnesses called by the [claimant], improve her "quality of life". It is not the test that the defendant should be required to pay by way of damages to the [claimant] consequent upon the unfortunate injuries resulting from the accident any sum which will simply make the [claimant] happier or more comfortable ... the provision must be one which is reasonably necessary to compensate for what she has lost, but also no more than is reasonably likely to be expended on her behalf in providing her with the substitute for what she has lost.

Mitigation of loss

The claimant is under a duty not to act unreasonably in failing to mitigate his or her loss.[25] Unreasonable failure to take such steps will result in the

---

21 In *Rahman v West Pennine HA* (18/18/02, QBD); LTL 13/5/03, McCombe J said at para [15]: 'I accept Mr Wingate-Saul's oral submission that the purpose of the award is to restore, so far as possible, this Claimant's quality of life'. Also, in *Manna v Central Manchester University Hospitals NHS Foundation Trust* [2015] EWHC9 (QB) Cox J said at [236]: 'The philosophy underpinning all the equipment recommended, including items of assistive technology which I deal with shortly, is the need to provide quality of life for [the claimant]...'.
22 In *Rialis v Mitchell* (1984) Times, 17 July, Stephenson LJ said at p 25 of the transcript: '... the court must not put the standard of reasonableness too high when considering what is being done to improve a plaintiff's condition or increase his enjoyment of life'.
23 See e.g. *Burton v Kingsbury* [2007] EWHC 2091 (QB), in which Flaux J stated when considering the claim for information technology: 'If such technology is available to give the Claimant a level of independence so that he does not have to summon a carer or his wife to switch on a light or a piece of equipment or to draw a curtain or blind, it seems to me that he should be entitled to it and to recover its cost from the Defendant'.
24 [2000] PIQR Q44.
25 Although see *The Solholt v Sameiet Solholt* [1983] 1 Lloyd's Rep 605, in which Lord Donaldson MR stated: 'A [claimant] is under no duty to mitigate his loss, despite the habitual use by lawyers of the phrase "duty to mitigate". He is completely free to act as he judges to be in his best interests. On the other hand, a defendant is not liable for all loss suffered by the claimant in consequence of his so acting. A defendant is only liable for such part of the [claimant's] loss as is properly to be regarded as caused by the defendant's breach of duty'.

claimant being limited to the damages which would have applied had those steps been taken. The burden is upon the defendant to prove that the claimant has failed to mitigate his or her loss.

The question of whether or not the claimant has failed to mitigate his or her loss is a question of fact not law for the trial judge to determine. The claimant's reasonable expenses in minimising his or her losses may be recovered, e.g. medication and treatment expenses; so too may the costs of retraining to equip the claimant for another job from which is practicable despite the injuries suffered. Should the mitigation prove unsuccessful or worsen the claimant's condition, assuming the steps taken were reasonable and the chain of causation has not been broken, the defendant will remain liable for the extent of the claimant's injuries including any deterioration.[26] Likewise, if the treatment takes longer than expected or the expense incurred in pursuit of mitigation is greater than first anticipated, assuming the claimant has not acted unreasonably and the chain of causation is not broken, any additional loss will be recoverable.[27] However, if the steps taken to mitigate loss are successful, the defendant is entitled to the benefit of the same.[28]

Importantly, the claimant needs only to act 'not unreasonably', having regard to all the circumstances.[29] The test for judging the claimant's actions is not high. The test is objective, i.e. what a reasonable man would have done in the claimant's position.[30] Account is only taken of matters known to the claimant at the time, and subsequent knowledge with the benefit of hindsight is ignored.[31] The claimant's impecuniosity is not to be held against him or her.[32] Further, a mistaken judgment may be considered a natural consequence for which the defendant is responsible.[33] In terms of past expenditure, the claimant need only select an option within the reasonable range of options to have acted reasonably in mitigating his or her loss.[34]

As regards loss of earnings and residual earning capacity, the court will take into account the claimant's pre-existing ambitions and interests. For example, a claimant is unlikely to be required to undertake a better-paid sedentary job if he had always wanted to work on a farm, assuming that this ambition was

---

26 *Rubens v Walker* [1946] SC 215; *Hoffberger v Ascot* (1976) 120 Sol Jo 130, CA.
27 *Mattocks v Mann* [1973] RTR 13; *Candlewood Navigation Corpn Ltd v Mitsui OSK Lines Ltd* [1986] 1 AC 1; *Lagden v O'Connor* [2003] UKHL 64.
28 *British Westinghouse Electric and Manufacturing Co Ltd v Underground Electric Railways Co of London Ltd* [1912] AC 673.
29 Richardson v Redpath Brown & Co Ltd [1944] AC 62.
30 *Morgan v T Wallis* [1974] 1 Lloyd's Rep 165.
31 See e.g. *Rubens v Walker* [1946] SC 215. See also *Morris v Richards* [2003] EWCA Civ 232.
32 *Lagden v O'Connor* [2003] UKHL 64.
33 Per Lord Haldane in *The Metagama* [1927] 29 Ll L Rep 253; *Morris v Richards* [2003] EWCA Civ 232.
34 See *Manna v Central Manchester University Hospitals NHS Foundation Trust* [2015] EWHC9 (QB) per Cox J at [14].

reasonable and could still be realised with assistance.[35] Likewise, the court will be slow to find a claimant has acted unreasonably by failing to move to another country in order to realise a higher earning capacity, especially if that would involve uprooting the claimant's whole family.[36]

As regards medical treatment, before the claimant can be held unreasonable in refusing to undergo any proposed treatment, it must be shown that there is a proven benefit on the balance of probabilities.[37] The claimant is not necessarily expected to submit to invasive medical treatment or surgery which carries with it significant risks or has an uncertain outcome.[38] Likewise, the claimant cannot be expected to undergo medical or psychological treatment where there is conflicting evidence about the likely benefit of the same.[39] The court will also take into account the circumstances and subjective qualities of the claimant.

It is important to note that each case is fact sensitive, and consideration must be given to the particular factors influencing the claimant to refuse particular treatment. Factors likely to be important include: (i) the prospects of success; (ii) the risk of complications (and their severity); (iii) the claimant's anxieties about the treatment (including any past adverse experiences of similar treatment); (iv) advice received from treating doctors about the treatment; (v) advice received from the claimant's GP; (vi) advice received from medico-legal experts; and (vii) whether or not the experts instructed in the case consider that it is reasonable for the claimant to refuse to undergo the treatment in all the circumstances. These factors should be considered cumulatively. Additional potentially relevant factors include the degree of understanding and education of the claimant, and whether the claimant has to pay (and can afford the treatment) or if it can be obtained free of charge on the NHS.

As regards the appropriate test to be applied, Sachs LJ said in *Melia v Key Terrain Ltd*:[40]

> As between a claimant and a tortfeasor the onus is on the latter to show that the former has unreasonably neglected to mitigate the damages. The standard of reasonable conduct required must take into account that a claimant in such circumstances is not to be unduly pressed at the instance of the tortfeasor. To adopt the words of Lord Macmillan in the well-known Waterlow case, the claimant's conduct ought not to be weighed in nice scales at the instance of the party which has occasioned the difficulty.

---

35 See eg *Woodrup v Nicol* [1992] PIQR Q104 per Russell LJ at Q111.
36 *Limbu v MOD* LTL 17/7/08.
37 *Morgan v T Wallis* [1974] 1 Lloyd's Rep 165.
38 See e.g. *Geest v Lansiquot* [2002] UKPC 48.
39 *McAuley v London Transport Executive* [1957] 2 Lloyd's Rep 500 at 505.
40 (1969) No 155B. These remarks were cited with approval by the Court of Appeal in *Morris v Richards* [2003] EWCA Civ 232.

For a good example of this test in action, it is worthwhile considering the facts of *Morris v Richards*.[41] The claimant was involved in a road traffic accident and was forced to give up her job as a radiographer. In an attempt to mitigate her loss, she took up a job as a marketing manager with Toshiba. Her new job paid much better than her old job but she struggled to perform her duties. It was the claimant's case that she did not possess the relevant skills or experience for her new job (which was accepted by the trial judge). She got wind that her new employers were about to dismiss her and decided to 'jump before she was pushed'. The Court of Appeal held that the issue in the case was correctly decided to be a question of mitigation rather than remoteness (as argued by the defendant). Since the trial judge had made a positive finding that the claimant did not have the required qualities for the Toshiba job, it was held not to have been unreasonable for her to resign. In the words of Keene LJ:[42]

> The liability of a tortfeasor is not to be reduced because the injured party, having lost employment because of the injury, takes a different job in an attempt to mitigate his or her damage but loses that job because it is beyond his or her capabilities.

Conscious exaggeration and malingering

In civil as well as criminal cases, there is a presumption of innocence.[43] The claimant's symptoms are assumed to be genuine unless the contrary is proved. However, in personal injury litigation, allegations of exaggeration and malingering are not infrequent – often supported by video surveillance evidence – and commonly arise in cases involving mild traumatic brain injury.

A distinction needs to be drawn between conscious and unconscious exaggeration. On the one hand, conscious exaggeration or malingering involves a deliberate decision by the claimant to feign his or her injuries or to make out that they are worse than they actually are. In the worst-case scenario the 'claimant' may have never suffered any injury at all. On the other hand, unconscious exaggeration may be totally unintended and may relate to a recognised psychiatric disorder such as anxiety/litigation/compensation neurosis, somatic disorder, a chronic pain disorder or depression. Where the exaggeration is due to an unconscious psychological reaction, the claimant will be entitled to recover the full extent of his or her losses.[44] There is a duty, however, to ensure that the claim is resolved as quickly as possible where there are any issues of functional overlay/malingering.[45]

---

41 [2003] EWCA Civ 232.
42 *Morris v Richards* [2003] EWCA Civ 232 at para [21].
43 *Constantine Line v Imperial Smelting* [1942] AC 154, per Lord Wright at 192; *Emanuel v Emanuel* [1946] P 115.
44 *Digby v Essex County Council* [1994] PIQR Q54; *Page v Smith* [1993] PIQR Q55.
45 *Blyth Valley Borough Council v Henderson* [1996] PIQR P64.

The claimant's representatives owe a duty to be on the look-out for exaggerated claims and may face a wasted costs order for not taking appropriate steps to prevent an unmeritorious claim from proceeding to trial. In practice, in the absence of conclusive objective evidence (such as appropriate video surveillance evidence), many cases are difficult to pigeon-hole. Assuming that the claimant's continuing symptoms cannot be explained organically, additional expert evidence (usually from a psychiatrist/neuropsychiatrist or psychologist/neuropsychologist) will be required to determine whether the claimant's symptoms may be genuinely related to the defendant's wrongdoing.

In some cases, it may well be that there are elements of both conscious and unconscious exaggeration. In such a case, it will be necessary for the court to make a finding as regards the extent of each and when, but for the conscious exaggeration, the claimant might have made a good recovery/returned to work etc.[46] The claimant's presentation to expert witnesses, demeanour in the witness box, and appearance in any video surveillance evidence or any other evidence there may be as to behaviour inconsistent with the claimed effects of the injuries will be crucial to this decision, as well as what the claimant tells people (e.g. employers) about his or her injuries and disability. Generally speaking, to establish the existence of conscious exaggeration – which is tantamount to an allegation of malingering or fraud – the evidence must be strong and cogent.[47] The onus is on the defendant to prove that the claimant is consciously exaggerating, malingering or fundamentally dishonest.[48] This does not mean that a different standard of proof applies. However, fraud is usually inherently less likely than other innocent explanations and 'cogent evidence is generally required to satisfy a civil tribunal that a person has been fraudulent'[49] and a court will 'look closely into the facts grounding an allegation of fraud before accepting that it has been established',[50] such that more persuasive evidence may be needed to satisfy that standard.

Where the defendant can prove that the claim is fundamentally dishonest, an application can be made to dismiss the claim which under section 57 of Criminal Justice and Courts Act 2015 the court must accede to (even if it

---

46 See e.g. *Smith v Rod Jenkins* [2003] EWHC 1356 (QB); and *Fletcher v Keatley* [2017] EWCA Civ 1540. See also *Shah v Wasim Ul-Haq and ors* [2009] EWCA Civ 542, in which Smith LJ said at para [20]: 'Of course, not all exaggerated claims entail dishonesty; sometimes exaggeration can be innocent, resulting from a subconscious preoccupation, even obsession, with the injury. Judges are always careful to take account of such effects when assessing damages'.
47 *Hornal v Neuberger Products Ltd* [1957] 1 QB 247; *Re Dellow's Wills Trusts* [1964] 1 WLR 451; and *Blyth v Blyth* [1966] 1 ALL ER 524, HL.
48 *Stojalowski v Imperial Smelting Corpn (NSC)* (1976) 121 SJ 118, CA; *Cooper v P&O Stena Line Ltd Ferries* [1999] 1 Lloyd's Rep 734.
49 *Secretary of State for the Home Department v Rehman* [2003] 1 AC 153, per Lord Hoffmann at para [55].
50 *Re Doherty* [2008] UKHL 33, per Lord Carswell at para [28].

would otherwise have been successful), unless it is satisfied that this would result in the claimant suffering substantial injustice.

Obviously, where the deception is blatant, such as a claimant who claims during a medical examination to have pain and difficulty walking but is later seen out of the examination room window running down the street, no psychological or psychiatric input may be needed. However, psychological or psychiatric evidence is often vital in cases where malingering is suspected. In particular, as explained above, there may be genuine reasons why a claimant unconsciously exaggerates his or her physical injuries, especially where the claimant suffers from psychiatric injuries or anxiety resulting from the ongoing litigation. Various tests have been developed by experts in order to assist with the assessment of whether or not claimed symptoms are genuine. For example, neuropsychologists use various 'validity' tests in order to distinguish between genuinely reduced cognitive performance following a head injury, and symptoms which may be simulated or exaggerated. Likewise, many orthopaedic surgeons use a variety of tests to attempt to catch out would-be malingerers. Perhaps the most famous of these are the tests developed by Waddell which include the 'compression test' (i.e. pressing down on the claimant's head) and the 'fake rotation test' (which involves rotating the claimant but not straining the claimant's spinal muscles).

Where the claimant is caught perverting the course of justice, e.g. by forging documents or bribing witnesses, the claimant is likely to be found fundamentally dishonest and his or her claim will be dismissed.[51] If the matter proceeds to trial and the judge makes findings of fact regarding dishonesty, it is likely that the court will refer the matter to the Director of Public Prosecutions for consideration as to whether the claimant should be prosecuted. Deliberate significant exaggeration of one or more claims in the claimant's schedule of loss is likely to be found fundamentally dishonest. Although, in the majority of cases, where the extent of the exaggeration is less severe, the judge must do his or her best to strip out the deliberately exaggerated elements so as to award appropriate compensation to reflect the actual level of injuries sustained.

Burden of proof

The general rule of evidence is that 'he who asserts must prove'.[52] Therefore, where a claimant asserts that he or she has suffered a particular head of loss as a result of the defendant's wrongdoing, for example loss of earnings, the claimant bears the burden of proving that he or she has in fact suffered

---

51 Criminal Justice and Courts Act 2015, s 57; Summers v Fairclough Homes Ltd [2012] UKSC 26.
52 *Robins v National Trust Co* [1927] AC 515; *Huyton-with-Roby UDC v Hunter* [1955] 1 WLR 603.

the alleged loss and the extent of the same.[53] Of course, to be recoverable the claimant must show that the loss suffered was a foreseeable type of damage which is recognised by the law and attributable to the defendant's wrongdoing.

The flip side is that where it is alleged that the claimant has failed to mitigate his or her loss, the defendant bears the burden of proving that the claimant has acted unreasonably.[54] Likewise, as above, the defendant bears the burden of proving an allegation of malingering, conscious exaggeration or fundamental dishonesty.

NHS or private care

Section 2(4) of the Law Reform (Personal Injuries) Act 1948 provides that:

> In an action for damages for personal injuries ... there shall be disregarded, in determining the reasonableness of any expenses the possibility of avoiding those expenses or part of them by taking advantage of facilities available under the National Health Service.

The claimant or the claimant's parent(s) where the claimant is a child or the claimant's litigation friend/deputy where the claimant is a protected party, has the right to elect whether they wish to receive care and treatment on the NHS or privately.[55] This applies even if the claimant has not received private services before the date of trial and for example has been residing in a care home funded by statutory services. In *Peters v East Midlands Strategic Health Authority and Nottingham CC*[56] Dyson LJ stated at [53]:

> We can see no reason in policy or principle which requires us to hold that a claimant who wishes to opt for self-funding and damages in preference to reliance on the statutory obligations of a public authority should not be entitled to do so as a matter of right. The claimant has suffered loss which has been caused by the wrongdoing of the defendants. She is entitled to have that loss made good, so far as this is possible, by the provision of accommodation and care.

---

53 *The Clarence* (1850) 2 W Rob (Adm) 283; *Bonham-Carter v Hyde Park Hotel* (1948) 64 TLR 178; *Ashcroft v Curtain* [1971] 1 WLR 1731; *Tate & Lyle Food and Distribution v GLC* [1982] 1 WLR 149; *Harrison v Leake* (1989) Times, 12 October, CA; *Hughes (Gordon Clifford) v Addis (John)* (23 March 2000, unreported), CA; Smith v McCrae [2003] EWCA Civ 505.
54 *Geest v Lansiquot* [2002] UKPC 48. See further *Froggatt v LEP International* [2002] EWCA Civ 600.
55 *Harman v East Kent Hospitals NHS Foundation Trust* [2015] EWHC 1662 (QB); see further *Peters v East Midlands Strategic HA* [2009] EWCA Civ 145.
56 [2009] EWCA Civ 145.

Since a claimant has a right to choose whether or not to accept state funded services, it is not an unreasonable failure to mitigate loss to fail to take up available statutory services. Where the claimant lacks capacity, it may be necessary for there to be a best interests decision regarding where the claimant should live and how this should be funded. As long as the trial judge finds there is a genuine desire and intention to pay for care and/or other needs privately in the future, it is not necessary to consider whether or not the claimant's preference is reasonable since he or she is entitled as of right to claim for the private costs.[57] It is for the claimant to prove on the balance of probabilities that he or she will pay for treatment privately rather than relying upon the NHS.[58]

The above principle equally applies to other heads of loss. For example, the claimant has a right to purchase an adapted vehicle,[59] prosthetics[60] or appropriate aids and equipment[61] privately, without needing to rely upon statutory provision. As long as it was reasonable to purchase the item in question, it is not relevant to the assessment of damages that the aid, appliance or item of equipment claimed may have been available on the NHS.

Future inflation

Medical costs often rise at a faster rate than other items of household expenditure. However, when assessing lump sum damages for future losses, save in exceptional circumstances, future inflation is ignored.[62] The reason is that future loss is calculated using multipliers which take into account inflation by reference to the Retail Prices Index (RPI). Arguably, future inflation should be taken into account for certain heads of loss which have historically risen significantly above the rate of RPI, e.g. the Hospital and Community Health Service Inflation rose 3.9% per annum from 1997 to 2002, compared with the rise in RPI over the same period of 2.3%. But this argument was rejected by the Court of Appeal in a group of test cases.[63] Although the Lord Chancellor has the power under the Damages Act 1996 to set a different discount rate for different classes of future pecuniary loss, to date this power has not been exercised.

A more accurate account can be taken of future inflation where damages for future pecuniary loss are awarded by way of periodical payments. This is

---

57 *Harman v East Kent Hospitals NHS Foundation Trust* [2015] EWHC 1662 (QB).
58 *Woodrup v Nicol* [1993] PIQR Q104, CA.
59 *Eagle v Chambers (No 2)* [2004] EWCA Civ 1033
60 *Pinnington v Crossleigh Construction* [2003] EWCA Civ 1684.
61 *Bishop v Hannaford* (21 December 1988, unreported), Otton J (as he then was); and *Parkhouse v North Devon Healthcare NHS Trust* [2002] Lloyd's Rep Med 100.
62 *Mallet v McMonagle* [1970] AC 166; *Taylor v O'Connor* [1971] AC 115; *Mitchell v Mulholland (No 2)* [1972] 1 QB 65; *Young v Percival* [1975] 1 WLR 17; *Cookson v Knowles* [1979] AC 556; *Lim Poh Choo v Camden and Islington Area Health Authority* [1980] AC 174; Auty v NCB [1985] 1 WLR 784; *Wells v Wells* [1999] 1 WLR 345.
63 *Cooke v United Bristol Health Care* [2003] EWCA Civ 1370.

because the court can choose the index or measure of inflation which most closely matches the head of loss in question. In particular, ASHE SOC (6115) is commonly used for uprating future and case management, [64] ASHE SOC (212) is used to uprate future therapy costs[65] and, in the absence of a more appropriate index, the default RPI measure is often used to uprate future deputyship costs.[66]

Generally speaking, this means that an award for periodical payments will more closely match the loss or expense in question since the payments will be upgraded by a measure which keeps pace with inflation most relevant to the head of loss in question.

Form of award

At present, once judgment has been entered, the court has five main options regarding the manner in which an award is to be made:

- Make a single lump sum award of damages.
- Make an award for provisional damages (assuming the same has been claimed).
- Make a non-variable periodical payments order.
- Make a variable periodical payments order.
- Adjourn and/or stay the assessment of some or all quantum issues until a later date (and in the meantime, if necessary, make one or more interim payments).

Lump sum damages

The general rule in English law is that damages are assessed on a once-and-for-all basis at the date of trial.[67] As regards future expenses and losses, a single lump sum is awarded of sufficient size so that, when the fund is invested, if capital is gradually drawn to make up income to the level of the continuing loss, the fund will last for precisely the period of the loss.[68] This is known as the annuity method, which was expressed in *Hodgson v Trapp*[69] by Lord Oliver of Aylmerton at para 826D as follows:

> Essentially what the court has to do is to calculate as best it can the sum of money which will on the one hand be adequate, by its capital and income, to provide annually for the injured person a sum equal to his

---

64 *Thompstone v Tameside and Glossop NHS Trust* [2008] EWCA Civ 5, [2008] 1 WLR 2207.
65 *Robshaw v United Lincolnshire Hospitals NHS Trust* [2015] EWHC 923 (QB).
66 *Robshaw v United Lincolnshire Hospitals NHS Trust* [2015] EWHC 923 (QB).
67 *Mulholland v Mitchell* [1971] AC 666; *Lim Poh Choo v Camden and Islington Area Health Authority* [1980] AC 174; *Wells v Wells* [1999] AC 345.
68 *Taylor v O'Connor* [1971] AC 115; *Lim Poh Choo v Camden and Islington Area Health Authority* [1980] AC 174; *Hodgson v Trapp* [1989] AC 807; *Wells v Wells* [1999] AC 345.
69 [1989] AC 807.

estimated annual loss over the whole of the period during which that loss is likely to continue, but which, on the other hand, will not, at the end of that period, leave him in a better financial position than he would have been apart from the accident.

Save where the claimant is a child or lacks capacity where the award must be approved by the court under Part 21 of the Civil Procedure Rules ('CPR') or where part of the award is to be paid to or held on trust for a third party, the award of a lump sum must be unconditional in the sense that the court cannot require the claimant to satisfy a condition before making the award of damages. Once made, the award is tax free.[70] Interest arising from investment, however, is taxable. Unless appropriate steps are taken, e.g. by setting up a trust, the claimant may lose his or her entitlement to means tested benefits and/or face recoupment in respect of accommodation provided by a local authority.

There are a number of advantages and disadvantages of the traditional method of awarding damages as a lump sum/annuity. On the plus side, the claimant and/or his deputy will have control over his or her damages and be able to spend as much or as little of it as and when desired. The most notable disadvantage is that, no matter how much care is taken to calculate the appropriate lump sum award, the figure may well prove to be too much or too little.[71] In particular, the claimant may die much sooner than expected or outlive the estimate of his or her life expectancy. Furthermore, there is the responsibility to invest the damages so that they last for the claimant's lifetime and this creates risk.

It should be noted that in certain cases, an additional lump sum may be recoverable on top of the pleaded claim in respect of a particular head of loss or generally, on the basis that there is a chance in the future that the costs for the item in question will increase. Such an award is often referred to as a 'contingency award'. Examples where such awards have been made include:

- The Court of Appeal awarded a lump sum of £15,000 in order to provide for the contingency that the claimant's girlfriend would not be able to continue providing housekeeping services.[72]
- An award of £100,000 was made for 'contingencies' to reflect increased costs in the event of marriage breakdown.[73] The claimant was hit by a drunken driver and suffered a very severe head injury. There was a high chance that the claimant would suffer from further episodes of psychiatric illness and that her marriage would break down. If her marriage broke down, she would be very vulnerable and would require a greater level of guidance and support.

---

70 Income and Corporation Taxes Act 1988, s 329(1).
71 *Wells v Wells* [1999] AC 345, per Lord Lloyd at 363 and *Islington Area Health Authority* [1980] AC 174 at 183, 'there is really only one certainty: the future will prove the award to be either too high or too low'.
72 *Bristow v Judd* [1993] PIQR Q143.
73 *Stuart v Martin* [2001] All ER (D) 401 (Oct).

- An increased multiplicand for annual costs was used in respect of the claimant's future care needs to reflect the chance that her current care regime might break down, requiring increased accommodation and care costs at a secure unit or a rehabilitation unit.[74]

Provisional damages

Under r. 41.2 of the CPR, the court may award provisional damages where such a claim has been pleaded and the court is satisfied that the conditions of s 32A of the Senior Courts Act 1981 or s 51 of the County Courts Act 1984 have been met. Section 32A(1) of the Senior Courts Act reads as follows:

> This section applies to an action for damages for personal injuries in which there is proved or admitted to be a chance that at some definite or indefinite time in the future the injured person will, as a result of the act or omission which gave rise to the cause of action, develop some serious disease or suffer some serious deterioration in his physical or mental condition.

In *Curi v Colina*[75] Roch LJ stated that there were three questions which needed to be asked in order to see whether or not an award for provisional damages was appropriate in any given case, namely:

- Is the chance of the claimant developing some disease or suffering some other deterioration in physical or mental condition measurable rather than fanciful?
- Can the disease or deterioration in physical or mental condition be described as serious?
- If the above two questions are answered in the affirmative, should the court go on to exercise its discretion to award provisional damages?

It should be noted that the claimant bears the burden of proving, on the balance of probabilities, that there is a measurable chance of the disease or deterioration materialising. There should be some clear-cut event which triggers entitlement to further compensation.[76] However, the fact that there may be a subsequent issue, as to whether the injury was actually causative of the deterioration in the claimant's condition which materialises, should not necessarily prevent the court from exercising its power to award provisional damages. Likewise, as long as it is measurable and not fanciful, the percentage risk of serious deterioration need not be high before the court will be persuaded to exercise its discretion to award provisional damages.[77]

---

74 *Kidd v Plymouth Health Authority* [2001] Lloyd's Law Rep Med 165 at 172.
75 [1998] EWCA Civ 1326.
76 *Wilson v Ministry of Defence* [1991] 1 All ER 638, per Scott Baker J at 644h.
77 In *Kotula v EDF Energy Networks & others* [2011] EWHC 1546 (QB) Irwin J (as he then was) made an order for provisional damages when the risk of the claimant developing really serious consequences from a syrinx was 0.1%.

As regards the exercise of the court's discretion, the courts have said that judges should not be 'very enthusiastic, [to exercise its power] save in the clearest case ...'.[78] In essence, the power should be confined to those cases where it is possible to describe with sufficient precision the event which has to occur before the claimant becomes entitled to seek further damages, and that the injury or deterioration which may occur in the future is not speculative or unclear. Further, the power should be used in a situation where paying a claimant at the date of trial, in respect of a risk he or she might suffer which in fact he or she may never suffer, would probably be to order a defendant to pay too much, yet if the risk were actually to materialise the amount would be insufficient to cover it.

Common examples of cases in which provisional damages have been awarded include the risk of the claimant developing epilepsy and the risk of developing syringomyelia. It may be more difficult to persuade the court that a psychological deterioration satisfies the necessary threshold for making a provisional damages award, especially if the evidence suggests that the psychological condition is likely to be treatable and therefore temporary.[79] However, provisional damages may be awarded for a risk of developing a serious deterioration due to a psychiatric condition such as depression where the evidence suggests that the condition could have a major debilitating impact on the claimant from which he or she is unable to cover and where the triggering event is expressed in terms of a resulting and substantial continuing loss of earnings.[80]

Variable and non-variable periodical payments

Since 2005 the courts have had the discretionary power to make an award for future pecuniary loss wholly or in part by way of periodical payments. Whenever the court is considering a claim for future pecuniary loss, the court must consider whether or not to make an award for periodical payments as opposed to a lump sum, and regard must be had to the factors set out in the CPR, para 1 of PD 41B, namely:

1. the scale of the annual payments taking into account any deduction for contributory negligence;
2. the form of award preferred by the claimant including
   a   the reasons for the claimant's preference; and
   b   the nature of any financial advice received by the claimant when considering the form of award; and
3. the form of award preferred by the defendant including the reasons for the defendant's preference.

---

78   In *Curi v Colina* [1998] EWCA Civ 1326 the Court of Appeal endorsed the approach taken in *Allott v Central Electricity Generating Board* (19 December 1988, unreported).
79   See e.g. *XX v Whittington Hospital NHS Trust* [2017] EWHC 2318 (QB).
80   See e.g. *H v Thomson Holidays Ltd* [2007] EWHC 850 (QB).

190 Loss, disability and impact

The level of periodical payments can increase or decrease in line with the claimant's anticipated needs. Periodical payments for care and case management will usually continue for life. However, periodical payments for other heads of loss such as loss of earnings will end on the claimant's retirement. The RPI is the default measure for uprating periodical payments, however, the court has the power to order that alternative measures be used instead and it is common for the court to select the most appropriate available index or measure to increase the periodical payments that most closely matches the loss in question.[81]

The court has the power to order that periodical payments are variable if there is specified improvement or deterioration in the claimant's condition which occurs at some point in the future. Often this power is used to vary periodical payments for the same trigger reasons which form the basis of an award for provisional damages. Common examples include developing a serious deterioration in condition due to intractable epilepsy or syringomyelia.

Adjournment, part adjournment and/or stay

CPR, Part 3 provides the court with the powers to order that any part of proceedings be dealt with as separate proceedings; to stay the whole or part of proceedings; and to try individual issues separately. Where some issues of quantum might be capable of resolution at the date of trial and others not, it is possible to adjourn and/or stay certain elements of the claim for future consideration.

For example, in *Cook v Cook and anor*,[82] the claimant was a 10-year-old child who was born prematurely as a result of a road traffic accident. She was rendered blind suffered a brain injury. Liability was admitted and it was agreed that she was likely to suffer some long-term problems. The claimant contended that it was too early to make a realistic assessment of her future needs and the costs of meeting the same. An application to adjourn the quantum trial was successful despite the defendant's objection. The claimant applied to limit the quantum trial to general damages and past losses up to the claimant's 16th birthday with all losses beyond that point to be adjourned. The application was supported by medical evidence which confirmed that it was too early to predict how the claimant would manage at school and too early to predict her psycho-social development and therefore how dependent she will be as an adult. Eady J granted the application given the complexity of the claim and the difficulty assessing the claimant's prognosis and long-term needs until she was older. He held it was plainly right to postpone the exercise

---

81 *Flora v Wakom (Heathrow) Ltd* [2006] EWCA Civ 1103; *Thompstone v Tameside and Glossop NHS Trust* [2008] EWCA Civ 5, [2008] 1 WLR 2207.
82 [2011] EWHC 1638 (QB).

of quantifying the claimant's long-term loss until such time as there was 'solid evidence available'.

Often if the claimant's medical prognosis is uncertain, the parties will agree to adjourn the assessment of damages until the position is clearer. Adjournments which are agreed by consent for this reason are often approved by the court. However, at some point the court will have to do its best to assess damages on the basis of the available evidence and sometimes the parties disagree as to whether the assessment of damages should be delayed. For example, in *Adan v Securicor Custodial Services*, [83] the claimant made an application to adjourn the assessment of his awards for future care and accommodation which was opposed by the defendant. The facts were that the claimant had been injured whilst being driven by the defendant to a court to be sentenced for a criminal offence. He suffered a severe head injury and was detained at Rampton Hospital under the Mental Health Act 1983 where he was likely to remain as an in-patient for the foreseeable future. The claimant sought to postpone the assessment of his claims for future care and accommodation in case he made an improvement such that he could be cared for in the community, in which case he would not be able to afford good care without the means to provide it, which he would have wished to have as part of his award. Eady J rejected the application, holding that there was nothing tangible to take the case out of the normal run of cases where it is still deemed appropriate, despite potential injustice, for the court to make a single award of damages to include the best assessment of future loss. Reliance was placed upon the observations made in several previous authorities[84] that the court's function was to bring an end to litigation, with the court doing its best to assess damages once and for all on the available evidence at trial, notwithstanding the fact that predictions have to be made about uncertainties in the future.

In appropriate cases the court may decide to adjourn the assessment of quantum on its own motion. For instance, the claimant in *Ahsan v University Hospitals Leicester NHS Trust*, who was in a persistent vegetative state, was being cared for in a private residential home funded by the local Primary Care Trust. The claimant's family wished for her to return home and be cared for at home with a private care regime. The judge declared that such a regime was reasonable and that damages should be assessed on this basis. But an interim payment was made and the case adjourned in order to allow a staged return so as to see whether, as a matter of fact, she was likely to return home for the rest of her life.

By virtue of Part 25 of the CPR, when the issue of quantum is adjourned or stayed in whole or in part, the court retains a general discretion to award one or more interim payments.

---

83 [2002] Lloyd's Rep Med 487.
84 Lord Pearce in *Murphy v Stone-Wallwork* [1969] 1 WLR 1023, Lord Hodson in *Mulholland v Mitchell* [1971] AC 666, and Phillips J (as he then was) in *Denny v Gooda Walker Ltd* [1995] 1 WLR 1206.

Procedure and the assessment process

Legal procedure is complex and often protracted. It is beyond the scope of this work to detail each procedural step. However, for the purposes of understanding how a claim moves from inception to conclusion, the following is a brief summary of the main elements of the process:

- Initial meeting with the client and agreement to take the case on.
- Funding organised (often by way of a conditional fee i.e. a no win, no fee agreement).
- Circumstances of claim investigated and evidence gathered.
- Court proceedings issued: particulars of claim and preliminary schedule of loss together with supporting expert evidence.
- Defence with preliminary counter-schedule and any expert evidence relied upon.
- Costs and case management conference at which directions are given to trial (assuming the claim is ready to be set down for trial otherwise there may be further case management conferences) and a cost budget may be set.
- Disclosure of relevant documents including medical records and support worker notes.
- Exchange of witness evidence.
- Exchange of expert evidence.
- Without prejudice discussion between opposing experts to prepare joint statements.
- Claimant's (updated) schedule of loss.
- Defendant's (updated) counter-schedule.
- Settlement/trial.

Most personal injury and clinical negligence claims involving adults are now subject to cost budgeting. Claims involving children are excluded from cost budgeting. Also, sometimes cost budgeting will be dispensed with in high value claims (over £10m) or those where the claimant's prognosis is uncertain.

Often liability is conceded at the outset or early into the litigation. However, liability may remain in issue throughout the process. Where liability is heavily contested, it may be sensible to try liability first as a preliminary issue, and if successful, to then move on to the assessment of quantum.

Procedurally, there is often a difference between personal injury and clinical actions claims when assessing quantum. Historically, in personal injury litigation expert reports are mutually exchanged ie the parties serve them at the same time. However, in clinical negligence actions, often the court will order sequential exchange. This means the claimant will serve his or her expert quantum evidence and schedule of loss first, to which the defendant responds (usually after a period of three–four months) with its expert quantum evidence and counter-schedule.

Legal principles of quantum 193

Inevitably, fighting to trial involves risk and uncertainty. The vast majority of personal injury and clinical negligence claims settle out of court. Settlement can be achieved in a number of ways. The parties can make oral or written offers to each other at any stage. However, in higher value claims, it is very common for claims to resolve following a round table meetings which can be held remotely using Zoom or Skype.

Competent solicitors will provide the experts with copies of all relevant documents in a well organised bundle. They will also keep their instructed experts fully appraised of the litigation process and supply copy court orders confirming the dates by which reports and joint statements must be provided. Ideally, where the cost budget allows, there will be close liaison between the litigation team and the instructed neuropsychologist whose input may be sought as follows:

- Prior to the issue of proceedings for the purposes of preparing a draft report.
- In conference with or without counsel to discuss the draft report (if necessary) prior to finalising the same for service with the particulars of claim or the defence.
- Prior to the costs and case management conference to provide an estimate of costs for budgeting purposes.
- Re-assessment of the claimant to prepare an updated report to be served in compliance with the court's deadline.
- In conference with or without counsel to discuss any amendments to the report with a view to finalising the report for disclosure.
- For comments on the witness and/or expert evidence served by the other parties.
- In conference with or without counsel to discuss the claim and issues before the without prejudice meetings with the opposing experts.
- In conference with or without counsel to discuss any clarification for further evidential steps required in light of the expert joint statements.
- In conference with or without counsel to discuss pros and cons, any additional evidential steps which need to be taken and tactics prior to making an offer or entering into settlement negotiations.
- In conference usually with counsel prior to trial.
- Attendance at trial and conferences with trial before or after court.

Input may be sought in writing (often by email) or by telephone or increasingly by videoconference. The extent of counsel's involvement depends on the value of the clam. In lower value cases, the solicitor will be responsible for most interaction and finalising the expert evidence. In catastrophic injury cases it is not uncommon for there to be two counsel, a silk or leading counsel and a junior counsel. Solicitors and counsel will work together as a team in order to progress the claim as effectively and efficiently as possible, whilst doing their best to stay within the confines of any costs budget set by the court.

Conclusion

The assessment of quantum in personal injury and clinical negligence cases is complex and time consuming. Fundamentally, so far as it is possible to do so financially, the court is concerned about putting the claimant back in the position he or she would have been in but for the injury. There are many competing principles which the practitioner has to bear in mind including reasonableness, causation and proportionality. Consideration also needs to be given to the most appropriate form of award and whether there might be reasons for seeking provisional damages. In the next chapter we look at practical aspects of assessing quantum and the types of claims that an expert neuropsychologist will often be asked to advise upon.

11 Practical applications of quantum principles

Andrew Worthington, William Latimer-Sayer and Andy Tyerman

Introduction

The previous chapter introduced the legal principles that underpin the assessment of quantum in the civil courts of England and Wales. In this chapter the focus turns to the practical application of the principles and the role of the expert neuropsychologist in the evaluation of quantum. In this chapter, we discuss specific heads of loss under which neuropsychological evidence is likely to have an important bearing in the assessment of personal injury claims.

General damages for pain, suffering and loss of amenity

In respect of pain, suffering and loss of amenity, conventionally tariffs have been set by the Court of Appeal[1] and every few years the Judicial College publishes a book entitled "Guidelines for the Assessment of General Damages in Personal Injury Cases" which provides brackets for the vast majority of injuries.

In order for the court to ensure that the claimant's injuries are assessed by reference to the appropriate category, it may be sensible for the neuropsychologist to comment upon the severity of the neurological injury. The contribution of neuropsychological testing to this process and the specific challenges associated with mild brain injury are discussed in the chapters by Worthington and Moore.

The guidelines distinguish between very severe, moderately severe, less severe and minor brain injuries. Within the individual categories, the size of the award will depend upon various factors. Relevant considerations, for which it may be helpful for neuropsychological evidence to comment upon in order to ensure that the court places the claimant in the correct category of the Judicial College guidelines, include the following:

- The extent and severity of the initial injury;
- The extent of any continuing disability and the prognosis for the same;

---

1 *Wright v British Railways Board* [1983] 2 AC 773; *Heil v Rankin* [2001] QB 272.

DOI: 10.4324/9781003105763-14

- The extent of the claimant's care needs and dependence on others;
- The extent of any intellectual deficit;
- The degree of insight, if any;
- Life expectancy;
- The extent of physical limitations;
- Requirement for gastrostomy for feeding;
- Sensory impairment;
- Ability to communicate with or without assistive technology;
- The extent of any personality change;
- The presence of any psychiatric disorder such as depression;
- Extent of any behavioural problems;
- The presence of risk or developing epilepsy;
- The presence or absence of headaches;
- The impact upon the claimant's ability to work;
- The impact on the claimant's ability to manage his or her finances;
- The impact on the claimant's leisure activities.

Some of these will be explicitly stated in a letter of instruction but the neuropsychologist is frequently asked to comment on any areas they consider to be within their field of expertise. Expert neuropsychological opinion on these matters will often provide helpful evidence for determining quantum, including prognosis and the prospects for rehabilitation and recovery.

Rehabilitation

Following severe injuries, initial treatment is almost invariably provided by the NHS. Discharge planning can be difficult and will often depend upon the funds available. Whilst initial transfer from hospital to a rehabilitation centre is usually funded by statutory services, the difficult next stage of transition back into the community for complex cases can lead to costly delays without an independent source of funding (Worthington & Oldham, 2006). Where liability is admitted, hopefully it should be possible to obtain interim payments in order to fund rehabilitation privately, which may not be readily available on the NHS.

In serious cases the need for rehabilitation may exceed the available statutory provision in intensity or duration. On occasion there may be a transition phase during which NHS therapists and independent practitioners both work with the claimant addressing different aspects of their injuries or during a brief handover period.

The neuropsychological legacies of brain injury can affect all aspects of a person's functioning. Especially relevant are executive dysfunction and related neurobehavioural disorders which can cause altered social behaviour with significant impact on ability to live safely and independently (see Wood & Worthington, 2017). Neuropsychologists play a crucial role in advising the court on the likely impact of brain injury on all aspect of a person's recovery, including treatments delivered by other disciplines. Consideration needs to be given to whether other therapists should receive training or be assisted by a neuropsychologist. Worthington et al. (1997), for example, reported two cases where physiotherapists adapted their treatment under neuropsychological guidance to overcome an impasse in therapy. In very severe brain injury where direct work with the injured party is not possible this may be the main role of a treating neuropsychologist.

Teamwork lies at the core of rehabilitation, but this sometimes leads to criticism for duplication of roles and proliferation of team meetings. Equally, therapists working in isolation may be unwittingly overlapping or pursuing conflicting objectives. In serious injury cases teamwork is essential but must have effective leadership, agreed objectives and efficient communication. The different stages of rehabilitation and models of provision within the medico-legal context have been addressed in detail by Worthington (2020).

Although intensive therapy may pay dividends early in rehabilitation it may be unnecessary or unhelpful in the later stages when people are living in the community. A balance must be reached between sufficient provision to promote learning and avoiding too much therapy, whether it be individual sessions being too long, too intense or too frequent. Consideration needs to be given to what a person can cope with at any given time in their recovery; opportunities for rest and consolidation are essential. An *intensive* rehabilitation regime may be contraindicated by a person's level of concentration and fatigue as well as recovery potential. This is distinct from an *extensive* regime which is a comprehensive programme addressing all aspects required to optimise recovery, one step at a time, at a practical and sustainable pace. Individual therapists operating in isolation may consider only their contribution when what is needed is an over-arching plan prioritising different therapies at different times.

An expert giving an opinion on the type and duration of rehabilitation and its likely benefits should make clear their professional experience in the field at the beginning of their report when setting out their credentials. This is because rehabilitation expertise varies amongst neuropsychologists and will assist the court in judging the merits of their views.

In addition to neuropsychology input, the expert neuropsychologist may well be asked to comment upon the benefit or otherwise of other forms of treatment and therapy such as hydrotherapy, occupational therapy, speech and language therapy, massage and music therapy. This is reasonable where such opinion is limited to the behavioural or psychological benefits. Where the claimant resides in a residential home, the neuropsychologist will often be asked to consider the reasonableness of the care, treatment and therapies provided. It may be that the claimant's needs are being fully met, in which case no further input is required. Alternatively, 'top up' input may be necessary in order to bring the level of services up to what would be considered reasonable provision.

198 *Loss, disability and impact*

Sometimes neuropsychologists will differ in terms of (a) issues within their respective fields of expertise and (b) whether they consider an issue is a matter for neuropsychology opinion. Conversely some experts opine beyond their area of practice. This is more likely to become apparent in a without prejudice joint discussion between experts. In the experience of one of us (AW) there are various ways of dealing with this as the following examples illustrate.

(i) It is reasonable to recommend an assessment by a professional in another field (much as one would recommend another expert) but not to recommend exactly what type or amount of treatment, if any, that professional should provide:

Expert B criticised Expert A's recommendation for a physiotherapy assessment but this was justified on the basis of the claimant's complaints and was not a recommendation for treatment.

(ii) It may be reasonable to provide a view on the psychological aspects of a physical condition even if that condition lies within another area of medical practice:

Expert B considered a skin condition a matter for dermatology but Expert A maintained that there was a significant psychological component – importantly this was also the view of the dermatology expert.

(iii) However, the neuropsychologist should avoid straying into details of treatment and prognosis if they do not have clinical experience in the condition:

Expert B gave an opinion on the prognosis of fibromyalgia despite not being involved in such cases clinically whereas Expert A deferred to a rheumatology opinion.

(iv) Neuropsychologists should adhere to a level of explanation in keeping with their training:

Expert B proposed that abnormal glomerular filtration rates underpinned the claimant's cognitive difficulties but was persuaded by Expert A that details of putative mechanisms was a matter for expert renal opinion.

Occasionally experts from different disciplines are asked to hold a without prejudice joint discussion, with a view to preparing a joint statement setting out the issues upon which they agree and those which are disputed.

This can lead to difficulties, for example an expert from another discipline declining to compete a joint statement with a psychologist or a psychologist feeling somewhat pressured by a psychiatrist into signing a statement they did not agree with.[2] Some neuropsychologists may feel uncomfortable with this but one of us has undertaken joint discussions with psychiatrists and rehabilitation physicians without difficulty based on a level of mutual respect. It is important to set out differences of professional training and to recognise what each party brings to assist the court. There are always exceptions such as the psychiatrist one of us encountered who administered a computerised cognitive test battery and carried out effort testing, claiming that although he was not a neuropsychologist, he had a higher level of training than a neuropsychologist. What is relevant is not the level of training but whether the person has the training necessary to carry out the examination they have conducted and interpret the results.

Treatment, therapies and neuropsychology input

An important element of the expert neuropsychologist's role is to advise upon the neuropsychology treatment which the claimant may have received, is continuing to receive at the date of assessment and reasonably needs in the future.

In rare cases, where the claimant has made an excellent recovery from his or her injuries or has been resistant to neuropsychological input, it may be that no ongoing treatment is warranted.

However, perhaps save in the mildest of cases, neuropsychological evidence should address and provide estimated costs assuming treatment on a private basis (assuming reasonably required as it usually is) for the following aspects of potential future input:

- Direct treatment of the claimant.
- Training and guidance for the claimant's family.
- Training and guidance for the claimant's carers.
- Ad hoc guidance, support and advice for the claimant's case manager.
- Liaison with the claimant's educational establishment or employer.
- Contingency input to assist with crisis management and significant life events.
- Attendance at multidisciplinary meetings (and where necessary to act as clinical lead).
- Undertaking neuropsychological assessments and report writing.
- Undertaking risk assessments – for example as regards the number of carers required to accompany the claimant whilst accessing the community.

The neuropsychologist is expected to give an opinion on the required duration of therapy. Whilst recommendations should take account of the research evidence this is often limited. Guidelines for optimum therapy sessions for

2 *Jones v Kaney* [2011] On appeal from [2010] EWHC 61 (QB).

mental health interventions may need adjusting upwards as well as adapting for people with brain injury. Teaching cognitive skills and emotional coping strategies involves having opportunities for consolidation and generalisation over many months, sometimes years. Rarely is education alone sufficient though it may be a good starting point.

At some point during this process therapy shifts from a focus on improving function to one of maintaining function. This typically entails a reduction in frequency of therapy, although sessions may have been reducing for some time as the pace of learning slowed. It is accompanied by a change in overall objectives to preventing deterioration. For psychological interventions this may involve relapse prevention work and 'stress-testing' the skills taught. This phase is also associated with increasing transfer of responsibility to support staff to carry out procedures and implement strategies necessary to sustain optimum functioning. This is a long-term objective and requires intermittent review by professional therapists to ensure input remains appropriate. This may involve training new staff, reviewing guidelines and adjusting interventions. This is not an absolute change, and experience has shown that as long as people are capable of learning, small incremental gains may continue to be made and accumulated over several years.

Where the claimant suffers from behavioural problems, it may be necessary to allow for behavioural management training courses for the claimant's support workers and family. Such courses may need to be repeated periodically, especially if there is a regular turnover of carers.

In more complex brain injury cases where the claimant is cared for in the community a neuropsychologist might be chosen to act as the clinical lead for the multidisciplinary team. This may involve additional costs in terms of goal setting and chairing meetings. The treating neuropsychologist may be asked to provide a prediction for the level of ongoing input as this will assist the medico-legal expert when advising upon the reasonable level of future input and confirming the reasonable level of future anticipated costs.

Claimants with prolonged disorders of consciousness

For claimants with a prolonged disorder of consciousness there may be a dispute as to the benefits of rehabilitation. Ideally a SMART assessment would be carried out by an independent assessor (Gill-Thwaites, 1997), although other forms of evaluation used in some services include the WHIM (Shiel et al., 2000) and STAR (Stokes et al., 2018). Where an expert is not SMART trained, they should utilise the information provided by a SMART report or consider recommending an assessment of this nature. One of us has been asked to explain the relevance of neuropsychology evidence in a claimant in low awareness state, which is easily satisfied by noting the behavioural nature of such evaluations, the role of neuropsychologists in their development and precedents for use of neuropsychological evidence in court proceedings (McMillan, 1996). There may be little formal neuropsychology input required clinically, but a recommendation to repeat SMART assessments periodically and a regime of care and sensory stimulation with a view to improving quality of life which may range from massage and music therapy to community visits.

Calculating costs

Properly funded, well-organised and skilfully delivered rehabilitation is not a cheap option but can be very cost-effective (Worthington et al., 2019). As regards the calculation of the likely future costs, there are two main methods. The first is to attempt to estimate the number of hours of input required in each of the different areas so as to be able to provide an estimated annual total. Often the estimate will be split into different phases over the claimant's lifetime, with the more intensive phases of treatment being required within the first few years of injury. After a few years, the level of input required may drop down to more of a 'maintenance' level.

The second method, often utilised where there may be a range of variable factors and it is difficult to be precise regarding the level of input required, is to give a broad estimate of the total likely number of total sessions for a given period or over the claimant's lifetime. The two methods can be combined. For example, where the claimant has moderate symptoms which are likely to respond to cognitive behaviour therapy, it may be reasonable to allow for an initial course of therapy together with a contingency allowance of a certain number of additional sessions which can be used as and when required to help cope with significant adverse life events in the future.

When providing an estimate of future anticipated neuropsychological costs, it is sensible to consider the applicable hourly rate for neuropsychologist/clinical psychologist. This will depend upon a number of factors including where the claimant lives, the complexity of the case in question and the level of skills, experience and training of the clinician required. At the time of writing and no doubt going forwards much work will be undertaken which is non-contact i.e. over the phone or using videoconferencing. However, where the treating clinician needs to travel to see the claimant and/or provide training, a suitable allowance should be made for travel time and mileage expenses that are likely to be incurred.

A realistic cost estimate must take into account hidden costs such as preparation of materials and reports, communications between sessions, liaison with a case manager or deputy. A breakdown of costs is helpful when calculating (and justifying) costs, but needs to be reasonable and proportionate and a move towards videoconferencing should be welcomed though it will not be suited for all cases. A basic template for cost calculations is provided in Table 11.1.

Table 11.1 Template for calculating therapy costs

Input	Unit Cost	Total Cost / Time
Treatment session		
Return travel time		
Return mileage		
Administration per session		
Attendance at MDT meetings		
Reports		
Miscellaneous emails, telephone calls, letters		

Care and support

The amount of care and support a claimant requires is fact-sensitive and varies from case to case. The court's assessment will be based upon a detailed consideration of all the evidence including witness evidence, expert evidence and documentary evidence. The court will undertake a three-stage assessment as follows:

(i) What are the claimant's needs?
(ii) How are those needs best met?
(iii) What is the likely cost of meeting those needs?

Neuropsychological evidence will be important as regards (i) and (ii). There may be significant disagreements and discrepancies between the experts. Usually, the care experts will deal with (iii) so this need not trouble the other experts.

Considerations regarding the assessment of long-term future care include:

- The number of support worker hours reasonably required.
- The number of carers reasonably required at any one time (and in particular whether two or more carers might be required at any one time due to manual handling issues or behavioural problems).
- Whether case management is reasonably required.
- The involvement of family or friends providing gratuitous care as opposed to having professional carers (including the likelihood of this breaking down and the anticipated consequences should this occur).
- The need for night care and whether this should be on a waking or sleep-in basis.
- How the claimant's prognosis might impact upon future care needs – for example, a reduction in care needs following successful rehabilitation or an increase in care needs due to physical or cognitive deterioration.
- Increased care needs during times of illness or ill-health.

- Increased care needs during times of crisis.
- Increased or reduced care as a result of starting a relationship or as a result of a relationship breakdown.
- Increased care needs as a result of having children.
- The need for assistance with domestic tasks (if any).
- The need for assistance with DIY, decorating, gardening etc (if any).

Disagreement sometimes arises about whether a person's needs would be best served in a residential or nursing home or in their own home with private care. There are arguments for both views and careful consideration must be given to the appropriate factors in each case. For example, if the person has rehabilitation potential it is important to determine which environment would be more conducive to their recovery. The risk and benefits of a larger care team versus a smaller bespoke team will depend on matters such as physical care needs, challenging behaviour and communication difficulties.

Fostering dependence versus facilitating independence

On behalf of defendants, it is often argued in brain injury cases that providing too much care may foster an unnecessary dependence on others. It is important to ensure that the primary purpose of the damages award is achieved. In particular, where possible, the claimant should be facilitated to return to activities he or she previously enjoyed. In order to undertake such activities, the claimant may well need some assistance. Those who suffered brain injuries often suffer from memory and concentration problems as well as fatigue and a lack of motivation. Diminished motivation or apathy is an under-recognised but common consequence of brain injury, often mistaken for depression (Worthington & Wood, 2018). They may need prompting or encouragement to assist them to organise and partake in everyday activities rather than being seen as 'fostering dependence', it may be that assistance from well-trained support workers is crucial to 'enabling independence' and ensuring that the claimant returns to as many previous activities as possible. Inadequate support, whether insufficient in amount or ineffective in delivery, risks an increased and ultimately unsustainable care burden on the family and other informal sources of assistance. It should be noted that brain injury is increasingly recognised as a significant risk factor for homelessness (Oddy et al., 2012; Topolovec-Vranic et al., 2012; Stubbs et al., 2020; Worthington et al., 2020).

Support may perform a scaffolding function which serves to provide the necessary structure and prompts for maximum independence. The support regime, often augmented by professional advice and coordinated by a brain injury case manager, provides a therapeutic milieu or prosthetic environment (Wood & Worthington, 2001) that extends far beyond the benefits of individual therapy sessions. In this regard, the support workers may be seen as a substitute for the loss of cognitive function suffered by the claimant.

Without such support some claimants may be reluctant to leave their homes and end up leading a very different and poorer quality existence than before their injuries.

Concern about over-provision of support may arise when there is no clear rationale for the level of input or a claimant is not demonstrating expected levels of autonomy. Opportunities to test out independence can be built in to support programmes and tend to be under-utilised by case managers. Too much care and support stifles progress, either breeding complacency or risking disengagement from support altogether. Too little support prevents recovery potential being fulfilled and may lead to increased costs in the longer term. Adoption of a hypothesis-testing approach to this issue would assist experts and ultimately the courts in determining an appropriate level of provision – what might informally be termed the Goldilocks standard. Comparisons can be made on days with and without support or experimenting with different levels of prompting during support hours, and either side of formal support. For example, depending on whether a person has difficulties primarily in initiation or seeing tasks through to completion, they can be set tasks to initiate prior to commencement of support or to complete in their own time tasks that have been initiated together. Where prospective memory is a problem (remembering to do things at a future time or place), a person can be given reminders in the form of prompts beforehand. Rather than such cues always being delivered in the same way at the same time, opportunities can be explored for prompting over increasing time intervals, gradually more distant from the time to carry out the action. Over time prompting can embrace tasks of increasing complexity or be faded out altogether.

Even when sufficient funding is available to pay privately, it can be very difficult to establish a full and well-functioning care regime. Sometimes, despite the best endeavours of the treating clinicians, the claimant may simply not want the level of care being recommended. In which case, the court's assessment regarding the claimant's long-term care will need to be realistic as regards the amount of care that the claimant is likely to accept and will in fact be implemented.[3] To this end, in order to form a balanced view when opining about the claimant's long-term care needs, it is important for neuropsychological experts to review carefully all the available evidence including:

- The witness evidence.
- The claimant's medical records.
- The claimant's educational and/or employment records.
- The claimant's support worker records.
- The claimant's case management records.
- The other expert evidence (on both sides).

---

3 See e.g. *Huntley v Simmonds* [2009] EWHC 405 (QB).

As with therapy, it may be possible to reduce hours of support over time to an effective maintenance level of scaffolding. This often has to be done very gradually, especially if support has been intensive and/or for a long period. Phased reductions in support should be carefully monitored with the proviso that hours may need to increase again if there are signs of deterioration. In one complex case Mr Justice Parker considered there should be a period of four years to reduce support from eight hours per day to four hours a day.[4]

Ageing and care needs

The main reason care needs increase with age is due to physical infirmity or cognitive decline, which may be associated with behaviour changes. Neuropsychologists are frequently instructed to provide an opinion on the likelihood of deterioration in the claimant's condition. This entails consideration of medical conditions in future which may have neuropsychological consequences such as the development of epilepsy. Neuropsychologists usually leave the quantification of risk of future decline to medical colleagues, for example the risk of epilepsy is the province of an expert neurologist, but are sometimes encouraged (usually by claimant solicitors) to comment on the possibility of dementia. Evidence suggests that rather than causing dementia, brain injury may lower the neural reserve and cause cognitive symptoms to manifest at an earlier stage (James et al., 2021).

Unless the neuropsychologist has particular expertise in this area it is advisable to avoid quantifying the risk and to focus instead on what difference such a diagnosis would make to support on neuropsychological grounds. For example, would it increase the amount of care, need for an additional carer, the type of care or entail a move from home into a more institutional setting?

Accommodation

In general, where the claimant has significant accommodation needs as a result of his or her injuries, the parties will instruct accommodation experts. Such experts will provide a detailed analysis of the claimant's accommodation needs and the costs of meeting the same. In the first instance, a decision needs to be taken as regards whether the claimant's home at the time of injury is still appropriate (with or without adaptations) or if the claimant requires alternative accommodation. Some of the main issues pertaining to accommodation that neuro psychologists are often asked to comment upon include the following:

- The size of the property and in particular the need to be able to have some privacy away from carers.
- Sufficient space for undertaking therapies and support worker activities away from other members of the household.

---

4 *Loughlin v Singh, Pama & Co Ltd, Churchill Insurance Co.* [2013] EWHC 1641 (QB).

- The positioning and location of the property – whether this should be in the countryside or close to a town or city to increase availability of activities or access to carers.
- The need for environmental controls to maintain a level of independence.
- Carers' facilities and how these should be arranged to maximise effectiveness.
- The reasonable need (if any) for safe outdoor space.
- The reasonable need (if any) for a workshop, snug or den.
- The reasonable need (if any) for a home hydrotherapy pool.
- Reasonable measures to reduce anxiety, psychological symptoms or epileptic triggers: for example, extra security measures or double glazing to reduce environmental noise.

The expert should consider environmental contributors to disability which could be ameliorated with a modified environment (Alderman et al., 2019). Neuropsychological difficulties that may be relevant to these issues include evidence of sensory overload, distractibility, memory loss, perceptual impairment, executive disorders, irritability, aggression, fatigue and sleep disturbance.

Aids and equipment

Occupational therapy experts are usually instructed to advise upon items of aids and equipment which the claimant might benefit from. For example, memory aids are often recommended, although many smartphones (which the claimant may have had in any event) now provide such facilities. This is an aspect of rehabilitation which is likely to see rapid growth in future and mainstream technologies will increasingly offer rehabilitative opportunities. This has a particular relevance for neuropsychology in relation to memory and executive deficits (Worthington, 2017) and further down the line for visual perceptual impairments (Worthington & Sudol, 2015). Whilst neuropsychologists will not necessarily be asked to comment upon the precise make or model of the recommended aids or equipment or be asked to provide an estimate of the likely costs and relevant replacement periods etc, their input may be valuable in terms of principle or overall support as follows:

- Confirmation regarding whether the claimant understands cause and effect e.g. for switch operated controls or for using a Smart wheelchair running on a predetermined track.
- Whether the claimant has sufficient cognitive function to be able to operate sophisticated environmental controls.
- Whether there may be untapped cognitive potential which has not been realised due to communication difficulties.
- Whether the claimant has or is likely to gain an adequate level of understanding and judgment to able to decide when and to whom they should open his or her front door.

- Whether the claimant has or is likely gain sufficient intellectual capacity and judgment to be able to control an electric wheelchair independently, with or without supervision.
- Whether a sensory room/Snoezelen is reasonably necessary.
- The prospect of improvement in the claimant's level of cognitive ability and understanding either with age or rehabilitative treatment such that more sophisticated assistive technology might be appropriate in the future.
- The need for more rugged or protective cases.
- The need for lockable doors or emergency alarms for carers to be able to call for help.

Loss of earnings and earning capacity

Whilst many clinicians will work within the terms of the Equality Act 2010, in a legal context where the claimant has suffered significant injuries which render him or her disabled, the Ogden definition is where the claimant meets the definition of disabled under the Disability Discrimination Act (DDA) 1995. Where the impairment is work-affecting by either limiting the kind or amount of work the claimant is able to do, loss of future earnings will be calculated using the Ogden approach.[5] This involves two separate calculations. Firstly, an assessment of the claimant's pre-injury earnings. Secondly, an assessment of the claimant's likely residual earning capacity. Extensive research has confirmed that disability has a considerable impact on an individual's earning capacity including making it harder for him or her to find work, increasing the time spent out of work in-between jobs and often leading to earlier retirement. This data is reflected in the application of higher discounts for contingencies other than mortality to residual earnings for those claimants who meet the Ogden definition of being disabled.

The Ogden definition of disability is defined as follows:

i. The person has an illness or a disability which has or is expected to last for over a year or is a progressive illness; and
ii. The DDA (1995) definition is satisfied in that the impact of the disability has a substantial i.e. non-trivial adverse effect on the person's ability to carry out normal day-to-day activities; and
iii. The effects of impairment limit either the kind or the amount of paid work he/she can do.

A key factor for neuropsychology evidence is the extent to which the claimant's brain injury impacts upon his or her ability to undertake daily activities

---

5 Latest edition is the 8th Ogden, which is available from the Government Actuary's website: https://www.gov.uk/government/publications/ogden-tables-actuarial-compensation-tables-for-injury-and-death.

and therefore the severity of the disability. Where the continuing impairment is very mild or does not meet the Ogden definition of disability, a more modest award is likely to be recoverable. This will probably be a low multiple of the claimant's annual earnings by way of a *Smith v Manchester*[6] or *Blamire*[7] award. Where the claimant is disabled under the Ogden definition, a detailed analysis will need to be undertaken regarding the claimant's likely career path and prospects before and after the injury.

Return-to-work and quantum

A return to previous or alternative work, education or training is a key component of quality of life, psychological well-being and life satisfaction for people with brain injury (Tyerman et al., 2020). Given the financial consequences, evaluation of past, current and anticipated future employment, career prospects and earnings is central to the assessment of quantum.

Understanding return-to-work

Whilst there is no specific information pertaining to those with brain injuries, data from the Labour Force Survey published by the Office of National Statistics have consistently shown that unemployment rates for those with mental impairments tend to be higher than for other health conditions. Return-to-work figures after traumatic brain injury (TBI) vary greatly (0–90%) across studies in systematic reviews (e.g. Kendal et al., 2006; Nightingale et al., 2007; Van Velzen et al., 2009b), compounded by variable subgroups in terms of nature/severity of injury, unclear work status (pre-injury and pre-rehabilitation), lack of detail of rehabilitation provided, differential time post-injury and variable definition of return-to-work (Tyerman, 2012). The latter varies from full-time competitive employment to more inclusive definitions which include paid, supported/sheltered work, voluntary work, vocational training, further education and home-making (Tyerman et al., 2020). Even for those in paid employment it is often unclear if this was in a previous or alternative role, with or without modifications, full- or part-time, at an equivalent or reduced level, with or without extra training and at a competitive level or not (Shames et al., 2007).

Overall, the evidence is that a minority of people with TBI return successfully to work – for example after excluding outliers with very high or very low rates, pooled return-to-work results for 4,709 participants with mild-severe TBI who were in paid employment or voluntary work at the time of injury ranged from 30–65% with an average rate of 41.7% at 1-year post-injury (Van Velzen et al., 2009b). However, it is important to note that

---

6 *Smith v Manchester Corporation* (1974) 17 KIR 1.
7 *Blamire v South Cumbria Health Authority* [1993] PIQR Q1.

this review was restricted to those in work at time of injury and the overall figure is based on just six USA studies (including mild TBI and one with over half the total participants) out of a total of 35 TBI studies reviewed from 10 countries. Historically, for people with TBI receiving neurorehabilitation in the UK, rates of open employment at follow-up have typically been lower, ranging from just 16% to a high of 44% for a group receiving specific return-to-work support. Changes in occupation and job demands are common after brain injury (Van Velzen et al., 2009b) and an initial return to work (or transition from education or training for those injured as children) does not mean a future career path consistent with pre-injury work history or expectations, or even long-term employability. The expectation of career progression, for example to a more challenging job role or even taking on additional duties within an existing job, can put a person's employment at risk after brain injury, as illustrated by the marked stress, anxiety and exhaustion experienced by a person with primary executive difficulties after TBI (see Example E; Tyerman, 2020) Some studies suggest a slight increase in return-to-work over time, but others have highlighted "job instability" and an early UK rehabilitation follow-up found no-one employed at on average seven years post-injury who was not already employed at two years (Oddy et al., 1985).

Problems in predicting return-to-work

A wide range of factors have been found to be associated with return-to-work after TBI including severity of injury, educational level, pre-injury work status, functional status at discharge, global cognitive function, perceptual ability, executive function, deficits in activities of daily living, length of stay in rehabilitation, receipt of vocational rehabilitation and emotional/psychiatric status (Tyerman, 2012; Tyerman et al., 2020). However, systematic reviews (e.g. Crepeau & Scherzer, 1993; Nightingale et al., 2007, Saltychev et al., 2013, van Veltzen, 2009a) cast doubt on establishing consistent, reliable and valid prognostic variables that predict return-to-work after brain injury on an empirical basis.

Even with methodological consensus, definitive prediction of return-to-work may remain elusive due to the complex interaction of differentially relevant factors relating to the individual, work situation at time of injury, nature of brain injury, rehabilitation received and specific job demands (Tyerman et al., 2020). As commented,

> people with a comparable brain injury who receive similar rehabilitation will likely be differentially restricted in their work prospects depending upon their profession and specific job role, whilst those with a similar job role will likely be differentially restricted depending upon the nature and severity of brain injury and the rehabilitation received. Prospects for those with a need for alternative employment will also likely vary

according to access to suitable vocational rehabilitation and the job market across occupational sectors, geographically and over time.

(Tyerman et al., 2020)

As such, providing an opinion of an individual's prospect of returning to work, education or training, of sustaining a job role and of progressing in their career over time after brain injury remains a matter of expert judgment, weighing up the positive and negative influences of all known relevant factors. One such factor is the nature of neuropsychological impairment and associated disability/disadvantage.

Neuropsychological constraints on return-to-work

Neuropsychological impairment has long been reported to be associated negatively with vocational outcome after TBI in individual studies. This has included both the extent of cognitive impairment in general and executive function (including cognitive flexibility, problem solving, self-awareness/acceptance) in particular, but also primary neurobehavioural/emotional difficulties and secondary psychological impact in the context of the person's work circumstances. However, a link between neuropsychological test results and return-to-work has not always been found, as was the case for the original specialist vocational assessment programme of "Working Out" (brain injury vocational rehabilitation programme), Community Head Injury Service, in Buckinghamshire. The original core assessment programme integrated vocational interviews, neuropsychological assessment, occupational therapy assessment, and observation of work attitude, performance and behaviour as observed on practical work activities and reported on vocational rating scales. Whilst those who returned to work scored higher on almost all neuropsychological tests, no statistically significant differences were found (Tyerman & Young, 1999, 2000). Whilst this may reflect the relatively low number of participants, the work attitude, performance and behaviour of those who returned to employment on programme completion were rated significantly more positively by staff on most factors. These ratings provide valuable indications in vocational rehabilitation about how the underlying difficulties on formal testing restrict people in a practical work environment, but also how they influence and are also influenced by factors such as productivity, concentration, fatigue, confidence and emotional state (Tyerman et al., 2020).

Models of vocational rehabilitation (VR) after brain injury to have emerged over the last 40 years include brain injury rehabilitation services with integrated or added vocational rehabilitation elements, VR models adapted for brain injury, case coordination models and consumer directed models (see Tyerman, 2012). In most cases, well over half the group returned to paid employment although few programmes have been evaluated through controlled or comparative studies. In a quantitative synthesis of 26 studies involving 3,688 adults with TBI, aggregated results indicated that VR programmes produced higher and quicker return-to-work than that reported in non-intervention follow-up studies (Kendall et al., 2006). A more recent review found "strong evidence" that work-directed interventions in combination with education/coaching are effective in promoting return-to-work and "indicative findings" for the effectiveness of work-directed interventions in combination with skills training and education/coaching (Donker-Cools et al., 2016).

In VR neuropsychological assessment plays an important role in guiding decision making about potential jobs and job tasks. On occasions this can highlight the need for a major change in career direction to fit strengths and weaknesses after brain injury, as illustrated for Example A over 15 years post-injury (Tyerman et al., 2017). However, extrapolating from this to long-term work prospects is complex and practical assessment of work attitude, performance and behaviour (e.g. in community VR activities and on work trials) may also be included, especially in relation to executive difficulties (Uomoto, 2000). In the context of VR, neuropsychological assessment may be just one component in a complex multi-faceted process. Stergiou-Kita et al. (2011) reviewed 35 key processes synthesised into seven key categories:

(1) identification of purpose and rationale;
(2) intake process including demographics, pre-injury history and medical/injury-related factors;
(3) assessment of the person (i.e. physical, neuropsychological/cognitive, psychosocial, communication, functional status/level of independence, general and work-related behaviours and the individual's perspective);
(4) assessment of the environment (i.e. physical workplace environment and workplace culture and supports, social support and services and economic factors);
(5) assessment of the occupation/job requirements;
(6) analysis and synthesis of results;
(7) development of evaluation recommendations.

Evidence from relevant stakeholders (i.e. the person, healthcare providers, employers, advocates and family) is advocated, alongside the need to understand the meaning of work for the individual, their VR goals and perceptions of work competence/readiness, anticipated challenges and available support (Stergiou-Kita et al., 2011, 2012).

Return-to-work in the context of litigation

In the medico-legal context, assessment of work capability and future career prospects will often be a more circumscribed process, conducted independently of exploration of a specific job role in the context of a VR programme. Clinical neuropsychologists may be asked their opinion on matters such as: the person's capacity for work; how close they may be to pre-injury work performance levels; the reasonableness or otherwise of the amount of time they had off work; the extent to which any injuries are disadvantageous to them in a work environment; what type of work they are capable of (both currently and in the future); potential loss of earnings; and any associated rehabilitation costs (Tyerman et al., 2020). The neuropsychologist should take into account not only the likelihood of a claimant of returning to their previous job role but any impact on their future career prospects, for example as a result of work-limiting fatigue, initiative and organisational skills. Personality change which manifests as increased susceptibility to stress, short-temper, reduced tolerance and social diplomacy can be equally as damaging to career advancement.

A specialist opinion from a VR practitioner or employment expert may also be sought when the work-related issues are complex and/or when a clinical neuropsychologist or other health expert does not have specialist experience of the specific work issues. This might include the following: absence of a clear work history, particularly if this is in the context of an atypical or inconsistent educational history; when there is an unusual discrepancy between apparent work potential and actual attainment; when people have unusual jobs without a clear career trajectory; and when people have highly demanding jobs, for which even subtle or mild difficulties may lead to significant disability within the workplace and or a have substantial impact on career advancement (Tyerman et al., 2020).

Neuropsychologists may believe that a person has an obligation to mitigate their losses in seeking employment but this is not the case. The claimant should not act unreasonably in failing to do so but consideration needs to be given to a person's previous occupation. A claimant seeking to return to a previous high level occupation should not be penalised for failing to consider lower paid work at a lower skill level. This point was made by Mr Justice Picken in dismissing the argument on behalf of the defendant that the claimant, Dr John, a GP, was not entitled to recover loss of earnings resulting from failure to find alternative employment due to being focussed on resuming his medical career:

> It seems to me that it was not unreasonable for Dr John to do what he could to achieve this aim, and that he should not be penalised, in effect, for doing so. [The defendant's] argument amounts essentially to a contention that Dr John has failed to mitigate, yet I do not consider that Dr John's conduct has been unreasonable.[8]

The complexity of judgments about work prospects is evidenced by numerous individual examples from the Working Out Programme of people who

---

[8] *Dr Sido John v Central Manchester and Manchester Children's University Hospitals NHS Foundation Trust* [2016] EWHC 407 (QB).

Practical applications of quantum principles 213

have not been as successful in return-to-work as was initially expected based on their skills, as well those who have exceeded expectations. The former includes people for whom headaches, fatigue and/or anxiety have precluded a build-up of work activity with a view to progressing to paid employment, but also those with intractable neurobehavioural or adjustment difficulties, particularly when combined with limited insight. For example, a former manager with significant but manageable cognitive difficulties demonstrated the skills to work in a design role, but who took his frustration of not working in a managerial capacity home to his wife and two young children. His legal claim enabled him to settle for a voluntary role over which he had control in an area of practical work that he enjoyed rather than struggle on in an employed role, which would have put the viability of his family situation at increased risk.

Other disappointing examples include a client who demonstrated the skills to work in an administration capacity but whose disinhibited, and at times verbally aggressive, behaviour was not tolerated in an office environment. For another client, disinhibited behaviour (including inappropriate sexual remarks) and very colourful language had a tendency to cause offence and was at times experienced as threatening, which had led to repeated loss of employment in spite of having the requisite work skills. Whilst assisted in developing increased awareness and control, his response to unpredictable situations will likely lead to repeated loss of employment without ongoing support. Another client with relatively moderate cognitive impairment was reluctant to accept the need for and to make use of memory management strategies, thereby limiting job prospects. Others have seemed to have made a successful return to previous or alternative work but been unable to maintain this in the long-term due to a wide variety of factors including build-up of fatigue and/or stress and anxiety (e.g. on increasing hours back towards pre-injury level), on taking on additional responsibilities, on development in the job, on introduction of new technology, in change to management or supervisory staff and a change to location requiring additional and prohibitive travel in terms of increased fatigue. As such, an initially successful return to work is not necessarily followed by long-term sustainable employment.

As a counter-balance to the above, a client with very severe TBI with limited insight, marked fatigue and memory impairment, irritability, disinhibition and emotional vulnerability was considered early in her recovery to have very little chance of a return to employment. However, with continuity of rehabilitation provision across in-patient, day, community and specialist VR, coupled with an extremely supportive family and an exceptionally supportive employer, she was eventually able to return to her former workplace in a voluntary capacity at around 20 months and back into paid employment at around 30 months post-injury. Other examples of people coping better than anticipated included a return to self-employment as a journalist (and subsequently completing a post-graduate degree), training as a healthcare professional in spite of marked fatigue, in managing seemingly prohibitive memory difficulties through job coaching and extensive use of coping strategies, a design job in spite of visuo-spatial and constructional difficulties and in sustaining supported employment over a period of 25 years in spite of major cognitive restrictions. However, it is interesting to note that none of the above examples had significant behavioural difficulties.

Whilst unexpectedly positive outcomes are obviously very welcome, it is essential that judgments about employment prospects do not overestimate the likelihood of ongoing paid employment. Positive outcomes may also be dependent both on specialist VR and ongoing support, as and when required, in many cases for years after initial return-to-work and in some cases on an ongoing basis in order to maintain employment. There is of course the potential for positive vocational outcomes to break down regardless of VR support and, as such, caution is warranted in predicting long-term employment without clear and convincing supporting evidence. Where paid work proves not to be viable, supporting (including funding as required) the person in finding alternative occupation (e.g. in education, voluntary, leisure, social or family roles) may be critical to the continued well-being of the person and family.

Whilst the above examples illustrate the complexity of such judgments, for many integration of detailed information from holistic vocational assessment has proved a good fit with VR needs/outcomes. As such, it would seem reasonable for conclusions drawn from specialist VR to be afforded significant weight in assessing work prospects. A significant proportion of people with TBI (including severe TBI) are able to return-to-work if sufficient and appropriate rehabilitation effort is invested (Shames et al., 2007). However, the vast majority of people seeking a return-to-work after brain injury in the UK do so without such assistance. In 2004 it was estimated that VR provision was less than 10% of that required with very few services geared specifically to brain injury (Deshpande & Turner-Stokes, 2004). A subsequent mapping exercise of VR provision for people with long-term neurological conditions reported that only 23% of the services identified were dedicated VR services, only 18% of services offered help with job seeking as well as job retention and most saw less than 10 people for VR per year (Playford et al., 2011). As such, it was concluded that VR services in England are under-resourced and do not meet the needs of people with neurological conditions including brain injury.

It is likely that the majority of people involved in litigation following brain injury will not have had access to specialist VR input from statutory services to assist in a return-to-work. Under these circumstances, referral to a specialist VR programme could potentially be funded through the legal claim, as illustrated by an example of surprisingly few legal referrals to the Working Out Programme. A former technician who lost his job on medical grounds 2.5 years after brain injury was unsuccessful in sustaining alternative employment, obtaining and losing six jobs over the next five years. Whilst he had been seen by the Disability Employment Advisor at his local job centre and had some VR of a generic nature, he had received no significant brain injury rehabilitation and no specialist VR. An independent case manager who assessed his care needs for a legal claim, recommended specialist VR. On initial assessment at 7.5 years post-injury, the client was resigning to not being able to sustain employment, commenting that he had just about given up – his confidence and self-belief were at rock bottom. After specialist inter-disciplinary assessment he completed an initial VR programme, progressed to a voluntary work trial and on to a paid work trial and full-time paid employment in a carefully selected role where his attention to detail and accuracy was an asset in spite of his slow speed and memory difficulties. This positive experience demonstrated employability and restored his confidence, provided of course that he continues to work in a role that plays to his strengths. Without specialist VR his prospects of sustained employment would have remained very low, risking further negative impact on his mental health and also on already strained family relationships.

Whilst this specific client developed a good understanding of his own support needs and the principles/process of VR, for many others (especially those with executive difficulties) this is not the case. As such, clients may run into difficulties when an informed and supportive manager or supervisor leaves, when the job changes or when the person seeks promotion or a change in job role. For this reason it is important to build in provision for further access to specialist VR advice and support, as and when required.

Experience highlights the potential benefit of referring people with brain injury to specialist VR programmes; However in the UK these remain few and far between. As such, maximising chances of return-to-work for those with brain injuries may potentially require the input of a case manager employed through a legal claim, sourcing and coordinating alternative occupational opportunities and/or VR including the services of a specialist independent vocational case manager and/or vocational support worker, as appropriate. Whilst this is dependent on there being sufficient staff with the required training and experience to fulfil specialist VR roles, one advantage of this approach is the possibility of building in provision for long-term intermittent or ongoing vocational support as required whereas referrals to some specialist VR programmes may be time limited. This may be particularly important where the claimant is unable to return to his or her previous occupation and needs to spend time finding or being assisted by VR practitioners in securing an alternative job or where various different types of job are tried without success. It is not uncommon for those with brain injuries to take many years to recognise the limitations of their residual difficulties and accept what they are and are not capable of doing. Even if retraining is undertaken and a suitable role found, further additional vocational support may well be required in the future if and when that job is lost or comes to an end.

Mental capacity

Mental capacity is addressed elsewhere in this volume, but many issues of this nature are directly relevant to quantum. Neuropsychological evidence and the results of psychometric testing will often be influential regarding the assessment of the claimant's capacity and the neuropsychologist may be asked to advise upon:

- The claimant's capacity to make decisions regarding where he or she lives and the need, if any, for a best interests decision or for welfare deputy to be appointed.
- How compliant or challenging as a result of the brain injury the claimant is likely to be and the prognosis for any continuing behavioural problems resulting in increased input from trustees or deputies.
- The claimant's capacity to form relationships and to raise a family.
- The (increased) risk of relationship breakdown.
- The propensity for engaging in dangerous or criminal activities.
- Behavioural difficulties and how easy these will be to manage.
- Whether the claimant is likely to have testamentary capacity.

The main scenarios regarding the ongoing management of the claimant's finances (in ascending order of level of protection) are as follows:

 (i) No help or assistance required;
 (ii) Gratuitous help from family and friends;
 (iii) A personal injury trust with lay trustees;
 (iv) A personal injury trust with professional trustees;
 (v) A deputyship with lay deputy;
 (vi) A shared deputyship with both lay and professional deputy;
(vii) A professional deputyship.

Out of these options, (iv) and (vii) are likely to be the most expensive because professional deputies – usually solicitors specialising in private client work – will charge by the hour for the work they do, albeit hopefully delegated to the lowest grade fee earner able to deal with the particular task. Furthermore, with options (v) to (vii), the Court of Protection charges annual management fees and there are additional costs in terms of assessing fees, security bonds and appointing deputies. Option (v) is unlikely to be accepted by the court in relation to a claim involving severe injuries where the damages are high, since the court almost invariably requires a professional deputy to be appointed.

Neuropsychologists can encounter difficulties in reaching a view on mental capacity for various reasons. Capacity is presumed unless there is evidence to the contrary (the functional test), but often there is little evidence of impulsive or reckless spending because a claimant may already be protected by their family or simply does not have access to sufficient funds. Careful consideration has to be given to whether all practicable assistance has been provided (about which there is often room for dispute), whether it would make any difference to the outcome and whether assistance provided enables a person to exercise capacity or merely substitutes for their own decision making. Decision making may also be impaired by virtue of emotional lability rather than intellectual impairment. Where a person performs well on cognitive testing but other evidence raises concerns about decision making the question of a 'frontal paradox' is often raised (see Worthington (2019) and Fisher-Hicks, Wood and Braithwaite this volume). Support records that detail budgetary competence and financial decision making are a rarity but may be valuable source of information about a person's fiscal competence on a day-to-day basis.

In 'borderline' or other appropriate cases where the court either approves the setting up of a trust or the claimant is deemed to have capacity with the benefit of (professional) trustees to assist with the management of finances, a personal injury trust may be considered to offer a sufficient level of protection. Much depends upon how compliant the claimant is and how willing and able he or she is as regards seeking and accepting advice. In reality, where there are professional trustees, the annual costs of running the trust may be similar to (albeit a bit less than) the costs of a professional deputyship. However, there may not be the same safeguards. In particular, the costs charged by the professional trustee are not assessed annually by the court and, depending on the type of trust set up on the claimant's behalf, he or she will be able to disband the trust and gain direct access to the damages.

Thought will need to be given to the claimant's prognosis. Whilst the claimant may not have capacity to manage his or her finances as at the time of assessment, consideration will need to be given as to prospects of the claimant gaining or regaining capacity in the future. Such predictions usually want for scientific data and opinions have to be based on the injury severity, prospects of neuropsychological recovery, how 'borderline' the issue is and the potential availability of assistance in future.

Likewise, the neuropsychologist may need to provide an estimate regarding when a claimant who currently has capacity to manage his or her affairs but has a deteriorating neurological condition is likely to benefit from a personal injury trust and/or their damages managed by a deputy in the Court of Protection.

The costs of the different levels of protection can be deferred to an expert in trusts/deputyship. The neuropsychologist must steer clear of offering financial advice but may be able to give some helpful guidance regarding the factors which might influence the activity level of the trust/deputyship and therefore the level of fees which is likely to be incurred.

Conclusion

Neuropsychological evidence has a central role in quantum considerations in serious brain injury cases. Expert opinion on severity of brain injury, extent of cognitive deficits, behavioural and personality changes and psychological sequelae informs the assessment of general damages. Neuropsychological insights into a claimant's condition are often helpful in determining factors other than brain injury which may be contributing to their disability or general presentation. Lawyers often draw upon such evidence to value a personal injury claim. Potential for employment is often an important element of a claim and neuropsychologists have key skills in assessing this aspect of prognosis, but outcomes are very variable and research evidence has to be carefully interpreted. Where an expert neuropsychologist is also experienced in therapy and rehabilitation their evidence can be especially helpful in costing treatment. Rehabilitation is cost-effective if properly resourced and case managed. The need to avoid over-provision of support often requires timely transition to a maintenance programme. The value of scaffolding should not be underestimated but a hypothesis-driven approach whereby support is tested out in different ways at intervals during the life of the claim is to be encouraged in order that, as far as possible, expert opinion on long-term needs is based on evidence on the ground. In serious brain injury cases neuropsychological expertise may well be called upon to assist the court to decide important mental capacity questions involving many decisions a person might need to make over the course of a lifetime. This includes not only capacity to manage property and financial affairs but may involve health-related decisions, those concerning personal relationships and testamentary capacity.

References

Alderman N, Wood R Ll & Worthington A (2019). Environmental and behavioral management. In: Silver J, McAllister T & Arciniegas D (Eds) *Textbook of Traumatic Brain Injury* (3rd edition). Washington: American Psychiatric Association, 853–877.

Crepeau, F & Scherzer, P (1993). Predictors and indicators of work status after traumatic brain injury: A meta-analysis. *Neuropsychological Rehabilitation, 3*, 5–35.

Deshpande, P & Turner Stokes, L (2004). Survey of vocational rehabilitation services available to people with acquired brain injury in the UK. In: A Tyerman & MJ Meehan (eds). *Vocational Assessment and Rehabilitation after Acquired Brain Injury. Inter-Agency Guidelines.* London: British Society of Rehabilitation Medicine, Jobcentre Plus and Royal College of Physicians.

Donker-Cools, BH, Daams, JG, Wind, H & Frings-Dresen, MH (2016). Effective return-to-work interventions after acquired brain injury: A systematic review. *Brain Injury, 30*, 113–131.

Gill-Thwaites H (1997) The sensory modality assessment rehabilitation technique – a tool for assessment and treatment of patients with severe brain injury in a vegetative state. *Brain Injury 11 (10)*: 723–734.

James S, Nicholas J, Lane C et al. (2021). A population-based study of head injury, cognitive function and pathological markers. *Annals of Clinical and Translational Neurology* 1–15.

Kendall, E, Muenchberger, H & Gee, T (2006). Vocational rehabilitation following traumatic brain injury: A quantitative synthesis of outcome studies. *Journal of Vocational Rehabilitation, 25*, 149–160.

McMillan TM (1996) Neuropsychological assessment after extremely severe head injury in a case of life or death. *Brain Injury 11 (7)*: 483–490.

Nightingale, EJ, Soo, CA & Tate, RL (2007). A systematic review of early prognostic factors for return to work after traumatic brain injury. *Brain Impairment*, *8*, 101–142.

Oddy, M, Coughlan, A, Tyerman, A & Jenkins, D (1985). Social adjustment after closed head injury: A further follow—up seven years after injury. *Journal of Neurology. Neurosurgery & Psychiatry*, *48*, 564–568.

Oddy M, Moir J, Fortescue D & Chadwock S (2012). The prevalence of traumatic brain injury in the homelessness community in a UK city. *Brain Injury 26 (9)*: 1058–1064.

Playford, ED, Radford, K, Burton, C, Gibson, A, Jellie, B, Sweetland, J & Waykins, C (2011). *Mapping Vocational Rehabilitation Services for People with Long-term Neurological Conditions*. Summary report. Available online: https://www.networks.nhs.uk/nhs-networks/vocational-rehabilitation/documents/FinalReport.pdf.

Saltychev, M., Eskola, M., Tenovuo, O. & Laimi, K. (2013). Return to work after traumatic brain injury: Systematic review. *Brain Injury*, *27 (13–14)*: 1516–1527.

Shames, J, Treger, I, Ring, H & Giaquinto, S (2007). Return to work following traumatic brain injury: Trends and challenges. *Disability & Rehabilitation*, *29*, 1387–1395.

Shiel A, Horn A, Wilson B, Watson M, Campbell M & McLellan D (2000) The Wessex Head Injury Matrix (WHIM) main scale: a preliminary report on a scale to assess and monitor patient recovery after severe head injury. *Clinical Rehabilitation 14*: 408–416.

Stergiou-Kita M, Dawson D & Rappolt R. (2011). An integrated review of the processes and factors relevant to vocational evaluation following traumatic brain injury. *Journal of Occupational Rehabilitation*, *21*, 374–394.

Stergiou-Kita M, Rappolt S & Dawson D (2012). Towards developing a guideline for vocational evaluation following traumatic brain injury: The qualitative synthesis of clients' perspectives. *Disability and Rehabilitation*, *34*,179–188.

Stokes V, Gunn S, Schouwenaars K & Badwan D (2018). Neurobehavioural assessment and diagnosis in disorders of consciousness: A preliminary study of the Sensory Tool to Assess Responsiveness (STAR). *Neuropsychological Rehabilitation*, *28 (6)*: 1–18.

Stubbs J, Thornton A, Sevick J, Silverberg N, Barr A, Honer W & Panenka W (2020). Traumatic brain injury in homeless and marginally housed individuals: A systematic review and meta-analysis. *Lancet Public Health 5 (1)*: e19–e32.

Topolovec-Vranic J, Ennis N, Colantonio A, Cusimano M, Hwang S, Kontos P, Ouchterlony D & Stergiopoulos V (2012). Traumatic brain injury among people who are homeless: a systematic review. *BMC Public Health 12*: 1059.

Tyerman, A (2012). Vocational rehabilitation after traumatic brain injury: Models and services. *Neurorehabilitation*, *31*, 51–62.

Tyerman A (2020). Vocational rehabilitation. In: V Dietz & Ward N (eds.). *Oxford Textbook of Neurorehabilitation*. Oxford: Oxford University Press, 399–446.

Tyerman A, King N & Hillier M (2020). Return to work and vocational rehabilitation. In: M Van Den Broek & S Sembi (eds). *Brain Injury Claims*. 2nd edition. London: Thomas Reuters, 399–446.

Tyerman A, Meehan M & Tyerman R (2017). Vocational and occupational rehabilitation. In: B Wilson, C van Heugten, J Winegardner & T Ownsworth (eds.) *Neuropsychological Rehabilitation: International Handbook*. Abingdon: Psychology Press, 378–388.

Tyerman, A & Young, K (1999). Vocational rehabilitation after severe traumatic brain injury: Evaluation of a specialist assessment programme. *Journal of the Application of Occupational Psychology to Employment & Disability*, 2: 31–41.

Tyerman, A & Young, K (2000). Vocational rehabilitation after severe traumatic brain injury: II Specialist interventions and outcomes. *Journal of the Application of Occupational Psychology to Employment & Disability*, 2: 13–20.

Uomoto, JM (2000). Application of the neuropsychological evaluation in vocational planning after brain injury. In: RT Fraser & DC Clemmons (Eds) *Traumatic Brain Injury: Practical Vocational, Neuropsychological and Psychotherapy Interventions*. Boca Raton: CRC Press, 1–94.

van Velzen, JM, van Bennekom, CAM, Edelaar, MJA, Sluiter, JK & Frings-Dresen, MHW (2009a). Prognostic factors of return to work after acquired brain injury: A systematic review. *Brain Injury*, 23 (5): 385–395.

van Velzen, JM, van Bennekom, CAM, Edelaar, MJA, Sluiter, JK, Frings-Dresen, MHW (2009b). How many people return to work after acquired brain injury?: A systematic review. *Brain Injury*, 23 (6): 473–488.

Wood R LL & Worthington A (2001). Neurobehavioural rehabilitation: A conceptual paradigm. In: Wood R Ll & McMillan TM (Eds) *Neurobehavioural Disability and Social Handicap Following Traumatic Brain Injury*. Hove: Psychology Press, 107–131.

Wood R Ll & Worthington A (2017). Neurobehavioural abnormalities associated with executive dysfunction after traumatic brain injury. *Frontiers in Behavioral Neuroscience*. doi.org/10.3389/fnbeh.2017.00195.

Worthington A (2017). Emerging technologies for the rehabilitation of executive dysfunction and action disorganisation. *Austin Journal of Clinical Neurology* 4 (4): 1116.

Worthington A (2019). Decision making and mental capacity: Resolving the frontal paradox. *The Neuropsychologist* 7: 31–35.

Worthington A (2020). Neurorehabilitation after acquired brain injury. In M van den Broek & S Sembi (Eds) *Brain Injury Claims* (2nd edition). London: Thomas Reuters, 283–334.

Worthington A & Oldham J B (2006). Delayed discharge from rehabilitation after brain injury. *Clinical Rehabilitation 20*: 79–82.

Worthington A & Sudol J (2015). Assistive technology for disorders of visual perception. In: O'Neill B & Gillespie A (Eds) *Assistive Technology for Cognition*. Hove: Psychology Press, 65–81.

Worthington A & Wood R Ll (2018). Apathy following traumatic brain injury: A review. *Neuropsychologia 118*: 40–47.

Worthington A, Williams C, Young K & Pownall J (1997). Re-training gait components for walking in the context of abulia. *Physiotherapy Theory and Practice 13* (4): 247–256.

Worthington A, da Silva Ramos S & Oddy M (2017). The cost effectiveness of neuropsychological rehabilitation. In: Wilson B, Winegardner J, van Heugten C, Ownsworth R et al. (Eds), *International Handbook of Neuropsychological Rehabilitation*. Abingdon, Oxon: Routledge, 469–479.

Worthington A, Edwards L & Joiner L (2020). Homelessness and head injury: Health, well-being and social integration in referrals to a neurocase management service. *The Neuropsychologist* 7: 47–54.

12 Conclusion

Formulating neuropsychological opinion in brain injury

Phil. S. Moore, Shereen Brifcani and Andrew Worthington

Through the process of editing, we have enjoyed many conversations with neuropsychologists and lawyers, and by doing so, have recognised the importance of sharing our respective professional positions and perspectives. This book was forged during a global pandemic. Whilst this undoubtedly brought challenges for medicolegal work, it also presented opportunities during periods of remote working for reflection, stimulating conversations amongst colleagues more widely and on broader issues than the specific cases typically discussed. It provided an opportunity to identify core topics, emerging topics and themes which deserve attention due to the immense complexity in brain injury litigation. We discuss some of these briefly within in this chapter.

When developing the remit of each chapter with contributors, it was clear how some areas of this work are relatively established and follow a clear narrative, whereas others – such as mild traumatic brain injury – are less straightforward, with research open to interpretation and differing clinical opinions. Negotiating these alternative narratives in order to understand and explain sequelae of traumatic brain injury (TBI) is challenging and has real consequences for litigants. It has been our objective both to acknowledge a range of opinion, but also to be clear where we believe the weight of evidence leads. In this way we hope to provide readers with a balanced appraisal of the issues, useful to both defendant and claimant lawyers as well as to clinicians.

Synthesis

Throughout the process of editing, we considered ways in which the neuropsychological and legal aspects of brain injury litigation could be synthesised. Structuring chapters in line with the key elements of a legal instruction, addressing in turn what would have occurred but for the injury, the claimant's condition and prognosis and their consequential losses and needs for care and rehabilitation was one way in which we attempted this, along with having co-authored chapters and descriptions of how neuropsychologists and lawyers can work together with the aim of thorough and meaningful assessment. Below, we set out the content of the book in the form of a formulation of neuropsychological assessment within brain injury litigation: a schematic

DOI: 10.4324/9781003105763-15

222 Conclusion

summary of an approach to neuropsychological evaluation for the Courts based upon the topics covered.

We have sought to identify key principles and highlight important scientific and legal issues in order to promote best practice in expert neuropsychological assessment. Areas included may be classified as responsibilities necessary

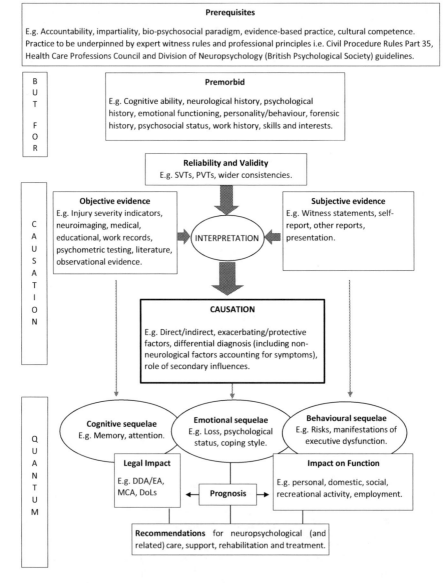

Figure 12.1 Formulation for neuropsychological opinion in brain injury
Source: Authors.

as fundamental to the expert witness role, and/or professional underpinnings of neuropsychology. Abiding by rules and guidelines that govern and regulate practice are a key prerequisite, with the following identified as central: Part 35 of the Civil Procedure Rules, professional guidelines primarily provided by the Health and Care Professions Council (HCPC, the regulatory body for practitioner psychologists), and the Division of Neuropsychology within the British Psychological Society.

A key part of the assessment is establishing how the individual was and would likely be, but for the index event. While 'Premorbid' often focusses upon cognitive and intellectual ability, establishing premorbid functioning is important across multiple domains. As described by Bunnage in his chapter 'creating a reliable picture of what someone was like before in terms of their cognitive function, emotions and behaviour/personality is difficult', and estimation in each area relies upon tools that have their scientific strengths and weaknesses. A key skill of the neuropsychologist is to synthesise multiple sources of data and information, and to present a balanced and evidenced view of premorbid ability. As outlined by Kent et al. the impact of brain injuries sustained during childhood has a bearing upon the trajectory of the child and increases risk of contact with the criminal justice system. The method associated with establishing premorbid functioning in children requires a somewhat different approach to that used with adults, for example relying upon information from school records and establishing abilities of close family members. While areas of focus for premorbid functioning may vary for different claimants, the framework above identifies key areas of consideration that are likely to be relevant in establishing a picture of the individual in the absence of the index event.

In the process of establishing causation, the editors have identified key areas of investigation, all of which have a bearing upon interpretation of the assessment data and findings. Central principles that underpin the assessment are reliability and validity. Whilst these terms have a technical meaning within neuropsychology relating to psychometric properties of assessment tools, they also apply in a broader sense and relate to the consistency of the evidence as a whole and the extent to which it represents the claimant's actual abilities and functioning. A fundamental part of the neuropsychological assessment is defining whether the client is able and willing to engage in the assessment process, so that reliable results can be obtained from psychometric testing which informs an understanding of their ability to function outside the clinic setting. Gerhand and colleagues demonstrate the crucial importance that measures of performance and symptom validity have in the neuropsychological examination in identifying potential issues with engagement and credibility. Viewing performance and symptom validity as part of the wider context (i.e. the claimant's previous and current characteristics, and the features of the assessment(s) utilised), and also rigorously checking for consistency alongside other evidence, are identified as important aspects of developing an opinion in this area of examination.

Objective evidence forms a crucial part of the neuropsychology assessment and includes data generated from sources such as medical records, psychometric testing and clinical observations, interpreted with a background knowledge of the scientific literature. As described by Worthington and Moore, psychometric testing – specifically use of standardised neuropsychological tests – is a key task for the assessing neuropsychologist. Neuropsychological testing requires careful thought applied to test selection (including psychometric properties of the tests), specific case complexities and the questions for which answers are being sought. Failure to appreciate the clinical complexities of a case, inappropriate tests for the job in hand or lack of understanding of the psychometric bases of interpretation will compromise the resulting neuropsychological opinion and undermine the credibility of the expert. One of the first tasks for experts involved in TBI cases, is to establish severity of the injury. In some cases this may be straightforward or may have already been established, which is more commonly the case in the moderate-severe range of injury. As described by Worthington and Moore however, mild TBI is one of the most contentious areas in brain injury litigation, and requires an enquiry that differs from more severe forms of injury, with an increased focus upon non-neurological factors. Subjective evidence, such as the way the claimant presents, their own description of changes they experience (and those of loved ones, professionals, etc.), and witness statements are also important in framing the objective evidence, recognising the impact of the injury sequelae from the claimant's perspective, and gaining an insight into daily life.

Central to the assessment findings is Causation, namely the extent to which presenting difficulties are linked to the injury: i.e. 'what has the injury caused?'. Answering this question requires the neuropsychologist to consider difficulties common to the nature and severity of the brain injury, while recognising that individual differences in biological, psychological and social (biopsychosocial) domains will have an impact upon how these difficulties present. Establishing causation involves a formulation of direct and indirect consequences of the injury, factors that exacerbate symptoms and protect against further difficulties, and recognition of the role of potential secondary influences. The process of considering causation in light of the evidence may also lead to the opinion that difficulties are related to non-neurological factors.

Integration of the information gathered during the assessment gives rise to an understanding of brain injury sequelae, including cognitive, emotional and behavioural aspects, all of which will have a reciprocal bearing upon each other. This requires the neuropsychologist to synthesise the full spectrum of information and view it within the context of the merits and shortcomings of the literature. Different weight may be given to different sources of information in different cases. The notion of a Frontal Paradox described by Fisher-Hicks and Wood may lead the expert to rely more heavily upon sources such as witness statements, or observations made in daily life. The bio-psychosocial formulation provides a coherent framework which allows the neuropsychologist to identify effects of the brain injury, and why particular difficulties have emerged for the claimant within the context of the nature of their injury.

A key outcome of a neuropsychological assessment is establishing how brain injury sequelae have an impact upon functioning for the claimant. This can include the development of an understanding of the current experience and daily routine of the claimant, how presenting difficulties are maintained, and a prognosis. This formulation generates recommendations for treatment, care and support. There will also be potential wider legal implications, where for example mental capacity is lacking, or where reasonable workplace adjustments are necessary. The neuropsychologist's opinion may be updated following a period of treatment and review, or if new evidence comes to light. Ultimately, the opinion of the neuropsychologist forms part of the wider legal process, which fundamentally is concerned with 'putting the claimant back in the position he or she would have been in but for the injury'.

Future directions

There were inevitably topics we would have liked to include but which, through want of space, expertise or research evidence, we were unable. Clinically, these include psychometric testing of disadvantaged and diverse groups and the need to consider linguistic and cultural influences on symptom presentation and disability. From the legal perspective we would have explored the challenges of acting for people injured abroad and across different legal systems, the influence of the legal system on attitudes to compensation, and means of supporting vulnerable claimants through litigation. These subjects and others will have to await a different book at another time.

It is hoped that the present volume will provide practitioners with a sound understanding of the legal background and scientific principles which form the bedrock upon which an expert neuropsychological opinion should be based. The framework outlines key tasks for the expert neuropsychologist, which is hoped will be a useful resource for clinicians and lawyers alike. It is the editors' and authors' desire that the book will contribute to the high standard of expert neuropsychological evidence which the courts require so that justice may be seen to be done.

Index

Note: **Bold** page numbers refer to tables; *italic* page numbers refer to figures and page numbers followed by "n" denote endnotes.

A, B and C v X,Y and Z (2012) 166n30
Abbreviated Injury Scale (AIS) 118
Abe, J. 56
Abeles, N. 129
abusive home environments, and paediatric TBI 67, 72
acceleration principle 177
Acceptance and Commitment Therapy (ACT) 130
accommodation needs, evaluation of quantum for 205–206
'acquired sociopathy' concept 142
Adan v Securicor Custodial Services (2002) 191
Aderemi v London & South Eastern Railway Ltd (2013) 11
ADHD (Attention Deficit Hyperactivity Disorder) 70
adjournment/part adjournment and/or stay 190–191
ageing, and care needs 205
aggravation/exacerbation principle 177
Agranovich, A.V. 56
Agrawal, N. 120
Ahsan v University Hospitals Leicester NHS Trust 191
aids and equipment, evaluation of quantum for 206–207
Alderman, N. 141, 151
Alexander, M. P. 148
Algina, J. 37
Ali v Caton & Anor (2013) 56, 167n33
Allen, L. M. 103
Allott v Central Electricity Generating Board (1988) 189n78

Alzheimer's disease 101, 102; *see also* dementia
Ambulance and Helicopter Emergency Medical Service, accident notes from 14
AMDC v AG and Anor (2020) 161n13
AMDC v AG and CI (2020) 159, 160n9
amenity *see* loss of amenity
American Academy of Clinical Neuropsychology 39, 97
American Congress of Rehabilitation Medicine 120
American Psychiatric Association *see* DSM-5; DSM-III; DSM-IV
amnesia, post-traumatic amnesia (PTA) 120–121
Anderson, T. 124
annuity method 186–187
Anti-social Behaviour, Crime and Policing Act (2014) 78
aphasia 53–54
Arden, Mary, Lady Justice 164–165
Arnett, P. 43
arterial spin labelling (ASL) 122
Ashcroft v Curtain (1971) 184n53
ASHE SOC (212) 186
ASHE SOC (6115) 186
Asken, B. 123
Association of Trial Lawyers 104
athletes 30
attention control, assessing 148–149
Attention Deficit Disorder 83
Attention Deficit Hyperactivity Disorder (ADHD) 70
Auerbach, Simon Joseph, HH Judge 9
Autism 83

Auty v NCB (1985) 185n62
award of damages: aim 5; annuity method 186–187; contingency awards 187–188; lump sum damages 186–188; periodical payments, variable and non-variable 189–190; provisional damages 188–189; stay and/or adjournment/part adjournment 190–191; *see also* expenses; losses; quantum, legal principles of (W. Latimer-Sayer); quantum principles, practical applications of (A. Worthington, W. Latimer-Sayer and A. Tyerman)
Axelrod, B. N. 93

B v A Local Authority (2019) 76n5, 163n23
BADS (Behavioural Assessment of the Dysexecutive Syndrome) 141, 145; Zoo Map subtest 141
BAE v Konczak (2017) 8–9
Bailey v MOD (2009) 7
Bailey v Warren (2006) 164–165
balance (in opinions) 2
balance of probabilities 5, 21
Barnett v Chelsea and Kensington Hospital Management Committee (1969) 176n16
Bechara, A. 150
Behavioural Assessment of the Dysexecutive Syndrome (BADS) 141, 145; Zoo Map subtest 141
behavioural management training courses 200
behavioural rating scales 151
Belanger, H. 128
bell curve (normal distribution) concept 26, 38, *39*
Benson, D. F. 144
Berkeley, G. 116n1
Bigler, E. D. 89, 104, 130, 153
Billett v MOD (2015) 11
Binder, L. M. 128
biopsychosocial framework 2, 126, *222*, 224, 225
Bishop v Hannaford (1988) 185n61
BISI (Brain Injury Screening Index) 71
Blackburn, Colin, Baron Blackburn 5n3
Blamire v South Cumbria Health Authority (1993) 208
Bloom, B. 129
Blyth v Blyth (1966) 182n47
Blyth Valley Borough Council v Henderson (1996) 181n45

Bonham-Carter v Hyde Park Hotel (1948) 184n53
Boone, K. B. 97
Booth, J. E. 101
Bourhill v Young (1943) 176n12
Bracewell, Joyanne, Justice 165
brain: brief description 64–65; developmental stages 65–66; myelination 67; neural plasticity 66, 67–68
Brain Injury Screening Index (BISI) 71
Braithwaite, Bill, frontal lobe paradox, legal perspective 151–152
breach of duty 5, 7, 8
Brifcani, Shereen *see* neuropsychological aspects of brain injury litigation (P. S. Moore, S. Brifcani and A. Worthington); neuropsychological opinion in brain injury (P. S. Moore, S. Brifcani and A. Worthington)
Bristow v Judd (1993) 187n72
British Psychological Society: Division of Neuropsychology 51, 223; Performance Validity Tests recommendations 97; 'What makes a good assessment of capacity' 162
British Westinghouse Electric and Manufacturing Co Ltd v Underground Electric Railways Co of London Ltd (1912) 179n28
Brockhaus, R. 100, 102
Brownhill, Ian P. 2; *see also* legal frameworks and offenders with brain injuries (Ian P. Brownhill); mental capacity in brain injury litigation (I. P. Brownhill)
Bryant, B. 118
Bryant, R. 127
Bunnage, Martin *see* premorbid abilities (M. Bunnage)
burden of proof 183–184
Burgess, P. W. 44, 141, 144, 147–148, 150
Burton, Michael, Justice 178
Burton v Kingsbury (2007) 178n23
Bush, S. S. 48
'but for' test 6–9, 40, 176

Candlewood Navigation Corpn Ltd v Mitsui OSK Lines Ltd (1986) 179n27
Canyock, E. M. 99
capacity 13–14, 46; *see also* mental capacity; mental capacity in brain injury litigation (I. P. Brownhill)
cardiac disease, cognitive effects of 43

care needs: and ageing 205; evaluation of prior to and after accident 12; evaluation of quantum for 202–203; facilitating independence 203–205; and formulation for neuropsychological opinion 225
carer records 15
Carragee, E. J. 23
Carson, A. 102
case management 4, 12; case management records 15, 52, 204
CATs (Cognitive Ability Tests) 84–85
causation 5, 176–177, *222*, 223, 224
cervical spine injury 117–118
Chadwick, John, Lord Justice 160, 163–164
Charles, Henry F. *see* legal principles in brain injury litigation (H. F. Charles and R. Johnson)
CHAT (Comprehensive Health Assessment Tool), TBI section 71
Chaytor, N. 50
children *see* paediatric outcomes after traumatic brain injury (H. Kent, J. Tonks, H. Williams)
Chovaz, C. J. 55
Civil Procedure Rules (CPR): para 1 of PD 41B 189; Part 3 190; Part 21 187; Part 25 191; Part 35 223; r. 41.2 188
The Clarence (1850) 184n53
clinical negligence 15, 45, 192, 193, 194
Clinical Psychology 85
cognition: cognitive functions, neurological basis of 36–37; cognitive functions to assess 36; cognitive impairment and depression 100–101, 103; cognitive impairment and formal neuropsychological tests 45; cognitive impairment and PTSD 101; cognitive tests 27–29, 40–41, 44, 129; health problems, cognitive effects of 43; modular cognition 36; *see also* executive functions
Cognitive Ability Tests (CATs) 84–85
cognitive behavioural therapy (CBT) 130
compensation claims: for railway injury (1870s) 117; *see also* expenses; losses; quantum, legal principles of (W. Latimer-Sayer); quantum principles, practical applications of (A. Worthington, W. Latimer-Sayer and A. Tyerman)

Comprehensive Health Assessment Tool (CHAT), TBI section 71
concussion: defining 123–124; post-concussion syndrome (PCS) 124–126, 130; 'spinal concussion' notion 117–118
Condit, D. C. 99
consciousness disorders: minimal conscious state (MCS) 55; prolonged disorders of consciousness 200–201
consent, and offenders with brain injuries 75–76, 77
Constantine Line v Imperial Smelting (1942) 181n43
contingency awards 187–188
conversion disorder 91
Cook v Cook and anor (2011) 190
Cooke v United Bristol Health Care 185n63
Cookson v Knowles (1979) 185n62
Cooper v P&O Stena Line Ltd Ferries (1999) 182n48
Corr v IBC Vehicles Ltd (2008) 175n10
cost calculations (for therapies) 201–202, **202**
County Courts Act (1984, s51) 188
Court of Appeal: 'but for' test 7–8; capacity to conduct proceedings 164–165; disability 11; future inflation 185; general damages for pain, suffering and loss of amenity 195; lump sum damages 187; mitigation of loss 180n40, 181; provisional damages 189n78
Court of Protection 32, 75, 76, 161, 216, 217
Covid-19, and loss of earnings 12
Cox, Laura, Justice 178n21, 179n34
CPR *see* Civil Procedure Rules (CPR)
credibility issue, and neuropsychological tests 17
Criminal Justice and Courts Act (2015, s 57) 182–183
criminal records 17, 52
criminality: and paediatric TBI 64, 69–71; *see also* legal frameworks and offenders with brain injuries (Ian P. Brownhill)
Crocker, L. 37
Crosby, R. D. 90, 104, 107, 109, 110
'cry for help' notion 92, 127
CT scanning 30, 121, 122
cultural differences, and neuropsychological testing 55–56
Curi v Colina (1998) 188, 189n78

damages *see* award of damages
Damages Act (1996) 185
Damasio, A. R. 141, 142, 150
Davies, R. C. 69
Davies v Frimley Health NHS Foundation Trust (2021) 9
De Koning, M. E. 127
Demakis, G. J. 101
dementia 27, 93, 97–98, 100, 205; Alzheimer's disease 101, 102
DenBoer, J. W. 103
Denny v Gooda Walker Ltd (1995) 191n84
depression 23, 25, 98, 100–101, 103
deputyship 14, 186, 216, 217; *see also* trustees
DEX (Dysexecutive Questionnaire) 141
DEX-O (Dysexecutive Questionnaire, proxy version) 150
diabetes, cognitive effects of 43
Dickins v O2 (2008) 8, 9
diffusion tensor imaging (DTI) 122, 123, 130
Digby v Essex County Council (1994) 181n44
disability: Disability Discrimination Act (1995) 9, 10–11, 207; identifying and classifying 9–11; Ogden definition of 207–208
disconnection syndromes 37
D-KEFS tests 41, 47
documentation *see* records
Domino, G. 54
Don, A. S. 23
Donker-Cools, B. H. 211
'dosages' (of TBI) 64, 71
Dot Counting Test 95
Dr Sido John v Central Manchester and Manchester Children's University Hospitals NHS Foundation Trust (2016) 212n8
Driver and Vehicle Licensing Agency (DVLA), MOT records 15
DSM-III, factitious disorder 92
DSM-IV, post-concussion syndrome (PCS) 125
DSM-5: diagnosis, dimensional approaches to 126; factitious disorder 92; Major and Mild Neurocognitive Disorder 125; Mild TBI 120; neurocognitive disorder 36; post-concussion syndrome (PCS) 125
DTI (diffusion tensor imaging) 122, 123, 130
Dunhill v Burgin (Nos 1 and 2) (2014) 166n29

DVLA (Driver and Vehicle Licensing Agency), MOT records 15
Dysexecutive Questionnaire (DEX) 141
Dysexecutive Questionnaire, proxy version (DEX-O) 150
dysgraphia 54
dyslexia 54, 83
Dyson, John, Lord Justice 184

Eady, David, Justice 190–191
Eagle v Chambers (No 2) (2004) 185n59
Early Years Foundation Curriculum (3-to-4 years) 83–84
earning capacity 32, 207–208; *see also* loss of earnings; return-to-work
Eastvold, A. 51
ecological validity (of neuropsychological testing) 49–50
educational and school records 22
educational psychology 54, 85
educational records 22, 52, 85, 204; school records 15, 22, 52, 83, 84, 129
EEG (electroencephalogram) imaging 65
effort testing and performance validity (S. Gerhand, C. A. Jones and D. Hacker): case studies (1-4) 104–110; chapter overview 2–3, 223; chapter summary and conclusions 111; concepts and terminology issues 89–90; context and consistency 97–100; effort, motivation and classification of invalid responses 90–91, *90*; Malingered Neurocognitive Dysfunction (MND) 98–99, 104, 106, 107, 109, 110; malingering and factitious disorder 91–93; malingering and interpreting effort test performance 97; malingering and performance validity tests 89–90, 98; Performance Validity Tests (PVTs) 89, 93–104, **95**; Symptom Validity Tests (SVTs) 89, 93–94, **95**, 97; 'validity measures' term 94; *see also* Performance Validity Tests (PVTs)
EG, R (On the Application Of) v The Parole Board of England and Wales (2020) 75n1
eggshell personality principle 176
eggshell skull rule 6, 31, 176
electroencephalogram (EEG) imaging 65
Ellison v University Hospitals of Morecambe Bay NHS Foundation Trust (2015) 174
Emanuel v Emanuel (1946) 181n43
emergency services, accident notes/ reports from 14
emotion, and Iowa Gambling Task (IGT) 150

employment records 15, 52, 129, 204
Englander, J. 128
Equality Act (2010) 11, 207
equipment and aids, evaluation of quantum for 206–207
Erichsen, John Eric, 1st Baronet 117–118
Eslinger, P. J. 142
Eth, S. 91
Ettenhofer, M. 129
evidence *see* neuropsychological evidence (general); neuropsychological evidence (specific areas)
evidence-based reasoning 2
exacerbation/aggravation principle 177
exaggeration, conscious *vs.* unconscious 181–183
executive functions: and attentional control 148–149; and Behavioural Assessment of the Dysexecutive Syndrome (BADS) 141; and language 144; and Iowa Gambling Task (IGT) 150; and MET (Multiple Errands Test) 141–142; and neuropsychological testing 43–44, 141–144
expenses: causation and pre-existing illness/ill-health 176–177; claimant's loss *vs.* third parties 175; foreseeability 175; future *vs.* past 172; *vs.* losses 172; mitigation of loss 179; proportionality 174–175; quality of life 177–178; reasonableness 172, 173–174; remoteness 175; *see also* award of damages
experts, and principle of independence 152, 162
Eye Movement Desensitisation Re-Processing (EMDR) 130

facial injury, and MTBI 118–119
factitious disorder 91, 92
Falk, Sarah, Justice 160–161
family environment, and paediatric TBI 67, 72, 74
Fee, C. 128
Feinstein, A. 124
Fernandes, M. 128
Fernandez, A. L. 56
Financial Deputy 32
Fisher, C. M. 117–118
Fisher-Hicks, Samantha *see* frontal lobe paradox (S. Fisher-Hicks, R. Ll. Wood and B. Braithwaite)
Fitzpatrick, P. J. 101
Flaro, L. 102
Flaux, Julian, Justice 178n23

Fletcher v Keatley (2017) 182n46
flight-path system 85
Flora v Wakom (Heathrow) Ltd (2006) 190n81
fMRI (functional Magnetic Resonance Imaging) scanning 122
Fodor, J. A. 36
Folks v Faizey (2006) 161
forced-choice tests **95**, 102
foreseeability, and losses/expenses 175
'formulation' process, and clinical neuropsychology 22
Foskett, David, High Court Judge 6–7, 173
Frederick, R. I. 90, 104, 107, 109, 110
freedom of information requests 15
Froggatt v LEP International (2002) 184n54
frontal lobe functions: and executive functions 43, 44; *see also* frontal lobe paradox (S. Fisher-Hicks, R. Ll. Wood and B. Braithwaite)
frontal lobe paradox (S. Fisher-Hicks, R. Ll. Wood and B. Braithwaite): chapter overview 2, 224–225; chapter summary and conclusions 153; community independence, assessing 140; executive function, prefrontal cortex and neuropsychological tests 140–144, 151, 153; language and 'knowing *vs.* doing' 144–147; legal perspective 151–152; MET (Multiple Errands Test) 141–142; office-based assessments, problems with 147–148; psychometrics and behavioural rating scales 151; reasoning, emotion and Iowa Gambling Task (IGT) 150; SASNOS assessment 151; temporal discounting and impulsive decision making 149–150; tests and attention control assessment 148–149; tests and intelligence 149
'fundamental dishonesty' concept 92–93

Gale v Esure Services Ltd (2019) 123n5
Garrick, T. 91
Geest v Lansiquot (2002) 180n38, 184n54
George, M. S. 153
Gerhand, Simon *see* effort testing and performance validity (S. Gerhand, C. A. Jones and D. Hacker)
Gervais, R. O. 101, 103
Gilbert, S. 153
Glasgow Coma Scale (GCS) score 120–121

Goldenberg, G. 54
Gordon, S. N. 101
Grafman, J. 149
Gray v Thames Trains Ltd v anor (2009) 176n15
Green, P. 100, 102, 103
Greiffenstein, M. F. 24
Guise, E., de 122
Gunstad, J. 128
'gut feelings' (somatic markers) 150

H v Thomson Holidays Ltd (2007) 189n80
Hacker, David *see* effort testing and performance validity (S. Gerhand, C. A. Jones and D. Hacker)
Haldane, Richard, 1st Viscount Haldane 179n33
Hall, S. 103
Hanks, R. A. 93
Harman v East Kent Hospitals NHS Foundation Trust (2015) 184n55, 185n57
Harrison v Leake (1989) 184n53
Harvey, A. 127
Hayden v Maidstone & Tunbridge Wells NHs Trust (2016) 177n18
head injury, and MTBI 118–119
Health and Care Professions Council (HCPC) 223
Health and Safety Executive (HSE), accident notes from 14
hearing impairment 54–55
Heil v Rankin (2001) 177n19, 195n1
Heilbronner, R. L. 96, 99
high-functioning individuals 30–31
Hilsabeck, R. C. 101
Hinduja v Hinduja & Ors (2020) 160–161
Hiployee, C. 124
Hodgson v Trapp (1989) 186–187, 186n68
Hodson, Charles, Baron Hodson 191n84
Hoffberger v Ascot (1976) 179n26
Hoffmann, Lennie, Baron Hoffmann 182n49
homelessness 203
Hornal v Neuberger Products Ltd (1957) 182n47
Hospital and Community Health Service Inflation 185
Hotson v East Berkshire Health Authority (1987) 176n16
Hou, R. 127
housing records 15
Howlett v Davies (2017) 92

Hughes (Gordon Clifford) v Addis (John) (2000) 184n53
Hughes v Lord Advocate (1963) 175n10
100% principle 172
Huntley v Simmonds (2009) 204n3
Hurt, G. 129
Hussein v William Hill Group (2004) 162n21
Huyton-with-Roby UDC v Hunter (1955) 183n52

ICD *see* International Classification of Diseases
Illes, J. 123
Illness Perceptions Questionnaire 127–128
illness/ill-health: cognitive effects of 43; pre-existing and causation 176–177
impartiality 2
impulsive decision making, measuring 149–150
Income and Corporation Taxes Act (1988), s 329(1) 187n70
independence (of brain injury sufferers): assessing 140; facilitating 203–205
independence (of experts) 152, 162
inflation: future inflation 185–186; Hospital and Community Health Service Inflation 185
innocence, presumption of 181
insurance companies 30
intelligence, and consulting room executive tests 149
'intermediate patients' concept 104
International Classification of Diseases, ICD-10 and ICD-11 on post-concussion syndrome 125
Iowa Gambling Task (IGT) 150
IQ tests 27–29, 40–41, 84, 150
Irwin, Stephen, Lord Justice 9, 188n77
Iverson, G. L. 103, 125, 126
Ivey v Genting Casinos (UK) Ltd (2017) 92

Jackson, H. 140
Jackson, Rupert, Lord Justice 11
Jenkins, P. O. 125
Jennett, B. 120
Jobling v Associated Dairies Ltd (1982) 176n15
Johnson, Ruth *see* legal principles in brain injury litigation (H. F. Charles and R. Johnson)

Jones, Chris A. *see* effort testing and performance validity (S. Gerhand, C. A. Jones and D. Hacker)
Jones v Kaney (2011) 199n2
Judicial College, *Guidelines for the Assessment of General Damages in Personal Injury Cases* 195

Kay, T. 42
Keene, David, Lord Justice 181
Keith, Brian, Justice 8
Kennedy, Paul, Lord Justice 164
Kent, Hope 69; *see also* paediatric outcomes after traumatic brain injury (H. Kent, J. Tonks, H. Williams)
Kenth v Heimdale Hotel Investments Ltd (2001) 176n15, 177n18
Kidd v Plymouth Health Authority (2001) 188n74
kidney disease, cognitive effects of 43
Killilea v Aviva Insurance UK Limited (2018) 32
King v The Wright Roofing Company Ltd (2020) 166n28
Kings College NHS Foundation Trust v C and V (2015) 162n22
Kirkish, P. 91
Knight, R. T. 144
'knowing *vs.* doing' 144, 145–147
Kotula v EDF Energy Networks & others (2011) 188n77
Kuncel, N. R. 23–24

Lagden v O'Connor (2003) 179n27, 179n32
language: and frontal lobe paradox 144–147; and neuropsychological testing 55–56
Larrabee, G. J. 89, 96, 130
lasting power of attorney (LPAs) 14
Latimer-Sayer, William *see* quantum, legal principles of (W. Latimer-Sayer); quantum principles, practical applications of (A. Worthington, W. Latimer-Sayer and A. Tyerman)
Law Reform (Personal Injuries) Act (1948), Section 2(4) 184
learning difficulties 83, 84
legal frameworks and offenders with brain injuries (Ian P. Brownhill): compulsion versus consent 75–76; no mental capacity to consent to restrictions 76–77; restrictions imposed despite brain injury 77–78; risk management, proactive *vs.* reactive 78
legal principles in brain injury litigation (H. F. Charles and R. Johnson): award of damages, aim of 5; balance of probabilities 5; breach of duty and causation 5, 7, 8; 'but for' test 6–9; capacity 13–14; care/therapies 12; chapter overview 2; credibility issue 17; eggshell skull rule 6; information required by lawyers 4–5; information to support neuropsychologists (records and witness statements) 14–17; loss of earnings (Ogden Tables and assessing disability) 9–12, 14–15; 'material contribution' concept 7–9; neuropsychologist's report 17; offers to settle 4; pre-action protocol letters 4–5
Lezak, M. D. 141
Lim Poh Choo v Camden and Islington Area Health Authority (1980) 185n62, 186n67, 186n68, 187n71
Limbu v MOD (2008) 180n36
Linck, J. F. 101
linkworkers 71
Liossi, C. 141
Lishman, W. A. 120
Little, D. 122
Livingstone v Rawyards Coal Co (1880) 5n3, 171n2
A Local Authority v JB (by his litigation friend, the Official Solicitor) (2020) 76n4
loss of amenity, general damages for 195–196
loss of earnings: identifying and classifying disability 9–11; multiple scenarios and Covid-19 example 11–12; Ogden Tables (8th ed.) 9, 10, 11, 207; and periodical payment award 190; and quantum assessment 207–208; urgency of issue 14–15; *see also* return-to-work
losses: causation and pre-existing illness or ill-health 176–177; claimant's loss *vs.* third parties 175; *vs.* expenses 172; foreseeability 175; future inflation 185–186; future *vs.* past 172; 100% principle 172; mitigation of loss 178–181; proportionality not applied 172, 174; quality of life 177–178; remoteness 175; *see also* award of damages; loss of amenity; loss of earnings

Loughlin v Singh, Pama & Co Ltd, Churchill Insurance Co. (2013) 205n4
lump sum damages 186–188
Luria, A. R. 144

McAuley v London Transport Executive (1957) 180n39
McCaffrey, R. 125
McCombe, Richard, Justice 178n21
McCullagh, S. 124
McGeorge, P. 141
McHugh, L. 149–150
McMillan, T. 128
McWirter, L. 101–102
Magnetic Resonance Imaging (MRI) scanning 30, 65, 119, 122, 123; fMRI (functional Magnetic Resonance Imaging) scanning 122
magnetic resonance spectroscopy (MRS) 122
magnetisation transfer imaging 122
Major Neurocognitive Disorder 125
Malcolm v Broadhurst (1970) 176n14
malingering: and effort tests 89–90, 98; and factitious disorder 91–93; and interpreting test performance (context and consistency) 97, 111; Malingered Cognitive Dysfunction 89; Malingered Neurocognitive Dysfunction (MND) 98–99, 104, 106, 107, 109, 110; in personal injury litigation 181–183; Test of Memory Malingering (TOMM) 55
Mallet v McMonagle (1970) 185n62
Manchester, D. 140, 142
Manna v Central Manchester University Hospitals NHS Foundation Trust (2015) 178n21, 179n34
Marshall, S. 130
Masterman-Lister v Brutton and Co (2002) 160, 161, 163–164, 166n32
Mateer, C. A. 141
'material contribution' concept 7–9
Mattocks v Mann (1973) 179n27
Mayo Clinic classification system, and mild TBI 120–121
Mayou, R. 118
Meadow v General Medical Council (2007) 162n20
Medical Disability Society, Working Party (1988) 120
medical records 14, 15, 22, 25, 52, 129, 204

medical treatment: and formulation for neuropsychological opinion 225; and mitigation of loss 180–181; NHS or private care 184–185; *see also* neuropsychological treatment; rehabilitation; therapies
medicolegal neuropsychology practice, paucity of literature 1
Melia v Key Terrain Ltd (1969) 180
Memory Complaints Inventory 94
mental capacity: and formulation for neuropsychological opinion 225; and quantum assessment 215–217; *see also* legal frameworks and offenders with brain injuries (Ian P. Brownhill); Mental Capacity Act (2005); mental capacity in brain injury litigation (I. P. Brownhill)
Mental Capacity Act (2005): assessing mental capacity 13, 14, 158, 168; fluctuating capacity 167; how to assess capacity 162; how to assess capacity to conduct proceedings 163; how to assess capacity to manage affairs/property 167; person's best interests *vs.* protection of the public 76; presumption of capacity 158–159; right to detain a person for assessment/treatment 78; who should assess capacity 159–160
Mental Capacity Casebook (T. Ryan-Morgan) 162
mental capacity in brain injury litigation (I. P. Brownhill): chapter overview 2; chapter summary and conclusion 168; fluctuating capacity 167; how to assess capacity 162–163; how to assess capacity to conduct proceedings 163–166; how to assess capacity to manage affairs/property 166–167; Mental Capacity Act (2005) 158–160, 162, 163, 167, 168; neuropsychological assessment, advantages of 161–162; presumption of capacity 158–159; restoration of capacity 167–168; who should assess capacity 159–161
Mental Health Act (1983) 78
Merten, T. 103
Mesulam, M. M. 141
MET (Multiple Errands Test) 141–142
The Metagama (1927) 179n33
Mickeviciene, D. 124
Mild Neurocognitive Disorder 125

mild traumatic brain injury: and formulation for neuropsychological opinion 224; and legal principles in litigation 14; and neuropsychological evidence 5; and neuropsychological testing 45; and Performance Validity Tests (PVTs) 98, 103, 104–106, 107–109; *see also* mild traumatic brain injury (MTBI) and persistent neuropsychological symptoms (A. Worthington and P. S. Moore)

mild traumatic brain injury (MTBI) and persistent neuropsychological symptoms (A. Worthington and P. S. Moore): chapter overview 3; chapter summary and conclusion 130–131; contentious area 116, 130; defining MTBI 119–122; head/facial injury 118–119; history and statistics 116–117; mechanisms (CT, MRI, DTI) 122–123; medicolegal neuropsychological evaluation 125–126, *126*; neuropsychological intervention 129–130; post-concussion syndrome issue 123–126; psychological/social factors and implications for assessment 126–129; 'significant' and 'subtle brain injury' notions 121–122; whiplash (cervical spine injury) 117–118

Miller, B. I. 101
Millis, S. R. 93, 96
Millon Clinical Multi-Axial Inventory 94
minimal conscious state (MCS) 55
Minnesota Multiphasic Personality Inventory 94
Mitchell v Mulholland (No 2) (1972) 185n62
mitigation of loss 178–181
Mittenberg, W. 99
Miyamoto, Y. 55
MND (Malingered Neurocognitive Dysfunction) *see* malingering
Modified Somatic Perceptions Questionnaire 94
modular cognition 36
Montijo, J. 100, 102
Moor, Philip, Justice 77
Moore, Phil S. *see* mild traumatic brain injury (MTBI) and persistent neuropsychological symptoms (A. Worthington and P. S. Moore); neuropsychological aspects of brain injury litigation (P. S. Moore, S. Brifcani and A. Worthington); neuropsychological opinion in brain injury (P. S. Moore, S. Brifcani and A. Worthington); neuropsychological testing in brain injury litigation (A. Worthington and P. S. Moore)

'more of the same' principle 177
Morgan, J. E. 96
Morgan v Millett (2001) 176n15
Morgan v T Wallis (1974) 179n30, 180n37
Morris v Richards (2003) 179n31, 180n40, 181
Morrow v Shrewsbury Rugby Union Football Club Limited (2020) 30–31
MOT records 15
motivation, and effort testing 90–91, *90*
MRI *see* Magnetic Resonance Imaging (MRI) scanning
Mulhern, S. 128
Mulholland v Mitchell (1971) 186n67, 191n84
Mullins v Gray (2004) 176n14
Multidisciplinary Team records 15
Multiple Errands Test (MET) 141–142
Munby, James, Justice 165
Murphy v Stone-Wallwork (1969) 191n84
Mustard v Flower et al 50
myelination 67

National Academy of Neuropsychology 104
National Foundation for Educational Research (NFER) reading tests 84
National Health Service *see* NHS (National Health Service)
Neile reading tests 84
neural plasticity 66, 67–68
'neurocognitive stall' phenomenon 68, 71
neuroinflammation 68, 72
neuropsychiatrists, opinions of as part of neuropsychological evidence 5
neuropsychological aspects of brain injury litigation (P. S. Moore, S. Brifcani and A. Worthington): central themes and differences of opinions 1–2; chapter structure and contributors 2–3; medicolegal neuropsychological literature, paucity of 1; *see also* neuropsychological opinion in brain injury (P. S. Moore, S. Brifcani and A. Worthington)

neuropsychological evidence (general): nature and timing of 5; receipt of report 17; records and witness statements to assist 14–17; solicitors' support and procedural steps 193; subjective *vs.* objective evidence *222*, 224–225

neuropsychological evidence (specific areas): accommodation needs 205–206; aids and equipment 206–207; 'but for' test 6, 7, 8, 9; capacity 13–14; care and support 12, 202–203; care needs and ageing 205; dependence/independence levels 204–205; disability assessment 11, 207–208; eggshell skull rule 6; general damages for pain, suffering and loss of amenity 195–196; loss of earnings 9, 11, 12; mental capacity assessment 161–162, 167–168, 216–217; neuropsychological treatment and therapies 12, 199–200; premorbid ability 223; prolonged disorders of consciousness 200–201; quantum assessment (overview) 217–218; rehabilitation needs 196–199; return-to-work 211–212

neuropsychological opinion in brain injury (P. S. Moore, S. Brifcani and A. Worthington): chapter overview 3; formulation for neuropsychological opinion 221–223, *222*; future directions 225; guidelines and rules 223; objective evidence *222*, 224; premorbid functioning *222*, 223; process of establishing causation *222*, 223, 224; psychometric testing 223, 224, 225; reliability and validity *222*, 223; subjective evidence *222*, 224–225; treatment, care and support 225

neuropsychological testing: credibility issue 17; and executive functions 43–44, 141–144, 153; and return-to-work 210; *see also* neuropsychological testing in brain injury litigation (A. Worthington and P. S. Moore)

neuropsychological testing in brain injury litigation (A. Worthington and P. S. Moore): chapter overview 2, 224; chapter summary and conclusion 56; clinical tools and legal instruction 35; cognition and modularity 36; cognitive functions, neurological basis of 36–37; cognitive functions to assess 36; complex medical cases (aphasia, apraxia, vision/hearing impairment, minimal conscious state) 53–55; 'ecological validity' issue 49–50; executive functions 43–44; neuropsychometric testing, basis of 38, *38*; non-English-speaking claimants 55–56; normal and within-person variability 40–41; older *vs.* newer neuropsychological tests 47–48; premorbid (pre-injury) function 40; psychological and health conditions, influence of 43; psychometric principles 37–40; psychometric test score conversion table 39, **61–63**; psychometric test scores, reliability of 40; recording of neuropsychological examinations 50–51; repeat assessments and appropriate intervals 48–49; test batteries, flexible versus fixed 46–47; test specificity and sensitivity 41–43; triangulation of evidence from neuropsychological examination 51–53, *52*; 'useful but not determinative' 56; uses of formal neuropsychological tests 44–46; *see also* effort testing and performance validity (S. Gerhand, C. A. Jones and D. Hacker)

neuropsychological treatment: evaluation of quantum for 199–200; methods to calculate costs 201–202, **202**; and MTBI 129–130

NFER (National Foundation for Educational Research) reading tests 84

NHS (National Health Service): or private medical care 184–185; rehabilitation statutory services 196

The NHS Trust v Ms T (2004) 165

Nisbett, R. E. 55

nocebo effect 127

'non-credible performance' term 93

non-English-speaking claimants 55–56

normal distribution (bell curve) concept 26, 38, *39*

normal variability, and neuropsychological testing 40–41

Norris, G. 141

Nowak, M. 75

office-based assessments, and frontal lobe paradox 147–151

Ogden Tables (8th ed.) 9, 10, 11, 207; definition of disability 207–208

Ogwo v Taylor (1988) 175n10

Oliver, Peter, Baron Oliver of Aylmerton 186–187
Ommaya, A. 117
oppositional defiance disorder 70
Overseas Tankship (UK) Ltd v Miller Steamship Co Pty (The Wagon Mound (No 2) (1967) 175n10
Ozen, L. 128

Paediatric Neuropsychology 85
paediatric outcomes after traumatic brain injury (H. Kent, J. Tonks, H. Williams): chapter overview 2, 223; childhood traumatic brain injury (TBI), criminalisation of 64; 'dosage' of injury and effects of childhood TBI 64; 'dosages' and assessment of paediatric TBI 71; need for multidisciplinary approach 74–75; normative development of the brain 64–66; paediatric TBI 66–68; paediatric TBI and criminal behaviour 69–71; pre-morbid function in children/ young people 71, 83–85; social issues following paediatric TBI 68–69; socioeconomic and familial factors 72–73, 74; young female case (client A) 73–74; *see also* legal frameworks and offenders with brain injuries (Ian P. Brownhill)
Page v Smith (1993) 181n44
Page v Smith (1996) 173n4, 175n11, 177n17, 177n19
pain, general damages for 195–196
Pandharipande, P. 119
Panter, A. 56
parenting, and paediatric TBI 67, 72, 74
Parker, Jonathan, Justice 205
Parkhouse v North Devon Healthcare NHS Trust (2002) 185n61
Pastorek, N. J. 101
Patton, C. 99
PBM v TGT & Anor (2019) 167n34
Pearce, Edward, Baron Pearce 191n84
Performance Validity Tests (PVTs): case study: mild TBI 104–106; case study: mild TBI with comorbidities 107–109; case study: severe TBI 106–107; case study: severe TBI and use of non-test data 109–110; concept 89–90, 93–94; context and consistency 97–100; cut-off scores 94–96; forced-choice tests **95**, 102; intermediate patients 104; methods and procedures **95**; number of tests to administer 96–97; PVT failure and depression 100–101, 103; PVT failure and PTSD 101; PVT failure and warning test takers 103–104; PVT failure with implausible explanations 103; PVT failure without external incentive 101–102; summary and conclusions 111; *see also* malingering
periodical payments (variable and non-variable) 189–190
Personality Assessment Inventory 94
PET (Positron Emission Topography) scans 30, 118
Peters v East Midlands Strategic HA (2009) 184, 184n55
Phillips, Stephen, Justice 191n84
Phillips v Symes (A Bankrupt) (2004) 162n19
Picken, Simon, Justice 212
Pinnington v Crossleigh Construction (2003) 185n60
Plaut, D. 36
police: accident reports from 14, 15, 52; and Social Services records 15
Ponsford, J. 140
Poole, Nigel, Justice 159, 161n13
Positron Emission Topography (PET) scans 30, 118
post-concussion syndrome (PCS) 123–126, 130
post-traumatic amnesia (PTA) 120–121
Post-Traumatic Stress Disorder (PTSD) 94, 100, 101, 127
pre-action protocol letters 4–5
Pre-Curriculum Level Descriptors 84
pre-existing illness/ill-health, and causation 176–177
prefrontal cortex 43–44, 70, 140–144; *see also* frontal lobe paradox (S. Fisher-Hicks, R. Ll. Wood and B. Braithwaite)
premorbid (pre-injury) function: in children and young people 71, 83–85, 223; and formulation for neuropsychological opinion 222, 223; and neuropsychological testing 40; *see also* premorbid abilities (M. Bunnage)
premorbid abilities (M. Bunnage): chapter overview 2, 223; clinical neuropsychology and 'formulation' process 22; cognition, emotion and behaviour (in adults) 21–22; current 'self-report' and 'others-report' about the past 22, 23–24; past contemporary reports 22, 24–25; scientifically

predicted ability (cognitive tests) 22, 27–29; statistical probability 22, 26–27, 28; Willems QC's legal perspective 29–33; *see also* paediatric outcomes after traumatic brain injury (H. Kent, J. Tonks, H. Williams)
pre-school records 83–84
presumption of innocence 181
presumption of mental capacity 158–159
Priestley, N. 43, 140, 142
Prins, M. 122
private medical care, or NHS 184–185
procedural steps 192–193
proportionality 172, 174–175
Protagoras, 'Man is the measure of all things' 35
provisional damages 188–189
PS, Abdi Dahir, CF v The Queen (2019) 75n2
psychological disorder, cognitive effects of 43
psychometric testing: and behavioural rating scales 151; and formulation for neuropsychological opinion 223, 224, 225; and measurement of neuropsychological function 35; principles of 37–40; reliability of 40, 223; and statistical probability 26–27; test score conversion table 39, **61–63**; *see also* neuropsychological testing in brain injury litigation (A. Worthington and P. S. Moore)
psychotherapy records 15
PTSD (Post-Traumatic Stress Disorder) 94, 100, 101, 127
PVTs *see* Performance Validity Tests (PVTs)

quality of life, and losses/expenses 177–178
quantum, legal principles of (W. Latimer-Sayer): chapter overview 3; chapter summary and conclusion 194; claimant's burden of proof 183–184; claimant's loss and third parties 175; exaggeration and malingering 181–183; foreseeability and remoteness 175; form of award 186–191; fundamental aim (restitutio in integrum) 171; future inflation 185–186; losses and expenses, past *vs.* future 172; losses *vs.* expenses 172; mitigation of loss 178–181; NHS or private care 184–185; pre-existing illness/ill-health and causation 176–177; procedure and assessment process 192–193; proportionality 172, 174–175; quality of life 177–178; reasonableness 172–174; *see also* award of damages
quantum principles, practical applications of (A. Worthington, W. Latimer-Sayer and A. Tyerman): chapter overview 3; chapter summary and conclusion 217–218; accommodation needs 205–206; aids and equipment 206–207; care and support 202–203; care needs and ageing 205; cost calculations 201–202, **202**; facilitating independence 203–205; general damages for pain, suffering and loss of amenity 195–196; loss of earnings and earning capacity 207–208; mental capacity 215–217; prolonged disorders of consciousness 200–201; rehabilitation 196–199; return-to-work 208–215; therapies and neuropsychological treatment 199–200; *see also* return-to-work

R. v Pabon (2018) 162n17
Rahman v West Pennine HA 178n21
'random variable' notion 37–38
Re Dellow's Wills Trusts (1967) 182n47
Re Doherty (2008) 182n50
reading tests 27–29, 83, 84
Reaney v University Hospital of North Staffordshire NHS Trust & Another (2015) 6–7, 177n20
reasonableness 172–174
reasoning processes: and consulting room executive tests 149; impulsive decision making 149–150; inductive (emotional) reasoning 150
records: carer records 15; case management records 15, 52, 204; criminal records 17, 52; educational (incl. school) records 15, 22, 52, 83, 84, 85, 129, 204; emergency services records 14; employment records 15, 52, 129, 204; housing records 15; medical records 14, 15, 22, 25, 52, 129, 204; MOT records 15; Multidisciplinary Team records 15; police reports 14, 15, 52; pre-school records 83–84; social media intelligence reports 17; Social Services records 15, 22, 52; support worker records 204; therapy records 15

rehabilitation: evaluation of quantum for 196–199; intensive *vs.* extensive 197; methods to calculate costs 201–202, **202**; for prolonged disorders of consciousness 200; vocational rehabilitation (VR) 209, 210–211, 213, 214–215
reliability 40, 222, 223
remoteness, and losses/expenses 175, 181
Resnick, P. J. 91
respiratory illness, cognitive effects of 43
restitutio in integrum 171
Retail Prices Index (RPI) 185, 186, 190
return-to-work: lack of clear statistics 208–209; minority of TBI sufferers successfully returning to work 208–209; neuropsychological constraints 210–211; predicting return-to-work 209–210; vocational rehabilitation (VR) 209, 210–211, 213, 214–215; work capability assessment in litigation context 211–215; "Working Out" (brain injury vocational rehabilitation programme) 210, 212–213, 214
reward-choice paradigms 149
Reynolds, S. 129
Rialis v Mitchell (1984) 173n6, 178n22
Richardson v Redpath Brown & Co Ltd (1944) 179n29
Rickards, T. 126
Ritchie, C. W. 101–102
Robins v National Trust Co (1927) 183n52
Robshaw v United Lincolnshire Hospitals NHS Trust (2015) 173, 186n65, 186n66
Roch, John, Lord Justice 188
Rohling, M. L. 101, 128
Romesser, J. M. 101
Royal Bank of Scotland Plc v AB (2020) 158–159
Royal Borough of Greenwich v CDM (Rev 1) (2019) 167n36
Rubens v Walker (1946) 179, 179n31
Rusnak, M. 64
Russell, E. 48
Russell, Patrick, Lord Justice 180n35
Rutherford, W. H. 124, 128
Rutterford, N. 143, 149
Ryan-Morgan, T., *Mental Capacity Casebook* 162

Sachs, Eric, Lord Justice 180
Salford reading tests 84

SASNOS (St Andrew's Swansea Neurobehavioural Outcome Scale) 151
SATs (Statutory Attainment Tests) 84, 85
Al Sayegh, A. 130
schizophrenia 98, 100
Schmitter-Edgecombe, M. 50
schools: flight-path system 85; reading and other ability tests 84–85; school records 15, 22, 52, 83, 84, 129
Secretary of State for the Home Department v Rehman (2003) 182n49
Seel, R. T. 55
self-reports: and mild TBI 129; and premorbid abilities 22, 23–24; and Symptom Validity Tests (SVTs) 93
SEM (Standard Error of Measurement) 39, 42
Senior Courts Act (1981), s 32A 188
Serious Injury Protocol 4n1
settlements: offers to settle 4; variety of ways 193
Shah v Wasim Ul-Haq and ors (2009) 182n46
Shallice, T. 147–148
Sharp, D. J. 125
Sheffield City Council v (1) E (2) S (2004) 165
Sherman, E. 97, 98
Shuren, J. E. 149
Siegel v Pummell (2014) 122n2, 123n3
'significant brain injury' notion 121
Sim, A. H. 101
Simmons v British Steel plc (2004) 173n4, 175n11
single-photon emission computed tomography (SPECT) 118
Sklair v Haycock (2009) 7
Slick, D. 99
SMART assessments 200, 201
Smith, D. H. 124
Smith, Peter, Lord Justice 182n46
Smith v Leech Brain & Co Ltd (1962) 6, 175n10, 176, 176n12
Smith v McCrae (2003) 184n53
Smith v Manchester Corporation (1974) 208
Smith v Rod Jenkins (2003) 182n46
Smithurst v Sealant Construction Services Ltd (2011) 177n18
Snell, D. 127–128
social media intelligence reports 17
Social Services records 15, 22, 52
Sohlberg, M. M. 141

240   Index

The Solholt v Sameiet Solholt (1983) 178n25
somatic markers (or 'gut feelings') 150
Sowden v Lodge (2004) 173n5, 173n6
Spearman, Charles 37
SPECT (single-photon emission computed tomography) 118
speech therapists 54
'spinal concussion' notion 117–118
Sreenivasan, S. 91
Standard Error of Measurement (SEM) 39, 42
STAR assessments 200
statistical probability, and premorbid abilities 22, 26–27, 28
Statutory Attainment Tests (SATs) 84, 85
stay and/or adjournment/part adjournment 190–191
Stephenson, John, Lord Justice 178n22
Stergiou-Kita, M. 211
Stewart, W. 124
Stojalowski v Imperial Smelting Corpn (NSC) (1976) 182n48
Stone, S. 102
Strategy Application Disorder 144
Stuart v Martin (2001) 187n73
Stuss, D.T. 43–44, 144, 148
'subtle brain injury' notion 121–122
suffering, general damages for 195–196
Suhr, J. 128
Summers v Fairclough Homes Ltd (2012) 183n51
supervening illnesses principle 176–177
support worker records 204
Sutherland v Hatton (2002) 8, 9
Sweet, J. J. 96
Swift, Caroline, Justice 174
Swift, Jonathan, Justice 158–159
Symptom Validity Tests (SVTs) 89, 93–94, **95**, 97, 111

'task impurity' concept 44
Tate, R. L. 141
Tate & Lyle Food and Distribution v GLC (1982) 184n53
Taylor v O'Connor (1971) 185n62, 186n68
Teasdale, G. 120
'temporal discounting' phenomenon 69–70, 149–150

Tess Garraway v Holland & Barrett Ltd 92
Test of Memory Malingering (TOMM) 55
test theory 37–39, *39*
testing *see* effort testing and performance validity (S. Gerhand, C. A. Jones and D. Hacker); neuropsychological testing; neuropsychological testing in brain injury litigation (A. Worthington and P. S. Moore)
Teuber, H. L. 145
Thaine v London School of Economics (2010) 8, 9
Theory of Mind (ToM) 66, 68, 69
therapies: evaluation of prior to and after accident 12; evaluation of quantum for 199–200; methods to calculate costs 201–202, **202**; therapy records 15
39 Essex Chambers, mental capacity law briefing updates 162
Thompstone v Tameside and Glossop NHS Trust (2008) 186n64, 190n81
Thrul v Ray (2000) 178
TOMM (Test of Memory Malingering) 55
Tonks, James *see* paediatric outcomes after traumatic brain injury (H. Kent, J. Tonks, H. Williams)
tort 171, 174
Touradji, P. 56
TRACK-TBI study 124
traumatic brain injury (TBI) *see* mild traumatic brain injury; mild traumatic brain injury (MTBI) and persistent neuropsychological symptoms (A. Worthington and P. S. Moore); paediatric outcomes after traumatic brain injury (H. Kent, J. Tonks, H. Williams)
treatment *see* medical treatment; neuropsychological treatment; rehabilitation; therapies
'true score' notion 37
trustees 216, 217; *see also* deputyship
Tyerman, Andy 210; *see also* quantum principles, practical applications of (A. Worthington, W. Latimer-Sayer and A. Tyerman)

United Nations, *The United Nations global study on children deprived of liberty* 75

validity: and formulation for neuropsychological opinion *222*, 223; 'validity measures' term 94; *see also* effort testing and performance validity (S. Gerhand, C. A. Jones and D. Hacker); Performance Validity Tests (PVTs)
Van Dyke, S. A. 93
Vanderploeg, R. 130
variability: normal and within-person variability 40–41; 'random variable' notion 37–38
Vernon v Bosley (1997) 177n17
Victoria, Queen 117
violent behaviour, and paediatric TBI 69–71
vision impairment 54–55
vocational rehabilitation (VR) 209, 210–211, 213, 214–215
Voormolen, D. 125

Waddell, Gordon 183
WAIS (Wechsler Adult Intelligence Scale) *see* Wechsler tests
Wallace, E. 123
Walsh, K. W. 140
Warby, Mark, Justice 174
Wechsler tests 26, 47; WAIS (Wechsler Adult Intelligence Scale) 84; WAIS-III (Wechsler Adult Intelligence Scale-III) 150; WAIS-IV (Wechsler Adult Intelligence Scale-IV) 40, 41; WISC (Wechsler Intelligence Scale for Children) 84; WISC-V (Wechsler Intelligence Scale for Children-V) 85; WMS-III (Wechsler Memory Scale-III) 145, 150; WMS-IV (Wechsler Memory Scale-IV) 41; WPPSI (Wechsler Preschool & Primary Scale of Intelligence) 84; WTAR (Wechsler Test of Adult Reading) 83
Wells v Wells (1999) 172, 185n62, 186n67, 186n68, 187n71
Wernicke Korsakoff syndrome 12
WHIM assessments 200
whiplash injury 117–118
White v Fell (1987) 166n31
Whiten v St George's Healthcare NHS Trust (2011) 174
Whittaker, R. 127
Wilde, E. 122
Willems, Marc, QC 2, 29–33

Williams, D. 121
Williams, Huw *see* paediatric outcomes after traumatic brain injury (H. Kent, J. Tonks, H. Williams)
Williams, W. H. 69
Williams v Jervis (2008) 123n4
Wilson v Ministry of Defence (1991) 188n76
WISC (Wechsler Intelligence Scale for Children) *see* Wechsler tests
Wisdom, N. M. 101
within-person variability, and neuropsychological testing 40–41
witness statements 16, 30, 32, 52, 204, 224–225
WMS (Wechsler Memory Scale) *see* Wechsler tests
Wood, Rodger Ll. 141, 143, 149–150, 153; *see also* frontal lobe paradox (S. Fisher-Hicks, R. Ll. Wood and B. Braithwaite)
Woodrup v Nicol (1993) 180n35, 185n58
word-reading tests 27–29
work *see* return-to-work
"Working Out" (brain injury vocational rehabilitation programme) 210, 212–213, 214
World Health Organization: task force on mild TBI 120, 121; *see also* International Classification of Diseases
Worthington, Andrew 197, 198; *see also* mild traumatic brain injury (MTBI) and persistent neuropsychological symptoms (A. Worthington and P. S. Moore); neuropsychological aspects of brain injury litigation (P. S. Moore, S. Brifcani and A. Worthington); neuropsychological opinion in brain injury (P. S. Moore, S. Brifcani and A. Worthington); neuropsychological testing in brain injury litigation (A. Worthington and P. S. Moore); quantum principles, practical applications of (A. Worthington, W. Latimer-Sayer and A. Tyerman)
WPPSI (Wechsler Preschool & Primary Scale of Intelligence) *see* Wechsler tests
Wright, Robert, Baron Wright 176n12
Wright v British Railways Board (1983) 195n1
WTAR (Wechsler Test of Adult Reading) *see* Wechsler tests

X, Y, Z v Portsmouth Hospitals NHS Trust [2011] 12
X Council v BB, CB, AB (by her litigation friend, The Official Solicitor), The NHS Trust (2021) 75n3
XX v Whittington Hospital NHS Trust (2017) 189n79

Y County Council and ZZ (2012) 77
young offenders: and paediatric TBI 69–71, 72; *see also* legal frameworks and offenders with brain injuries (Ian P. Brownhill)
Young v Percival (1975) 185n62

Zasler, N. 55
Zoo Map 141

Printed in the United States
by Baker & Taylor Publisher Services